3   4 x 7/15

1/13

6/11

Praise for *Aspirations of Greatness*

"If you are one of the thousands of 'suddenly searching' achievers wading through the aftermath of a major, unexpected failure or loss, Jim Warner's *Aspirations of Greatness* was written for you. Using real case histories, the author is a clear-thinking and insightful guide through the aftershock, fear, rage, self-doubt, and chaotic frustration of midlife disillusionment. Jim introduces the reader to a new and healing way of thinking and living that leads to Reality and to a more solid and grounded kind of greatness . . . with love."
— J. Keith Miller, author of *The Secret Life of the Soul,*
The Taste of New Wine, and *Compelled to Control*

"I consider this book mandatory reading for anyone who has achieved career success but isn't fully satisfied with the result. Warner offers been-there-and-back insights along with a realistic path for seeking a more fulfilling life."
— Jimmy Calano, founder and former CEO of Career Track

"In reading *Aspirations of Greatness* I have revisited my struggles as a husband, father, lawyer, and businessman. The book affirms that, although the individual stories may vary, the American dream of success is totally empty without deep human and spiritual connection. The book will help every reader find that the joy of life ultimately comes from a surrender of self and communion with God."
— Mike Timmis, vice chairman of Talon LLC and
chairman of Prison Fellowship International

"An outstanding book on the soul of leadership. *Aspirations of Greatness* belongs on the must-read list of every executive."
— Mo Siegel, founder and CEO of Celestial Seasonings

"I wish I'd read *Aspirations of Greatness* thirty years ago when I was building my own 'tower' in the religious publishing world. Warner shows how executives, professionals, and people in ministry can wise up, face their blind spots, and avoid a personal train wreck. I highly recommend this book."
— Lyman Coleman, writer and publisher

"Jim's unique experience, compassion, brilliance and faith have led him to transform the lives of other high-powered executives, professionals and leaders who are seeking a new commitment and focus in their lives."

—Mrs. Kenneth W. Starr, Washington, D.C.

"Warner's insights into the confusion and challenges facing successful leaders are remarkable. The book has helped me step off the treadmill and begin to address the really important life questions that I've always known were there."

—John Heller, chairman and CEO
of Heller Seasonings and Ingredients, Inc.

"Beware! *Aspirations of Greatness* will challenge supposedly successful people who are tired of living on the surface. You may not agree with everything he says—I didn't—but I'll bet my house that you'll be stirred to pursue your own journey with greater intensity."

—Dan Webster, president of Authentic Leadership, Inc., and author
of *The Real Deal: Becoming More Authentic in Life and Leadership*

"Jim Warner's 'must read' book pierces through to the core of life transition issues and provides the navigation needed for true breakthrough possibilities!"

—Bill Jacobs, president of Bill Jacobs Automotive Group,
Chicago, Illinois

ASPIRATIONS OF GREATNESS

Mapping the Midlife Leader's Reconnection to Self and Soul

Jim Warner

JOHN WILEY & SONS, INC.

Published by John Wiley & Sons, Inc., New York
Published simultaneously in Canada.

Scripture taken from the *Holy Bible, New International Version®*. Copyright © 1973, 1978, 1984 by International Bible Society. Used by permission of Zondervan Publishing House. All rights reserved.

The "NIV" and "New International Version" trademarks are registered in the United States Patent and Trademark Office by International Bible Society. Use of either trademark requires the permission of the International Bible Society.

This publication is designed to provide accurate and authoritative information in regard to the subject matter covered. It is sold with the understanding that the publisher is not engaged in rendering professional services. If professional advice or other expert assistance is required, the services of a competent professional person should be sought.

Designations used by companies to distinguish their products are often claimed as trademarks. In all instances where the author or publisher is aware of a claim, the product names appear in Initial Capital letters. Readers, however, should contact the appropriate companies for more complete information regarding trademarks and registration.

Library of Congress Cataloging-in-Publication Data:

Warner, Jim, 1950–
    Aspirations of greatness: mapping the midlife leader's reconnection to self and soul/ Jim Warner
      p. cm.
    Includes index.
    ISBN 0-471-44398-0 (alk. paper)
    1. Leadership. 2. Leadership—Case studies. I. Title.
HD57.7 .W37 2001
658.4'092—dc21   2001036642

Printed in the United States of America.
10 9 8 7 6 5 4 3 2 1

In memory of my father, Robert Warner—
a great man.

CONTENTS

PREFACE

In 1992 I sold my once-thriving, then-struggling software business that I had founded 13 years earlier. As you'll see in my story, I was running on fumes, recovering from depression and ready for some rest, relaxation, and repotting. At first I was tempted to jump back into the race by buying or building a new company. The silent phone and empty pages in my daily planner reminded me of my vocational void, and how much my job had become intertwined with my identity. But after running at full throttle for 13 years, the time had come to examine both my engine and the racecourse—to look at my identity and mission.

At 43 years old I entered a wilderness period, seeking to rediscover lost passion and perhaps find a sense of destiny. I had been an extrovert my entire adult life, and this sabbatical period allowed my quiet, introverted, spiritual side to emerge for the first time. I wanted to find out who I was and what my life was for.

I took psychometric tests, attended "personal design" workshops, and immersed myself in self-discovery, be-all-that-you-can-be books. The real epiphanies came during group retreats, where I came face-to-face with both my giftedness and my dark side. These retreats allowed me to explore the uncharted terrain of my heart and emotions in a safe community of other wounded men and women. I made peace with my past, both reclaiming lost energy and reconnecting with God. Refreshed and alive after these retreats, I felt destined to help others reclaim their lives.

For three years after the sale of my company I coached entrepreneurs, family-business owners, executives, professionals, and ministers who were still in "the game," striving to find some blend of success and significance in their vocations and relationships. Usually we would meet over a meal to discuss a knotty business problem. Invariably, our conversation would turn to personal issues: a rebellious teen, a marriage in neutral, navigating a life without a compass, an internal emptiness. These executives had lots of friends, but few, if any, confidants with whom they could share their uncertainties and fears. I became a coach and confessor, someone who had walked in their shoes as a business owner and was willing to listen to their stories without judgment—without trying to "fix" them. With no therapist pedigree and no formal spiritual training, I became a counselor/minister-at-large.

During the last seven years of my business I had participated in and moderated Young Presidents' Organization forums—groups of six to a dozen company presidents who met monthly to discuss business and personal issues in a confidential setting. In 1994 three YPO friends who were familiar with my group work asked me to facilitate their annual three-day forum retreat. As we explored their deep-seated personal issues, I sensed that these high-profile leaders yearned for a safe place to put down their masks and open their souls. Fortunately, that's exactly what I was able to provide. They shared their stories of disillusionment and dilemmas, and I facilitated interaction, feedback, and accountability. They got closer as a group and many had personal breakthroughs on how to reinvigorate either their careers or their marriages.

Within six months, thanks to word-of-mouth referrals, I was vocationally regenerated as a "midlife transitions consultant," "personal coach," and "retreat facilitator." Far different from the boardrooms, bank meetings, and contract negotiations of my days as a company president, I attended training sessions in group dynamics, shadow psychology, and family systems. With my own self-exploration so fresh at hand, I was eager to be a catalyst for others—like opening a restaurant because I liked to eat. After my three-year sabbatical, I had replanted myself in a totally different role—and I loved it.

In the years since then, I have led many intimate executive retreats and transition seminars, hearing the stories of more than five hundred CEOs, executives, professionals, ministers, and spouses in midlife (ages 35 to 60). Causal patterns began to emerge among these leaders enduring vocational, marital, financial, relational, and spiritual angst, and also paths for them out of the desert into a life of passion, fulfillment, connection, and peace. The urge to write about these patterns and paths led to this book.

This book tracks the stories of seven successful midlife leaders, as well as my own story—case studies of successful men and women facing difficult transitional and personal issues, who want a deeper engagement with life, with others, with themselves, and with God. The stories of the seven protagonists have been masked to protect their identities, while maintaining the essence of their life journeys. Several other characters are interwoven throughout the book. Their vignettes capture the common issues of men and women in midlife malaise. If you think one of them is you, on a surface, conscious level you're wrong, but at a deeper, subconscious level, you're probably right.

The four parts of the book follow a natural progression, and the latter sections build on the stories, research models, and examples presented in prior sections. Nonetheless, recognizing that many readers choose a path through a book based on their reading style and interests, consider the following reading order options. If you engage with the stories of others, start with Part I, which profiles the primary protagonists. If you like to review the research, you might begin with Part II, which presents the causal patterns of people in midlife malaise. If you prefer to read about underlying concepts, you might skip to Part III, which presents several models for understanding how these patterns develop. If your primary interest is tools and solutions, read Part IV first, which outlines specific action steps for reconnecting with yourself, with others, and with God. Regardless of your standard approach, I encourage you to at least read the Introduction, which provides a quick sketch of the entire book.

Ninety percent of the participants in my retreat and coaching work are men. The split between male and female protagonists and vignettes follows this percentage, and, for consistency and easier reading, I've used the male pronouns when referring to individual characters. However, the patterns, models, examples, transformational tools, and conclusions apply to both men and women.

In summary, the main message of this book is:

> If your life is not working,
>   and you want a truthful, loving, full life—
>   you are not alone.
>   A path exists.
>   The path is difficult.
>   Here is the map.
>   Start the journey, now.

ACKNOWLEDGMENTS

Many other pilgrims and guides accompanied me during the nine-year journey that led to the birth of this book. I am grateful to:

> ➤ The five hundred YPOers, WPOers, TEC members, professionals, and spouses whose personal stories provided the primary spark for this book.
> ➤ My "Inspiration Team," the men and women who encouraged me during the conception and birthing of this book: Jimmy Calano, Delynn Copley, Father David Denny, Jim Dethmer, Keith Fairmont, Mark Gerzon, Jim Kochalka, Father Richard Rohr, Jeff Salzman, Bob Sloan, and Dan Webster.
> ➤ The facilitators, guides, and transition zealots who have dedicated much of their life to this work: Cliff Barry, Mary Ellen Blandford, Jude Blitz, Tom Daly, Jeffrey Duvall, Bill Evans, Brian Gast, Reneé Kauffman, Rachael Kessler, Frieder and Pernille Krups, Jan Lightfoot, Ann Marks, Kevin McHugh, Ashok and Manju Melwani, Steve Mountjoy, Tom Pitner, Dan Raker, Gary Sanfacon, Jeffrey and Cindy Ullman.
> ➤ My personal advisory board, small group accountability partners, and life mentors: Dave Bloom, Dan Bowdey, Edson Bueno, Bob Buford, Rich Case, Doug Coe, Duane Hermanson, Robert

Kulhawy, Scott Lynn, Paul Oerter, Brendan O'Reilly, Mike Regan, Michael Romano, Beat Steiner, David Turner, Bill Warner, and Jack Willome.

➤ Loma Huh, for her outstanding editorial teamwork on many, many drafts, and her soul-level belief in my vision for this book.

➤ Kaley Warner, for her careful transcription, insightful suggestions, and unwavering support from inception to publication.

➤ Rajan Kose, for his creative genius and professional graphics.

➤ Mike Hamilton, for championing this book within Wiley.

➤ Linda Indig, for overseeing the project at Wiley, with the help of Cape Cod Compositors.

➤ The other members of my production and review team: Henry Poirot and John Thompson.

➤ My family, who encouraged me during those long nights at the keyboard: Judy Wells Warner, Courtney Warner, and Paul Warner.

➤ The protagonists, who graciously agreed to lengthy interviews and review cycles and whose candid stories form the fabric of the book: You know who you are.

INTRODUCTION

Six men and one woman sit in a circle of lounge chairs on the deck of a hillside Caribbean villa. The sea breeze is soothing and the views of the nearby harbor are majestic. These three company presidents, two former chief executives, a prominent physician, and a minister are entering the third day of a life transition retreat, sharing their stories, issues, and wounds, interwoven with their dreams for a fulfilling, passion-filled life. The cell phones have been off for two days, and the conversation ranges from fearful to angry to hopeful.

Peter, 48, is the czar of an 87-year-old family distribution company. His father died three months ago, and the reins have fallen into Peter's ambivalent hands. Unmotivated financially—he amassed his "I don't need to work anymore" money years ago—Peter labors to maintain the oft-tainted family legacy. The business is in cruise control, like Peter's life. After 26 years in the company he longs for a vocational overhaul, but what would he do? The business is all he has ever known. And as he's the glue of the company, his departure would almost surely lead to a gradual but relentless decline in sales, morale, and return to the remaining shareholders—his uncles and

1

cousins, who, like Peter, have been at the company their entire working lives. Like Peter, it's all they know.

Peter reflects on his early 20s—his love for teaching and history, his competitive fire in golf, and the adventure of international travel. He then snaps back to the boredom in his life today. Pegged from birth to run this business, if he leaves now, he will defame the image of his father and betray his relatives. Now he's the patriarch; he's responsible.

Marty is associate pastor at a suburban megachurch, where he oversees the lay ministry. A gifted communicator and counselor, he has breathed intimacy and relevant teaching into a comatose congregation, launched a vibrant contemporary service, and now coaches 100 small-group leaders in the dynamics of community building by living the Word of God.

While Marty sees the life changes spawned in his ministry, he's bored and longs for more pulpit time. His leadership and creative skills, honed over 15 years working with teen groups, are now dormant as he endures pointless staff meetings, classroom juggling, and capital fund drives for the new sanctuary. But his salary is steady, and he's more secure than five years ago when the funding for his paraministry dried up, leaving him on the street with no money and two young children. His wife regularly reminds him of this.

At 42, Marty yearns to marry the reckless, attack-the-world attitude of his juvenile delinquent youth with the street-level preaching, leadership skills, and love for Jesus that he has developed over the past 20 years. While he has the vision, it's a big risk to start a new church. It will further strain his already fragile marriage and will almost certainly engender bad blood with this church's leadership. But something's got to change. This isn't working.

Thad is on the sidelines—again—this time of his own choosing. He's just finished a three-year turnaround assignment with a second-tier regional insurance firm, where he was the hired-gun president trying to save a family business gone awry. The company's chairman and great-grandson of the founder refused Thad's requests for stock options and overruled his plans for much-needed plant expansion and modernization, opting for higher cash flow and return to stockholders. Thad wanted to grow the business; the owners wanted to milk it. He spent most of the last year creating his own exit, but would have willingly left without a severance package—that's how frustrating the job had become.

Now 40, Thad has invested the past 14 years bailing out institutional investors, nursing silver-spoon family-business heirs, and making other guys rich. While he's accumulated a reasonable nest egg, he's always been the professional manager, never the owner.

Thad has the rare combination of deal wizardry and a motivational management style that make him the ideal executive team player. But now he wants to form and coach his own team. The money doesn't really matter, nor the time commitment—he has vast reservoirs of untapped energy, and he and Rachael are childless, though not by choice.

Thad loves to be the guy out front. He got his first taste of the spotlight as writer, producer, director, and star of the graduate school follies. In later assignments he inspired his staff at quarterly all-company meetings and held court at industry conclaves with his quick wit and repertoire of stories. But his relational gifts have been shelved during the past three years of dismantling and asset sheltering.

With over two years' worth of cash tucked away, he doesn't have to take the next job offer. He feels blessed that Rachael wants him to rediscover his passion in whatever time it takes. But a wary voice in Thad's head keeps resonating, "Get a secure job as a professional manager. You're good at this. It's what you know. It's *all* you know. Play it safe."

Larry identifies with the gulls circling overhead—his life is in a holding pattern. He has the office on the 36th floor, the panoramic view of the city, all the trappings, but no sense of purpose. He has paid his dues over the past 26 years as a gofer, manager, entrepreneur, sales and marketing wizard, and visionary in the eclectic blend of information services and real estate. Now, after a horrific divorce from his land development partners and its lingering bad blood, he ruminates about his destiny. He was wooed to his current job—business development vice president for a corporate intrapreneurship—a few short months after the split from his partners. He'd had some cash, but not enough to start his own firm, and a bird in the hand was better than. . . . So he jumped, similar to the knee-jerk way he took his first job as a programmer right out of engineering college.

Larry's life has been a tapestry of spontaneous "Sure, why not?" decisions. Inevitably each time the champagne went flat, he stayed too long and exited with acrimony. But now, at least, he is *seeing* the pattern. A quick study and corporately astute, he could ride this current meal ticket indefinitely, comfortably covering his family's cash burn rate. But his inner voice is calling him to pursue a sense of life purpose beyond the financial rewards and perks. He recalls his love for teaching, children, and sports, and wonders if some undiscovered calling awaits him that blends his giftedness in these areas. Larry's wife is supportive and would welcome both a downsizing of their lifestyle and more of Larry's time for her and their two teens.

He again follows the gulls in their circling pattern, hoping to see one break ranks and follow its own course.

For two days the men have been on eggshells around Susan. This woman is angry!—and exhausted and fragile. Her practice as a neurologist is booming. She speaks often at conferences, sits on local nonprofit boards, and reads bedtime stories to her three young children in her meager spare time. Her husband, who has been duped by both family members and an unscrupulous partner in two prior business ventures, looks for new opportunities while siphoning her hefty income to pay litigation expenses. But, no matter how glamorous her specialty, medicine is a piecework business, and if she doesn't practice they don't have income.

Most galling has been the strain with both her husband and in-laws. Communication is at a standstill with her husband, who closes down or escapes to the golf course when she confronts him about actively resuming his career, or at least standing up to his father and brothers. Her in-laws view her as the pariah who wooed away their number-one son and should be home with her children.

With no local support community, a reclusive husband, and ever-mounting responsibilities, her life is unraveling. And beneath all of this she yearns to tend her neglected flower beds, curl up with the great literature she escaped into as a child, and just hang out with her kids. In these three days with seven other leaders navigating treacherous midlife waters, it's no wonder her anger, sadness, and helplessness have begun to seep out and then overflow. She needs help, fast.

Stan's divorce, his second, is now final. He has come to the Caribbean to clear his head and ponder what might be next. The divorce was ugly and crippled him financially. The last three years of her bitterness, verbal abuse, and spending sprees have taken a huge toll on his energy and self-worth.

As a seasoned business strategist who has invested his career in reading symptoms, offering diagnoses, and rendering care to ailing businesses, why wasn't he able to apply the same approach to his marriage? How did marital Act II become a replay of Act I?

Perhaps it was his immersion in his company's growth, or slogging through, with due diligence, its sale to a larger competitor. Maybe it was the two-year earn-out period where he was the mediator, working 80-hour weeks trying to merge disparate cultures in a way that both satisfied their customers and returned a profit to the parent company.

Stan has always immersed himself in his work. He learned it from his dad, a giant of a leader and man who, in Stan's eyes, was the model executive, community figure, and father. Since his dad's death 16 years ago, Stan has felt driven to succeed but personally rudderless. He longs for his father's counsel now as he tries to piece his empty life back together.

Along with the lack of relationships, Stan is adrift vocationally. He dabbles in some investments and is operationally involved in a couple of start-ups, but he has little zest for his work. Despite the divorce settlement he could coast financially for at least a few years, so he can focus on a strategy for his "second half." Yet his whole life has been driven by "focus." For once, maybe he is being called to let go.

For the first two days of this retreat, Fletcher suppressed his welling frustration at the neediness of the others. "Why can't these people just suck it up and get a life?" he stewed. The consummate entrepreneur-competitor, he has grown his one-van office equipment installation and maintenance business into the premier service and supply network in the region, with $12 million in annual sales and healthy profitability. As 100 percent owner of his Subchapter S corporation, he takes home over $1 million annually.

Fletcher's life is almost perfect. He vacations around the world, flies his own plane, and has his pick of women. The company has healthy cash flow and ready buyers in the wings the moment he chooses to sell. At 38 and single, he can hardly ask for more, except perhaps a serious, not-just-for-sex relationship. But as he hears the marriage-collapse story of Stan, and the relational influenza of the others, why would he want to screw up a good thing?

Yet his defenses have begun to dissolve over the past two days. He is beginning to notice glimmers of his own hedonism and selfishness, which disgust him. An inner voice counters with conscience-soothing stories of his employee education programs and profit sharing, his low turnover and employee loyalty. "C'mon, you're benevolent and charitable; you give a lot to your people. They love you. You deserve to take care of yourself a little bit, too. You've earned it!" But now Fletcher yearns for intimate connection—to give and receive love.

The openness of the discussion also highlights the spiritual void in his life. He checked out on religion long ago, but he longs for a sense of peace and blessing without having to control everything. In the safety of the group he finds himself receptive to the "God stuff."

This is new territory for Fletcher, another new adventure. And for once he can't predict the outcome. He's not in control—and he's scared.

Over the past five years I have heard the life stories and vocational, relational, personal, and spiritual malaise of over five hundred company presidents, corporate executives, professionals, entrepreneurs, family business owners, and ministry leaders. These seven vignettes typify the angst and disillusionment of midlife leaders who at first glance seem to have it all, but are actually yearning for connection, peace, purpose, and "aliveness." Their lives aren't working, and they are open to change.

Most of my research has come from 60 intensive, multiday retreats with chief executive officers (CEOs) and their spouses, which I facilitated over a five-year span. Prior to a retreat, each participant completes "homework" that asks direct questions about the individual's personal, vocational, marital, relational, and spiritual issues. A summary of these leaders' most pressing issues is reproduced in Appendix A. Each participant is then interviewed confidentially about his or her life story and the concern areas identified in the homework. Often in the telephone interviews, these leaders express their confusion, anger, uncertainty, yearnings, and loneliness, highlighting their desperate need to connect, to confess, to be in community, and to be seen.

Most of these CEOs and spouses have never been in a safe environment for telling their stories and sharing their fears. Because of this, we typically invest the first day of each retreat in trust-building exercises, where the participants can experiment in taking down their masks and discover that they will not be judged or shamed by either the retreat leaders or the other participants. Often the emotional dam will burst for one individual who shares past betrayals or shaming and the current wounds that inhibit his or her relationships and dampen vocational passion. Over the course of the retreat the men and women begin to bond and the personal stories begin to flow.

Does Anybody See Me?

As the research base has grown, the patterns of disillusionment and unease among these leaders have begun to crystallize. Perhaps most prominent is their inherent loneliness. Most of these leaders are visible, powerful, successful men and women. They have the stature, twinkle in the eye, or charisma to capture and hold an audience or to be the life of the party. They live in glass houses and know how to dress the part while on display. Yet the recognition, affirmation, and adulation hold them hostage in isolation. Although they are recognized and followed by others, few feel genuinely acknowledged. Often, not even their spouses really know them.

Most believe they are approved of only when they perform and succeed, creating a perception of conditional acceptance by those around them—and by themselves. They fear, "If I don't deliver, I'll be rejected." They take pains to avoid or rationalize failure, and because their worth seems tied to excellence of performance, they are terrified of being ordinary.

Most carry deep wounds of insecurity. They long to share their vulnerabilities and fears with contemporaries without being judged or ostracized. In a word, they seek *friends*. Seasoned business, professional, or ministry veterans, they are rookies at cultivating relationships. They are comfortable in business, intellectual, recreational, and social milieus, and perhaps in mentoring others, but not in sharing their own anxieties, wounds, and dreams. They'll receive counsel from hired advisors, including attorneys, board members, and church elders, but they have no one to guide and befriend them during bouts of depression and loneliness.

I'm both surprised and saddened by the rampant low self-esteem among these corporate chieftains. Many mask their loneliness and yearning to connect behind a facade of wealth and notoriety. They are gracious, convivial, even stately when greeted, but underneath their aura of gentility and power, many, if not most, are clueless about their identity, their value without their trappings, and their worthiness to be leaders.

Few of these friendless men and women have felt love freely given in their lives. Almost all affirmations in their lives have had a price tag—an "if." If you get good grades, you'll get a car. If you make the varsity, we'll attend your games. If you make your sales target, you'll get promoted. Early in life many of these hard-charging executives, like Fletcher, were thrust into roles of responsibility, either in support of their families or, literally, to survive.

Constant activity, both within their businesses and through community or charitable affiliations, feeds their need for recognition. Driven to set aggressive targets, they take little time to bask in their accomplishments, always setting the target higher. And rather than face the erosion in their lives outside of work, they simply immerse themselves in new whirlwinds of vocational activity. While they complain about living life on a treadmill and about excessive demands on their time, few consider solitude or reflection time a high priority. They claim to be happy most of the time, but their eyes express a longing for connection with other hearts, beyond the realm of power lunches and industry receptions.

Where Am I Going?

Though viewed as successful by their peers, community, and, occasionally, their families, few of these leaders have a clear sense of life purpose or destiny. For 20, 30, even 40 years, these executives have invested in expanding their careers and maintaining control of their lives. As Richard Rohr says, they've been "building their towers."[1] Most have succeeded far beyond the dreams of their 20s, yet there is an aching hollowness to their success.

They have wealth, notoriety, and power. However, most confess to having little sense of mission, direction, or significance in their lives outside their businesses, professions, or ministries. To describe what eludes them, they use words like *destiny*, *fulfillment*, *passion*, *legacy*, and *connection*—something beyond the wealth and recognition they've already achieved.

Over 50 percent feel they have untapped or underutilized talent. But to explore these skills or to risk a totally different adventure might diminish or defuse their career trajectory. So they smother their artistic, teaching, musical, mentoring, or craftsmanship talents, choosing instead to push forward at full throttle in their careers.

How Much Money Is Enough?

Fully 70 percent of these leaders are driven to achieve a level of financial security that covers their lifetime needs so they won't have to work for an income or depend on others for support. The "enough" in the question "How much is enough?" ranges from $1 million to $100 million and, in most cases, "30 to 70 percent more than I have right now."

Most senior executives and professionals, especially those in their 40s and 50s, have far exceeded the net worth targets that they set 10 or 20 years previously, even when adjusted for inflation. Over the course of their careers they have repeatedly ratcheted their financial expectations higher, keeping with the 30 to 70 percent axiom. Yet most derive little fulfillment from their substantial possessions. They speak with hollow pride about the expensive new boat or the vacation abroad, often drawing comparisons with, and expressing envy for, their peers' toys. This questing and comparison dulls any memory of the contentment they might have had in their earlier years, when they had little money but a lot more happiness.

The interviewed executives are strafed in the crossfire of two overlapping fears: "I won't have enough money" and "I'll lose the money I have." These fears are most evident among those leaders who were raised in either dysfunctional or financially strapped home environments. They believe financial independence will distance them from the pain, obscurity or abuse of their youth. So, at an early age, they equate wealth with self-worth: "The more I have, the more I'm accepted and the better person I am." As their net worth expands, so do their lifestyles and the associated expectations of their peer groups, until what was originally escape from dysfunction or poverty turns into hubris and an insatiable lust for more.

Where Did the Love Go?

As evidenced by Stan's vignette, flat marriages or even divorces are prevalent among midlife leaders. Occasionally money is the reason. Caught up in the myth that more is better, the spouse drives the executive breadwinner toward an ever-escalating lifestyle until debt or other pressures burst the marriage.

More often, the spouse supports the executive during the career-building years, focusing on stability at home. In the dual-career family, like Susan and her husband, lives are run out of a common Day-Timer with the sterility of paying bills out of a common checkbook. The children are elements in a rotating schedule of day-care management, car shuttles, and it's-your-turn-to-go-to-the-soccer-game. Heaven help us if one of them gets sick.

The seeds of divorce are all too common. The executive invests his or her entire life in career pursuits and has little energy left for the marriage or family. Any free time goes to kids' events or obligatory entertainment. The executive views the home as a subsidiary: Time with the spouse (subsidiary manager) focuses on home to-do lists (operations), vacation planning (strategy), or the next major lifestyle purchase (capital expansion). After courtship and perhaps the early years of marriage, the couple have lost the ability to communicate from the heart. Sexual activity becomes a weekly, monthly, or less frequent occurrence with little romance.

Unspoken friction arises between the husband and wife. Fed by the recognition and perks at work, the executive schedules more road time or hunkers down in the office rather than absorb the verbal assaults or cold shoulder at home. The first affair, by either party, might lead to a flood of tears, pleas for forgiveness, and extended marital counseling. But the wounds are rarely cleaned out fully, and the patterns reemerge. After one last shot at reconciliation, the lawyers are called in, launching a lengthy gauntlet of lose-lose hell.

While divorce is painful, at least a decision has been made and the parties can get on with their lives. Of equal and often greater pain are the marriages where the executives work hard to lead balanced lives, seeking the best for both their marriages and their vocations. Career growth is desired, but not at the sacrifice of the family. A simpler lifestyle is accepted. However, except for the shrewd investor or trust-funder, these executives don't have early-retirement options; they have to work. It is a rare entrepreneur with exceptional boundaries who can maintain a balanced, healthy family life while leading a profitable, growing business. And for executives in corporate environments, devotion to family and marriage marks them as nonclimbers, and they become expendable by their companies during hard times.

Where Is God?

Nearly all the leaders over 40 that I've interviewed hear a small inner voice asking, "What's it all about?" These men and women seek a safe harbor, a place where they don't have to perform to know that they are approved or accepted. Beyond simple recognition, they hunger for a spiritual connection. Sadly, many speak of the impersonal or judgmental religious experiences they had as children. They bemoan the forced memorizations and tedious, irrelevant services. Having scorned the duplicity of parents, elders, and clergy who didn't walk their talk, when the first opportunity came—

usually in college—many shelved their spirituality and checked out of any organized religion. After that, the idols of career advancement and financial security often numbed any spiritual yearnings. Belief in a Higher Power was for the weak. They chose control.

Later—usually in midlife—a relational heartbreak, the death of a loved one, a divorce, or, as with Fletcher, an emerging sense that more money and women are not the answer, reopens a longing for connection and intimacy—a sense of some unconditionally loving Power, both beyond and within themselves. Some return to the religious traditions of their youth with a new maturity that allows them to reconnect. Others, still leery of the judgments and duplicity, avoid organized religion and seek community in recovery groups or awareness movements.

They desire to address an emptiness that possessions, accomplishments, and shallow relationships can't fill. They're looking for a "primary loyalty" in their lives—a place where they can be innocent, childlike, forgiven, and blessed.

This book is about the midlife leader's journey toward *aliveness*—a connection with self, others, God, and reality; a paradoxical sense of total, loving support while accepting our utter powerlessness; an unobstructed flow of energy through our beings, grounded in surrender to a Higher Power, fueled by a clear life purpose, and manifested to the world through loving service.

I emphasize and will often repeat this mantra of *aliveness*, because my research indicates that most apparently successful executives and leaders are "dead men walking." While the research comes from the stories of leaders, including eight primary protagonists profiled in Part I (Chapters 1 through 8), the principles apply to anyone who has lost his or her internal compass and feels lost, confused, lonely, or unloved. They long to feel good again, to feel whole.

The first stage of the journey is the realization that "My life isn't working." It often starts as a creeping doubt: "I'm devoted to a cause (career advancement, a happy family, wealth accumulation, winning souls, planetary restoration, a free world, pleasing God), and diligent in my efforts, but *something is not working*." For most leaders the disappointment boils down to "If I'm so successful, why do I feel so unfulfilled?" After 20 to 40 years of commitment and focus, these midlife nomads are often gridlocked within a litany of woes:

> ➤ I'm not using my true talents.
> ➤ I have no goals with real meaning or significance.
> ➤ I don't know where I'm going, but if I stop now I'll be a failure.
> ➤ All my preparation and training are for nothing.
> ➤ I follow all the rules and traditions of my religion, but I don't feel close to God.
> ➤ Other people view me as successful, but I don't feel my life has any significance or fulfillment.
> ➤ I feel like I'm living a lie.
> ➤ I don't know what to do with my life.

Rather than address the fears behind these issues, most disillusioned achievers either ignore the voices of discontent or deny the visual symptoms of malaise (lackluster marriage, deteriorating health), and retreat to the familiarity of their current situation. They rationalize: "It's not so bad here. I just need to try/study/work/pray harder."

Over time, as the breakdowns increase in intensity and no action is taken to face the reality of a life gone awry, the midlife wayfarer slips into one or more eddies. The most common path is to "defeat" the fears by diversions and escapes. Rationalizing that "My life is so miserable, I'll just keep sampling other 'lives' until I find one that works," the person becomes a dilettante, flitting from one vocation, relationship, or source of temporary pleasure to another, trying to stay a step ahead of the meaninglessness demon. Others escape into their work or divert themselves with hubris, hedonism, or their addiction du jour (alcohol, food, sex).

Eventually most of these escape artists, no matter how cunning, become haunted by an inner voice that screams, *"Wake up! This isn't working!"*—and they go numb. Somewhere in their being they grab this voice by the neck and exclaim, "I know this isn't working! I see that! But I don't know any other way! So I'll pretend I'm okay and continue with my current patterns and lifestyle. Yes, inner voice of discontent, I hear you—and I choose to ignore you."

And that's the day they die. They may physically take in breaths and plod around the planet a few more years, but their soul-level life-support systems are disconnected. Their outward satisfaction and confidence swathe, like a shroud, their inner unworthiness and desperation. They drift from coma, where at least there is a spiritual pulse, into the void of the living dead.

Another route out of denial, escape, and diversion is explosion, when outside forces (the seemingly out-of-the-blue divorce, a major health wake-up call, the death of a child, bankruptcy) thrust the person back to the *Wake up!* edge. Often, such a personal train wreck is the only way back into the world of the spiritually alive. It's like affixing those huge electrodes to the chest of a person whose heart has stopped and turning on the juice. That's why many alcoholics say that acknowledging their alcoholism is the greatest gift they ever received.

Part II (Chapters 9 through 12) expands on these midlife meltdowns, examining the commitment, disillusionment, confusion, and breakdown periods of the eight protagonists and other midlife leaders, and how they muster the courage to face and deal with their pain.

Part III (Chapters 13 through 19) introduces several models and metaphors for mapping the soul, offering glimpses into the labyrinth of the subconscious. Aliveness pilgrims begin to learn about the psychology, patterns, archetypes, and energy drains of *why* they feel so bad. The soul is presented as an endless maze of wounds and disowned parts, while simultaneously a vault of precious jewels: latent creativity and innocence, healthy sexuality, a life purpose, and a sense of destiny. Interspersed with the brittle shale of the wounds is the priceless gold of life.

Part IV (Chapters 20 through 22) describes the actions, antidotes, amplifiers, affinities, and attitudes that underlie aliveness and greatness. Beyond understanding the soul, earnest truth seekers must enter the dark, uncharted mines of their inner selves. In virtually all of my experiential work with men and women who pierce the darkness and encounter their disowned selves, they find a lonely child who longs to be safe, seen, held, and loved without judgment or condemnation. When this can occur at a visceral, even cellular level, the miracle of transformation and healing can begin. Chapter 20 describes the inner work process to excavate, encounter, and transform our shadows, along with specific action steps for reclaiming lost energy.

The transformed tunneler recognizes and accepts his powerlessness. He surrenders *all* of himself—the light and the dark, the conscious and the subconscious, the known and the disowned, his soul and spirit—to a Higher Power. He allows himself to receive grace—the unmerited love of God—and accepts that "all is as it is meant to be." He acknowledges the complexity of the world while living a simple life, grounded in gratitude, forgiveness, and compassion.

Chapter 21 expands on this place of surrender and gratitude, and offers strategies and tactics for addressing and overcoming the five primary midlife struggles: identity and purpose, money and materialism, balance and boundaries, marriage and family relationships, spiritual connection.

Chapter 22 explains how our true greatness emerges from the use of our innate giftedness—our genius—in loving service to others. Yet aliveness and true genius are often antithetical to the world's agenda. To be selfless and welcome reality often isolates us from others and begets aloneness. The faithful steward often serves anonymously. The cause supersedes comfort, recognition, and approval. The only way to stay in the fire of genius is through surrender of ego, embracing the mind-heart-soul mantra of "It's not about me. Thy will be done." In so doing we allow the spirit of peace to flow upward and outward through us, as we live out the genius ordained for our lives. Having navigated the downward and inward tunneling, and bathing in an oasis of grace, we can find joy in the light and be patient, hopeful, and alert in the dark.

Our world is hungry for people who demonstrate deep, genuine commitment to "the good of the realm" rather than to personal power, wealth, recognition, or success. The finest leadership exemplifies this type of commitment, which is rare among Western culture men and women who avoid soul-level exploration. It is my hope that through the models, examples, and stories in this book, more leaders will open themselves to the journey toward greatness and let their lives become nourishment for a starving world.

I

The FELLOWSHIP
of the BROKEN

1

The AUTHOR'S
RISE and FALL

I was the youngest of three children in a quiet, respectful home in south-west Michigan. Dad was a forty-year accountant in the hometown manu-facturing firm. My mother, a well-educated, intense, highly capable woman—born 40 years too soon—was a housewife. My siblings were seven and nine years older and left home right after high school. We had little contact with extended family.

Blessed with my mother's mind and athleticism, I excelled in acade-mics and sports. I also inherited her drive and will to succeed, gifts she was never allowed to develop and use. Raised in rural poverty, she escaped at age 16 to enter college, where she earned her teaching degree. But in the late 1920s she was trapped again, in society's discounting of women.

As a male growing up in the 1950s, I had few such constraints. I dom-inated my studies, made the all-star teams, and became an Eagle Scout. I had inherited my father's diplomacy and relational gifts, and was equally comfortable noodling with the brainy kids or hanging with the jocks. While seeking the limelight in accomplishments—scouting, academics, and athletics—I relaxed into a sidekick role with childhood friends, and few were allowed into the recesses of my heart.

Although gifted with mental acuity, physical strength, and relational adeptness, I abhorred confrontation. A smooth communicator and big for my age, I adopted a chameleon-like behavior, buddying with the school bullies while teasing or ridiculing less gifted classmates. In those years I had the mind, muscles, and presence of a leader, but lacked mature integrity.

Religious education and church attendance were central in our family life. Transferring from the local public school to the Catholic school in fifth grade, I became enthralled with the mystery and ritual of religious traditions. God was a Wizard of Oz presence, powerful and demanding, and if I played by the rules, He might even be loving. The members of the religious orders (brothers and nuns) were God's emissaries and gatekeepers, berating, filtering, and occasionally encouraging the unwashed, like me, so we might measure up to God's high standards.

Despite the flaws in the transmission, the presence and awe of God was conveyed to me. Sometimes in church I would imagine myself sitting in the lap of Jesus, and feel a flood of peace through my body. This feeling, even though it became very small at times, has never left me.

I learned how to appease people in authority, so I was rarely scolded or ridiculed, but I saw how my classmates were shamed for their curiosity, spontaneity, and creativity—for just being kids. Eventually, either the rebel in them ran wild and they were expelled or they were broken by the system and went numb. I felt sad watching the life being snuffed out of many of my friends—and I never wanted that to happen to me. So I suppressed my mischievous, exploratory side and did the authority-figure dance.

My parents encouraged and honored my activities. Whether I was learning chess or building a sailboat, my father, a wise and gentle man who didn't need center stage, always let me do it myself. This bred in me a deep self-confidence and independence that would carry me through my mid-30s.

While this quiet teaching from my father fueled my self-worth, I had no role models for relationships with girls. As a testosterone-filled adolescent, I perceived my parents as leading bland, antiseptic lives, and I wanted more. As a result, high school girls became targets for sexual exploration and exploitation. I would lure relationally starved girls into the backseat of the Chevy and pretend to be masculine.

My Depression-era parents' frugality had been instilled in me, and although I never worried about money, I was always aware of it. I had to find the best deal, and I negotiated everything. I was also influenced by my father's work ethic and had jobs from an early age. Paper routes, lawn mowing, and busboy jobs provided plenty of money for gas, dates, and independence throughout my school years.

Itching to escape from the small-town parochial-school environment, I immersed myself in the college scene—fraternity, girls, bars, sports. Surrounded by bright, worldly classmates, I ratcheted up my commitment level and excelled in computer science courses and intramural sports. I expanded my double life as the math whiz by day and jock/pub crawler by night and on weekends.

I loved computers. Unbeknownst to my athlete friends, I spent hours holed up in the computer lab creating and debugging complex programs. I found myself "in the zone," losing track of time as I wrote and tuned labyrinths of computer code that eventually yielded the right answer. Yet on short notice I could be shooting hoops or pounding down beers at the local bar with friends who didn't know a punch card from a punch bowl. I loved this diversity.

Girls were a new competitive playing field. Relational batting practice in high school evolved into scoring and "sport sex" with the current conquest in college. Falling in love my junior year led to my first taste of emotional intimacy, even the glimmers of a spiritual connection—but I wasn't ready. Over a series of months, Eros trampled Agape as she devolved into yet another pleasure target. Eventually she saw my shallow intentions and dumped me.

At 23 I fell in love for real. I saw in Judy the indefatigable spirit and insight of my mother interwoven with the compassion, relational depth, and steadiness of my father. An insightful, winsome woman, she made it safe for me to go beyond physical and emotional intensity into that place of Spirit I had hidden, out of fear of rejection, from all the others. She loved me for more than my brains and body, and called me on "my stuff." I felt free. Judy wisely and gently rejected my immature marriage proposal at the three-month mark of our courtship. Three years later she gave me the "marry me or move on" ultimatum as I was starting to slip back into my old selfish patterns. We just celebrated our silver wedding anniversary.

After college I entered my work life with a sense of confidence and invincibility. My strong academic credentials and connections led me to a plum programming job at a Colorado university. Ever the manipulator, I finessed my work assignments so they could be completed in only a few hours a week. During the remaining work hours I immersed myself in the then-emerging technology of computer graphics, developing complex yet practical programs to render images on an electronic canvas.

After six years in this academic-technology cocoon, my playground for exploration and creativity had become predictable and boring. Many of my colleagues had left to join fledgling high-tech firms and were becoming wealthy through their stock options. The time seemed right for a new adventure. So, with a hastily sketched business plan, an infant daughter, a newly retired-to-stay-home-with-the-baby wife, and a modest grubstake borrowed from my father, I became an entrepreneur.

It was perfect timing. The software company was profitable within six months and doubled in size for seven consecutive years, reaching $20 million in sales. Tapping my father's relational skills, I maintained a "family" culture as the company expanded to two hundred employees, three management layers, and several domestic and international sales offices. I was a winner yet again, enjoying a leadership position in a high-profile niche of the swashbuckling software industry, loyal customers, and a young, vibrant corps of employees. I reveled in the recognition, being courted by investment bankers and touted as a technology wizard in a hot market segment.

Nonetheless, at 37 I was still only a few years removed from my sheltered years in academia. I needed guidance and a new set of skills for business, so I wooed an outside board of directors and attended the Harvard Business School's Owner-President Management Program—"entrepreneur charm school"—with 120 other small-company presidents. I discovered I was just as smart as they were, and over a four-year span transitioned from technical founder to salesman and marketer, and finally to general manager and chief executive.

Then the hard times hit. Enamored with my transition from programmer to executive, I abdicated research on our customers' evolving product needs to a zealous but inexperienced development group. As a result, misdirected R&D efforts ravaged our balance sheet, yielding disappointing or stillborn products.

As sales flattened and profit went negative, I sensed it was time to get out and retained a merger and acquisitions broker who specialized in our industry. Enticed by the heady price/earning multiples other boutique technology companies generated, and blinded by my greed, we overpriced the company, resulting in few lookers and no serious offers. With no new products, revenue declined and cash tightened, leading to several rounds of layoffs. My once-hot company was now yesterday's news and slipping fast. Valued members of the employee "family" were leaving for greener, more dependable pastures. There was no choice but to enter a period of grim retrenchment and a desperate search for an exit—any exit.

On the personal side, endless weeks on the road had drained my once-bottomless energy and threatened both my marriage and my relationship with our three young children. Beneath the daily "game face" that I put on for employees and customers, my emotional and physical health were shot. At night I would be jolted awake at 3:00 A.M. by nightmares about mass resignations, gestapo-like bank meetings, or outright bankruptcy. I went into weekly therapy and took medication for depression. I felt like I was in a downward-spiraling whirlpool that was sucking the life out of me.

The rudest awakening came from a savvy board member and friend who told me, "If you didn't own more than half the stock, we'd fire you." My job environment had turned from sandbox to cesspool. People told me that turnaround artists *love* this challenge—but I was a builder and I hated it. For me, the thrill was gone, and I wanted out!

2

The BETRAYED EXECUTIVE

Thad's grandparents owned every kid's dream: a dime store with a candy counter. As the first grandchild, he was the apple of their eye who could do no wrong. He loved receiving their trinket gifts and being the center of attention at family gatherings. The cloister and ethnic traditions of his neighborhood led him to believe that all white people were Jewish. He lived a blissful childhood.

Thad's blue-collar father was in the throes of building his own business, and the family moved to a suburban neighborhood when Thad was eight. His parents drove him to excel in his studies, and his natural aptitudes took him quickly to the top of his class. Yet, as the new kid in town, Thad desperately wanted to make friends. He just wanted to be liked, to be average, but he was soon labeled as Thad the Thinker, to whom all the other kids went for help in their studies.

With his dad's immersion in business, he became a mama's boy—and she became a boy's mama. She had left the workforce at 20 to become a full-time mother, and her life revolved around her son. He reciprocated by comforting her during times of fear and sorrow, from adolescence to the present. Meanwhile, his father was oblivious to his mother's desperate need for connection, fulfilled through Thad.

In order to be liked, Thad became the chameleon conformist, doing other kids' homework and being nice. Teased for being small, he avoided all confrontation, except for the time when another Jewish boy was being mis-treated and Thad, terrified, faced down the school bullies. He was living the first of what would eventually become many dual identities: superior smart kid and inferior short weakling.

Thad's father, a strapping, aggressive six-footer, pushed him into foot-ball and scouting. Though Thad was fleet-footed, football was a disaster be-cause of his size. In scouting, he quickly navigated the ranks, but quit after an anti-Semitic remark by the scoutmaster. He made light of the incident with his parents, masking his shame; but the real hurt came when his father wanted him to conform, to "put up with it" and "don't be a quitter." While Dad wanted to be able to brag about his Eagle Scout son, Thad wanted his dad to approach the scoutmaster and stand up for him and the sacredness of the family's traditions. Thad also longed for his dad's encouragement to fol-low his heart and, when necessary, to defy authority.

During his teen years Thad became involved with the Jewish youth group at his synagogue, where he felt comfortable and secure. The mask of conformance melted away as he took a leader-spokesman role among his peers. He quickly moved into chapter-level and then district-level leader-ship positions. He became outgoing, even flashy, and became a hot item among the Jewish girls. He returned from weekend conclaves feeling exhil-arated and important.

The youth group experience buoyed his confidence in high school. He traded athletics for drama and became an instant hit as a thespian. Being onstage filled him with energy—he felt six feet tall—and gave him a new way to connect with his non-Jewish classmates.

Yet, while he liked performing and being seen, he also cherished his solo time. At school a new duality had set in: He loved performing in front of hundreds of people, but outside of the floodlights he liked being alone. His "connection space" was in the Jewish youth group. He played roles in both realms, but never felt he had an identity of his own. He never really knew which world was "real"—or which was the "real" Thad. He longed to bring the confidence and presence of the youth group world to his school life. "Why can't I strut down the hall with my head high? Wouldn't it be cool if they could see me in my other life?"

While Thad's grandparents led simple, unpretentious lives, money and notoriety were important to his parents, who tended to be more showy and lived just beyond their means. Desiring to escape vicariously their blue-collar heritage, his parents pushed him to become a professional—the physician, attorney, or executive about whom they could gloat to their friends. But Thad tended toward the frugality of his grandparents. Though the money seemed to flow when he was a child, he became indifferent toward possessions and always felt he had more than he needed. Influenced by his grandfather, he rarely spent the money he earned, putting it away instead in savings accounts or even mutual funds. He invested the monetary gifts from his bar mitzvah in the stock market, an investment that later became the down payment for his first home. He had what he wanted, and the family was comfortable. Not until college did he realize that there were rich people in the world.

Thad graduated fifth in his high school class of five hundred and attended the nearby state university, intending to pursue a law degree after his undergraduate studies. He majored in business to hedge his bets, in case he couldn't fulfill the coveted dream of his parents—to enter law school. He shed his childhood "Thinker" role and collapsed the dual lives of his high school years into a single college identity.

Academics came easily, and he cruised through both undergraduate and law school. His showman alter ego, birthed in the Jewish youth group and seasoned in the high school plays, wowed his classmates as he wrote, produced, directed, and starred in the law school review. He also had a natural penchant for business. He transformed a failing university nightclub into a thriving cash cow—his first turnaround. He reveled in his newfound independence, paying his own expenses and never needing money from home. At 25, with a law degree and pockets full of money and confidence, he was ready to take on the world.

Thad had met Rachael the first day of law school. They started out as best friends, and he consoled and helped her as she broke up with her old boyfriend. Romance blossomed after a year, and they were married in four. "She's observant, honest, witty, and knows me better than I know myself. I love her deeply."

Following law school Thad entered 18 months of indentured servitude at a big-city law firm. In a classic bait-and-switch move, the partners enticed him with the promise of litigation work—where he could again be onstage—and then deployed him in their corporate department to plug a vacancy. Since it was his first job, he dutifully complied, resigning himself to the 80-hour-a-week partner track for who-knows-how-many years until he "made it." The die was cast.

Happy in her own firm, Rachael saw the life being squeezed out of her husband. "You shouldn't be in law. You're going through the motions," she chided him. His nature was to gladly conform, to be the teacher's pet. Rachael's love and candor helped him see how he had sold out to the system and lost his zest for life.

A college classmate, experiencing similar frustration in his own firm, approached Thad with a feast-or-famine start-up idea. Within two months they both resigned from their law firms and launched their underfunded "international trading corporation." Having no outside capital, they took odd jobs to pay the rent and fund business development, and used the time zones in their favor fishing for business.

Their grand scheme never materialized; they never landed any customers. The months of negative cash flow continued to roll by, and Thad again felt the dead-end desperation first experienced in the law firm. He internalized his deep sense of shame after already "failing" at the law firm, and hid his sense of embarrassment from Rachael, fearing she would reject him.

His lifeline this time was one of their few prospective customers, who saw Thad's potential and offered him an entry-level job as the president's executive assistant in an international insurance firm. He told Rachael this would be a temporary move, until he could garner enough capital to again become an entrepreneur. But his business skills were valued by the founder of this family business, and both his salary and responsibilities rose quickly. The holding pattern became a career, and within five years he was chief operating officer of a $1 billion international company. Still, though well paid—almost $1 million a year—he had received no equity in the company.

A new duality crept into his life. In one moment he would pitch the stodgy company founders on his vision and strategy for growth, and in the next breath endear himself to the rank-and-file troops, who saw him as their champion battling the despot founders. In his own eyes he had become bigger than the owners and, simultaneously, the voice of the workers—the righteous buffer between management and labor. He was at the height of his ego and saw himself as wiser than his bosses. He changed policies, overturned their directives, and called his own shots.

The next-generation business heirs initiated his downfall. They resented reporting to him, earning less than him, and being treated as staff people rather than heirs. They betrayed him to the family matriarch, who in turn berated the owners to dismiss "the alien heretic." The owners recognized his talents and wanted him to stay as a "valued player," but with less responsibility, a lower salary, eventually reporting to heirs, and still with no equity. Guilt-ridden for being caught and fearful of an ignominious firing, he endured another six months before exiting quietly with a one-year severance.

Thad had enough cash to weather multiple years without an active income. Still working in her original law firm, Rachael would support anything he wanted to do. He cherished the memories of his high school plays, the law school review, and the spontaneous parody of the partners he had engineered at the law firm's Christmas party. He toyed with the idea of entering film school—but balked at the prospect of yet another failure. When a headhunter wooed him to take another turnaround assignment, with an equity kicker but a reduced salary, 1,200 miles away, he accepted.

Thad needed time to regroup. He wanted to distance himself from the "failures" of the law firm, the aborted entrepreneurship, and the demotion within the family business. He had still not "made it." Worse, he didn't know who he was. In a sense he was still mama's little boy and had underachieved in the eyes of his demanding father. He needed both geographical distance and time to sort through his identity and destiny.

Though far from a perfect fit, this turnaround, also in the insurance industry, would give him time to reflect while still letting him be a mensch within his family. Uncertain of his future, he wanted to do the tough inner work necessary to avoid future failures.

Now in their late 30s, Thad and Rachael were childless, their plans for a big family thwarted by Thad's low sperm count. The topic had become taboo as they both focused on their work. Their sex life suffered—what was the use?—and Thad denied the grief about the most wounded part of his life: that he was unable to sire a child, and therefore was not a real man.

3

The BREAKAWAY
ENTREPRENEUR

Five-year-old Stan followed his father around the yard, pushing his small plastic lawn mower. Then he'd go to the backyard and help Dad plant the new shrubs. Doing man's work, shadowing his father—what more could a boy ask for!

To Stan, his father was a demigod. Though he traveled extensively as a sales manager and eventually president of the local manufacturing company, Stan's dad had an electric, affectionate presence. He jockeyed his schedule so as to make all of Stan's games, especially the hockey games, where Stan excelled. And as the family grew in affluence, he gently reminded Stan, "We're no better than any other people. We're fortunate to be where we are." Given these values and his dad's work ethic and stature in the community, little Stan, adolescent Stan, and young adult Stan idolized his father.

Stan was the golden boy in his small town. Intelligent and athletically gifted, he excelled in all sports and was the first-chair student in the advanced classes. Even as a youth he was consumed with an insatiable drive to succeed, to be the very best. Stung by the "little rich boy" taunts of his peers, he pushed himself in his studies and at practice, in effect saying, "Nobody is going to give me anything."

But his dad refused to let Stan work, saying he'd be taking income from someone else who needed a job. With his ample allowance, Stan was never deprived, yet he also felt he was not pulling his own weight. He yearned to break away and stand on his own.

While Stan's father was the benevolent patriarch, Mom was the quiet, behind-the-scenes homemaker—and manipulator. Stan was her "special son" who either complied with her wishes or endured her verbal abuse and whippings, always done in secret. They must portray a serene, loving household, a facade to placate Dad, whose own upbringing had been unstable and violent.

Over Stan's feeble objections she demanded that he take agonizing violin lessons. She carefully monitored his friends. Faced with the bigotry of her Appalachian upbringing, Stan could not invite his black friends over to his home. If Dad was his cheerleader, Mom was his jailer.

While Stan was forced to suppress all emotions at home, a rage burned within him. Painfully shy, he became an animal on both the football field and the hockey rink, wanting to hit people, to hurt them. Sports became the acceptable outlet for his anger. The "A" student and athlete by day became a vandal and street fighter at night. When the older girl he dated in high school cheated on him, he totaled his car in a rage.

After high school his father finally freed him to work, and arranged laborer jobs for him, hoping that this would motivate him to do well in his studies. Released from the parental controls and small-town influence, Stan became a renegade in college, indulging in wild parties, pot, alcohol, and sex. He became a user—of alcohol, drugs, women, the system. He continued with his sports outlet, too. A walk-on hockey player, he became a starter his junior year, when his Division II college played for the national championship. As cocaptain his senior year, he was devastated when his team blew a one-goal lead in the final minutes of his second championship game and lost in overtime.

After the four-year cakewalk through undergraduate school, he had no vision for what to do with his life. Again Dad intervened: "If you don't know what you want, keep going to school." So he dutifully entered graduate school to become "more mature." Sensing opportunities in the Sunbelt, he entered an MBA program in Arizona. He had no driving passion for business, but since Dad was in manufacturing he thought that somehow he would eventually own a manufacturing company.

As he entered his second year of graduate school, Stan's life collapsed. Only days before a scheduled appointment with a cardiologist, a massive heart attack felled his father. His anchor gone, Stan numbly finished graduate school and entered the work world as a software engineer for a major international company. His father's death was Stan's harsh rite of passage into adulthood.

Stan channeled the irrepressible competitive drive from athletics into his vocation. For two years he was a nose-to-the-grindstone programmer within a tightly controlled pyramid structure. The corporate powers saw his potential and put him on a managerial track. Yet, similar to his parents, these new authorities in his life wanted a follow-the-rules worker who completed his work and didn't make waves. While he liked the meetings with clients and the problem solving, the bureaucracy was sapping him.

After five years of business boot camp, he was assigned to yet another anal, pedantic partner. Desperate for a change, he brainstormed his exit with a coworker, submitted his resignation, and opened up his own custom programming operation.

Perhaps the best incentive he could receive came from the closed-minded partner, who characterized Stan's planned start-up as "the dumbest thing I've ever heard. You'll be a huge failure. There's no way you'll ever be successful." His competitive juices flowing, Stan would now chew through steel to prove the man wrong.

Staying lean and mean, the entrepreneurial pair invested long hours delivering products on schedule with superior customer service. Still stinging from the indifference of their previous employer, the partners vowed to create a worker-friendly environment, virtually unknown at the time in custom software development. Their congenial, open-door culture lured the top people from both his stodgy, old organization and several competitors. The founding duo took modest salaries and plowed profits back into the business. Stan and his partner worked 14-hour days and they loved it. They believed in and lived their model, and it worked. Within eight years they had bootstrapped the business into a $35 million, highly profitable boutique software firm.

During his late 20s Stan dated Juliet, a vivacious, volatile woman. Their turbulent courtship was physically incredible. While he sensed this was not the woman of his dreams, he measured his love for her by his endurance in bed, and they became engaged. "We've been together so long, I guess we're supposed to be married," he rationalized. Besides, his father had always taught him to follow through on his commitments. And his mother, always portraying the no-fuss, see-our-happy-home illusion, would have been horrified if Stan had fled at the altar. So, though he knew it was wrong, he married Juliet—not for love, but out of obligation, honor, and lust.

His timing couldn't have been worse, coincident with his new business start-up. Juliet wanted a doting, trophy husband who gave up his friends, worked eight-to-five, and was home every evening. He wanted to immerse himself in the expanding business. Rather than face her tirades at home, he spent most evenings in the safe haven of the office. Workaholism became his primary anesthetic for the strife at home.

When he did spend time at home it was always the same: He'd try to be nice, and Juliet would erupt. He'd go numb and close down. She'd become more volatile. Occasionally, and very secretively, he sought solace with prostitutes. He and Juliet entered obligatory counseling after four years of marriage and divorced, childless, after six.

Stan's business continued to rocket. As he and his partner were planning a national expansion, which would again require them to reinvest all their assets, they were wooed by a national-level competitor with the promise of money off the table, capital for expansion, and autonomy in their operation. They jumped. With flush bank accounts and a significant upside if the merger went smoothly, Stan began the grueling two-year project of uniting two disparate cultures.

But he soon realized that the buyers didn't really want a swashbuckling, independent regional entity, no matter how profitable. They conspired to reshape Stan's company into their own image. In contrast to the promise of "merging" the two companies, Stan's responsibilities boiled down to "make your numbers." The family-like culture he and his partner had labored to build was to be reshaped into the by-the-rules hierarchy he had escaped from years earlier.

Wary of possible repercussions from Stan and his partner, the buyers drove a competitive wedge between them, offering a single chunk of earn-out money that they would split based on their individual performances—against each other. So much for loyalty; his partner betrayed Stan to get most of the cash.

As the divorce proceedings with Juliet neared closure and the consolidation torture at the company escalated, Stan had no oasis in his life. So when Linda took an interest in him, listened to his sorrows, and eased his loneliness, he quickly "fell in love." They dated exclusively for the next year. While his mother had been critical of Juliet, she openly loathed Linda. Yet for Stan, on the rebound, this was the "real love" that had eluded him before, and without misgivings he married her during the waning days of the earn-out.

Their problems began almost immediately, as if in dé-jà vu. Linda demanded his time and body, and berated him for his lame-duck commitment to the company over her. While they frolicked in bed—well, at least the sex was okay—her constant verbal abuse emasculated him. Tensions heightened between Linda and Stan's family until, at one pinnacle moment, she forced him to choose between her and his family. Fearing another divorce, he chose to stay in the marriage and became estranged from his mother and sister.

Even with the betrayals from both his partner and his new company, Stan planned to stay with the parent company after the earn-out. This was the only industry he had ever known, and he felt bound to honor the loyalty of his former employees. But Linda's demands and taunting became unbearable. She threatened to leave him unless he quit. He already felt shame from his family for his first divorce, and was terrified of becoming a two-time divorcé. So Stan reluctantly gave his boss six months' notice and worked diligently until the end. He could easily have taken a glide path out, but he would not compromise his father's values. Meanwhile, as in his teen years, he stuffed his anger and wallowed in depression. Escape evenings with call girls became frequent.

At 42, wealthy beyond his dreams, in his second volatile marriage, childless, and void of life purpose, Stan was gridlocked. A divorce would crush his already fragile ego and halve his net worth. To seek reinvigoration through a new business, especially a start-up, would almost certainly kill his marriage. Yet to Stan, retirement, living Linda's hedonistic lifestyle, was anathema both to his father's work ethic and his own self-worth.

4

The PROFESSIONAL

With four brothers, only boys in the neighborhood, and an adventurer father, Susan had to be up on the "boy" thing. Her physician-father was one of two doctors in the Pacific Northwest in his specialty. He traveled extensively, practicing and teaching, and exuded both compassion and toughness. Susan's grandfather had pioneered the Yukon at the beginning of the twentieth century. She had the genes of perseverance, resilience, and tenderness.

Reared in New England, Susan's mother was equally at ease at the opera or at a quilting bee. They had a solid marriage and fostered a safe, loving home where anything could be brought to the table. Open discussions (abortion, sex, war) and relationships were encouraged. Love and truth thwarted any attempts at gamesmanship. Yet Susan perceived little tenderness in her parents' relationship. As he served his patients and she raised her children, they rarely took time for their marriage.

Susan excelled in school, with interests spanning literature, the sciences, and the arts, especially music. While she had been the heartthrob of fourth grade, she lost interest in her childhood friends when the drinking and cattiness started in high school. A late bloomer physically, she felt insecure and awkward around boys, and was not worldly enough to have many female friends. Her interests in biology, the celebrated composers, and great literature didn't jibe with going to the Friday night kegger. She became a loner and invested most of her high school years in preparation for college.

Having never been away from home, except with relatives, the outdoors girl experienced a major culture shock attending the blue-blood, all-women college in the Northeast. She endured a new form of ostracism among her sophisticated, prep-schooled classmates. Over her head academically—only 40 percent of her high school class had gone on to college—she suffered early academic failings, the first of her life, and thought about going home. But her innate toughness caused her to persevere, make the grades, and, by her junior year, embrace her school. Success-through-persistence-and-discipline became her mantra for transcending adversity.

Bred in the competitive cauldron of a diligent, professional father and four tough brothers, she invested long hours in the lab or library, with occasional sojourns at the piano. She was torn between music and the biological sciences as her major, but eventually opted for biology. She hated the jealousy, infighting, and politics of the music program. Besides, she was sure she'd never be an accomplished performer or musician, at least not as a career.

In her first year of biology graduate school she saw that the politics extended beyond music and pervaded every department. Sobered by her classmates' calculated approaches to life—most just wanted a profession to make money—she eventually transferred to medical school, following in the footsteps of her father. Medicine provided greater income potential and independence, and was also more stimulating and challenging. She witnessed, too, the deep gratitude of her father's patients, and wished to work in an environment where she would be recognized, even honored, for making a difference in a person's life.

After infrequent, mostly platonic dating in both high school and college, she fell in love with a musically inclined lab partner during medical school. Deeply hurt when he broke off the two-year relationship ("You'll be a rich doctor and I can't compete"), she again retreated into her studies, pouring her soul out over the piano keys with occasional nights out at the symphony. Most of her classmates were now married, and again she was alone.

Susan had entered the deep tunnel of delayed gratification all too familiar to aspiring physicians. While most of her undergraduate friends started careers or families, bought homes, and made money, she slept at the hospital every fourth night, took grueling exams every few years, and accrued daunting debts. The goal of neurologist seemed like a mere pinpoint of light at the end of this tunnel—about the same size as her ego.

Seeing the intense competition for the premier residencies in her specialty, she accepted an assignment at a smaller Bible Belt hospital, planning on a five-year purgatory before entering private practice somewhere in her beloved mountains. Three years into her residency fate introduced other plans. On her blind date with John she sensed a kind, transparent, gracious man, so different from her medical peers with their indifference and arrogance. She had finally met someone who endorsed her interest in medicine, yet had a life away from the hospital. He spirited her away from the sterile hell of the laboratory and showed her a bigger world. He conceived creative diversions, and she appreciated his company. Yet she knew the residency, especially in this godforsaken town, was simply a way station in her life. Endure two more years, and she could return to the geography and culture that fed both her mind and soul. She abruptly broke off the relationship.

She was surprised by her own insensitivity, remembering the way *she* had been dumped in graduate school. So she opened the door again with John, planning to let him down gradually this time—and found herself falling in love. Figuring that she could one day convince him to move to the mountains, she agreed to be married after an 18-month courtship.

During the courtship she had assumed that they came from similar backgrounds. Both his parents went to church, seemed affable, and gave the impression of being a solid, supporting couple. She took them at face value and did little homework on her future in-laws. Only after they became engaged did the real truth begin to hit her, like staccato bricks in the face. The eldest son in a rancorous family business, John worked long hours as the glue in the company, massaging the fragile egos of his father (who owned all the stock) and his two misfit brothers. Most of his hometown friends were similarly shackled to their birthrights and obligations, running their families' businesses. Leaving town for Susan to open a medical practice in the Northwest would be both an embarrassment and a betrayal to John's family—out of the question.

During her adolescent years back home, the mothers of her classmates had all wanted their sons to marry a girl like Susan. But her soon-to-be in-laws wanted her barefoot and pregnant, the doting handmaid to their country club son. With her $90,000 medical school debt, they also saw her as a potential extortionist, intent on pillaging the family fortune. She had never dreamed that her prospective in-laws, so docile during the courtship with John, actually hated her guts. Still, she loved John, and she longed to be in a family environment—even this bag of nuts—so she went ahead with the marriage, convinced that her perseverance would eventually be rewarded, as it always had been.

After 28 years of education Susan was eager to go to work. She treated medicine as an art form, and her practice was her studio. She valued her patients, who in turn rewarded her with referrals that led to a burgeoning practice.

After multiple miscarriages and being rebuffed in adoption attempts, Susan eventually conceived again—not once, but thrice. The last pregnancy kept her bedridden for nearly nine months, during which she closed her medical practice, but continued paying employees as well as paying off her educational loans. Unfortunately, five years after launching her practice, her naïveté in money matters led to an embezzlement by the office manager and cost her a year's income.

Concurrently, John's life began to unravel. Ousted from the family business by his younger brothers' coup, he and a partner bought a low-tech manufacturing firm that depleted their reserves and demanded all his time. Susan's track record for enduring and eventually turning around difficult situations was in jeopardy. "John calls me the most important thing in his life, but I don't feel it. Where do I fit into his life? I'm not seeing a partnership." At age 39, with three children under age four, she found herself estranged from her in-laws, distant from John, and nearly out of cash.

Yet, like her grandfather in the Yukon, Susan was a survivor. She viewed her youngest daughter's birth as a hard-fought victory. Her new-found resolve pushed her to "do it all." Soon her practice flourished again, and she recommitted to national roles in specialty societies. She read bedtime stories each evening and played with her kids on the weekends. Ever responsible to those around her, she maintained a frenetic pace, wearing the multiple hats of physician, mom, manager, and mediator.

Her marital problems worsened. A chronic conflict avoider, John escaped to the golf course as multiple litigations in his company drained their money. Susan's practice was the cash engine for the family, a burning irony to her since her in-laws expected her to be the submissive mother-home-maker. But what grieved and angered her most was John's unwillingness to communicate. "Face your problems and deal with them," her father had imbued in her. So when John refused to confront the reality of his situation, Susan raged inside. Her superwoman heroics were not saving her marriage, and his closure caused her to feel empty and alone. Had they been childless, she would have left him, accepting the stigma of a failed marriage over the quicksand of her current state. But she felt responsible to keep the family hinged together. Their three young children needed the foundational love of a two-parent family like she had been blessed with as a child. She must endure.

After weighing every option, she was at the nadir of her existence. If the marriage died, they would decimate three little people. But the current situation was emotional suicide. If they didn't have a communication breakthrough soon, she would have to file for divorce.

5

The FAMILY
BUSINESS HEIR

Peter learned early in life not to rock the boat. Other than with his sister, whom he picked on regularly, he was the "nice boy" in school, at church, and around the home. He knew how to fit in, to have people in power like him. It was how he survived.

Peter's father was an imposing, intimidating man. Dutifully continuing the legacy of his family's business, he would often depart for work before dawn, arriving back home after 10:00 P.M. It wasn't that he worked that late; his normal routine was to stop off for a couple—well, several—drinks, before coming home in a near stupor and enraged. His parents' arguments were loud and terrifying to a seven-year-old boy trembling under the covers, clutching a teddy bear. Still, they maintained a public mask of normalcy, pretending they had a harmonious marriage, though he sensed no love between them. Their denial caused Peter both to doubt himself and to deny his own feelings: "It feels real, but I must be wrong."

Secrecy, fear, and denial were the norms in Peter's family. His mother moved out of the house and in with her parents when he was in fifth grade, under the ruse of having headaches and needing a quiet place. In reality she had demanded a divorce, anathema in their Catholic home. His father's drinking, violence, and multiple affairs had finally driven his mother, a feisty shrew who had never walked away from a fight, to draw a hard boundary to protect herself—to save her life.

His father, enraged that she would leave him and break up his "happy family," vowed to make her pay. He retained a vicious attorney who negotiated full custody of the children and meager alimony payments to Peter's mother. His father never really wanted the kids; he just didn't want *her* to raise them. Winning was more important than the well-being of his children. Refusing to live with his father, Peter was banished to a nearby boarding school where he became the quiet kid who "did things right" and "fit in." He dreaded Sundays, visiting day, when his father would want to take him out—to "connect."

After the purgatory of boarding school, his father pulled strings to get Peter into a premier private high school, his own alma mater, in their hometown. But Peter was totally unprepared and too immature for the steamroller, college-prep environment, and his grades plummeted. Intimidated by the teachers and feeling ugly and inferior around his classmates, he was an emotional wreck. Neither parent intervened; nothing happened. During his freshman year, he escaped in the fantasy world of professional sports, avidly tracking teams and players, to forget the reality of the loneliness he felt around his classmates. His life took on a sense of futility as he spiraled downward in adolescent depression. He desperately prayed that someone would discover him, see him. No one did, and he often contemplated suicide.

Finally, his father, accompanied by the pit bull attorney, orchestrated Peter's move to a less demanding school and a repeat of his freshman year. Given this lifeline, Peter reflected on his existence and concluded, "I'm the only one who can improve my life." The following year he made the honor roll.

Earlier, Peter had been enamored with the Catholic traditions and rituals, and in grade school he had even aspired to be a priest. But by high school he had walked away from the church. He had felt abandoned by God when he was shipped to boarding school. Nevertheless, at the turning point when he realized he must take responsibility for his life, he felt bathed in a shaft of grace and sensed that "Someone" had rescued him. The spiritual embers from early childhood were never fully extinguished.

However, though he was now considered to be one of the "smart kids," he never felt smart. He discounted his successes, and a critical voice inside his head kept telling him that he was inferior and ugly. He cruised through the following uneventful three years, making adequate grades. Only when pressured, sensing the acrid smell of impending failure, did he emerge from academic cruise control and apply himself. Throughout high school, riddled with shame and guilt about his intellect and appearance, Peter was awkward around girls and never dated. Masturbation was his sexual release.

During this time his mother had remarried, and Peter, now at an age where he could choose where he lived, moved in with her and his new stepfather. As with his father, Peter felt helpless around this powerful brute of a man, as he watched him verbally and physically assault his mother. She refused to leave, not wanting to be a two-time loser. Seeing this rerun of his childhood, Peter felt trapped.

After high school he enrolled in the nearby private university. He had no compelling reason; it was close to home, small, an easy choice. He lied about his sports credentials to be accepted into a fraternity. He should have been blackballed when they found out, but they gave him the benefit of the doubt and forgave him. This was a major event in his life: "cool guys" accepting him in his naked failure.

They convinced him to try out for the lacrosse team, a sport he had never played. He was content to be the backup goalie, grateful just to be on the team, to belong. When the team's goalie transferred to another school, Peter stepped in as the starting varsity goalie. Terrified of failing, especially in front of his new friends, he conditioned his body and immersed himself in the sport, leading his squad to two championships and selection to the all-conference team. Sports had allowed him, for the first time, to become a "somebody." He was ecstatic when he heard, indirectly, that his dad was proud of his accomplishments—the first accolades from his father in his life.

An academic dilettante during college, Peter had no concept of adulthood and work after graduation. The combination of repeating freshman year in high school and a high draft number kept him out of Vietnam. As the only son, his unspoken destiny was always to enter the family business. Since he showed no sense of purpose or excitement toward any other careers, his father waited quietly for this to happen. When Peter floated his possible move into a teaching career, his father quickly squelched the idea and offered him an entry-level job in the company. Though drawn to teaching, Peter acceded to his father's wishes and took the warehouse job.

For several years he drank at the trough of nepotism, living a playboy lifestyle while loathing his work. Finally his coworkers blew the whistle on

Peter's incompetence. Furious, his father threatened to throw him out of the business. Knowing he had a good thing going, Peter groveled and accepted a sales territory. He hated sales, but he needed the financial security to maintain his lifestyle.

Now that team sports were impractical, he switched from lacrosse to golf and became dedicated to improving his game. He found that when he applied himself he would often succeed, like when he bolstered his high school grades. He had a similar experience with Toastmasters, a training forum for public speakers. He became a gifted speaker and found he could succeed in sales even though he never liked selling. He began to develop a small base of self-confidence.

Unbeknownst to Peter the playboy, he had been pegged from birth to succeed his father in running the company. His father only cared about the transfer of the business to the next generation through Peter. Whether or not Peter had a life outside of the business was irrelevant.

His mother had warned him, "Don't ever go into your father's business. It destroyed your father. It will destroy you." She told Peter how his grandfather had dominated and belittled his father. His father had been a loving, spiritual man who, having fallen in love after World War II, was prepared to break away from the family orbit and live in Florida. But Peter's grandfather had lured him back into the family fold using the yoke of "family responsibility." He had acquiesced to the will of the patriarch and, over time, became hard, began to drink and carouse—began to die. And now the pattern was recurring through Peter.

Ten years younger than Peter, Jennifer was grounded, assertive, and optimistic. Her parents loved Peter's family and introduced the two young people at a family wedding. Somehow he came across as confident and fun. She was only 18, and he became her first—and only—serious relationship. They married two years later. Though monogamous, Peter otherwise maintained his selfish, single lifestyle. Still, through all his immaturity, Jennifer saw shreds of potential in her man. She suffered through his behavior but stayed by his side.

As with many small distribution companies, Peter's family business was dependent on keeping the lines of two major suppliers. During the mid-1980s, when Peter was still in sales, both these principals threatened to pull their lines from Peter's company. Both the nepotism at the top and the incompetence of the veteran, back-slapping sales manager bred an indifference among company leadership that, if maintained, would eventually decimate the business. Peter was the sole sentinel to his father:

"Dad, we're going out of business!" At Peter's urging they hired a management consultant who confirmed the ineptness of the current management team and urged them to bring in fresh, outside professional managers to run the business. But his father and uncle were adamant that no outsider would ever lead *their* business. So, by default, they offered the top job to Peter.

The fear-based competitive spark lit during Peter's college lacrosse years helped ignite his career. He found that if he could care about something, like the respect of his teammates, the success of the team, or the survival of his family's legacy, his leadership and strategy skills were formidable.

Fearing that the business would fail under his watch, Peter took charge and immersed himself in all aspects of the operations. He loved the challenge, the action, the passion of spearheading a company turnaround. He salvaged the two suppliers who had threatened to leave. After diligent preparation he gave riveting presentations to other potential suppliers and added several more significant lines. Within two years Peter's zeal had catapulted the fourth-generation, third-tier, sleepy distribution company into a regional powerhouse.

Over the next decade Peter became entrenched as the company leader and chief strategist. His father and uncle continued as semiretired advisors, and his cousins and nephews ran operations. Peter was still the go-to guy for impassioned sales presentations and delicate negotiations, but he had little to do with the mechanics of the business.

Now, in his late 40s and independently wealthy, he had lost passion for the business—the fire had gone out, and he'd run out of matches. He trudged into the office every morning out of guilt, and escaped most afternoons to the golf course. He longed to cash in his chips and exit, but there was no heir apparent among his cousins and nephews to run the business in his stead. Potential buyers approached him regularly, offering a lucrative payday that would provide financial independence throughout his extended family. But if he sold the business he would become the family Judas, selling out an 87-year legacy and defiling the life and work of his recently deceased father.

With no dragons to slay in the company and no voices of affirmation or encouragement to assure him that he was valued, the demons of guilt, selfishness, and unworthiness attacked Peter with a vengeance. Nothing he did was ever right, noble, wholesome, or pure. He anguished over a life misspent, wondering if he had been better cast as a teacher or coach. His sexual drive waned and he felt clumsy and incompetent around his children. Jennifer remained faithful, supportive, and accepting, but the marriage had become comfortable—and stale. His faith had returned following his marriage and parenthood, and he fervently sought solace in prayer and irregular Mass attendance. Yet he still heard the steady, pounding self-accusation, "You fool, you've squandered your life."

6

The MAVERICK

Fletcher could fix anything. Cars, lawn mowers, air-conditioning systems, home appliances—he had the mechanical dexterity and electronics insight to get broken things to work. From early childhood he was fascinated by tools and loved to hang out with his dad fixing things—whenever his dad was around.

He lived with an older brother and sister, a younger sister, and his parents in a series of tough, blue-collar neighborhoods. His father, a 30-year military man, moved his family every three to four years, so they never established any roots. His older brother was the rebel in the family and typically "got his ass beat by Dad." Most of Fletcher's friends were his brother's age and always in trouble; today many are either dead or in prison.

His parents endured a listless marriage and for the most part lived independent lives. His mother earned a modest livelihood in various office jobs, tended her house during the evenings, and seemed angry about her life. To gain his parents' attention and affirmation Fletcher became the "little hero" around the house, doing all the family odd jobs and yard work. Thirsting for praise, he performed more, piled higher, worked longer, finished sooner than his siblings, or anyone else. This be-better-than pattern became woven into his being.

He entered vocational school at 14 and worked at outside jobs 20, then 40 hours a week. He became hooked on making money and the independence it gave him. He would press the bills with an iron so they looked fresh and new, then he'd save them.

At 15 he was the top student in the entire school, and a whiz in electronics repair. He traveled alone by bus to the state electronics competition and finished third. As he received his award and saw that there were no family or friends in the audience to share this moment with him, he vowed, "If it's going to be, it's up to me. I'll do my own thing." He stuffed all sense of loneliness and medicated himself with a drive to succeed at work.

His unquenchable energy to be the best drove him to finish both trade school and high school one year early, while still laboring 40-hour weeks. He invested a year in a special out-of-state training program and, of course, finished first in his class. A loyal, hard worker, he returned to his hometown and was hired at the local electronics repair shop, where the owner had recognized his talents. Soon the business revolved around Fletcher's amazing speed and accuracy in the installation and repair of complex electronic equipment. The store flourished, and at 19 he was promoted to vice president, making $35,000 a year. He had his own apartment and a foreign convertible, and felt like a king. Awash in cash, yet greedy for more, he invested heavily in get-rich-quick futures markets.

The early 1980s recession stripped him back to bare metal financially—he lost it all. Yet he was undeterred. He simply wouldn't be as gullible next time, and he'd hedge his bets. He knew he would make it all, and more, again. He had erased the concept of failure from his mind. Out of loyalty he stayed another year with his employer, but then quit out of boredom. After traveling the country and delivering newspapers for six months, he started his own electronics installation and maintenance business.

With no plan, minimal business training, and very little money, Fletcher sought his first customers. After typing a resume he borrowed a car, briefcase, and sport coat, and made a cold call on the operations manager of the largest bank in the region. His soon-to-be competitors, national-level service providers, considered this a plum account, to be serviced by a battalion of technicians, wooed by multimedia sales presentations, nurtured on the golf courses of private country clubs, and won over cigars and cognac at five-star restaurants. Fletcher simply told the manager what he could do with a sincerity that is felt more than heard, without all the sales fluff and bluff. Fletcher got the account.

Beyond his prodigious capacity for work, Fletcher could also lure and motivate good people. Within a few years his single panel truck had grown to a fleet of vehicles and he employed 50 trained, loyal technicians. He underpriced and outperformed the national service chains. His parents went to computer technician school and joined his company, as did his brother. While generous with his staff and family, he retained 100 percent ownership and iron-fist control over all aspects of the business. He was becoming a legend in the region, and, by his standards, wealthy.

When he was 17 and naive, Fletcher's first girlfriend had cheated on him and left him devastated. "Who needs women?!" he felt. Later, however, with a bachelor apartment and a fast car, he had hooked up with a savvy seductress who took him to sexuality graduate school. During the next 15 years, into his late 30s, he leveraged his amazing stamina to drive his business during the day and party until dawn most nights. He flew his own airplanes, drove motorcycles, and satiated himself with the pleasures and vices of life. Anything worth doing was worth overdoing.

A couple of relationships lasted multiple years, but as soon as she hinted at permanence, he bolted. He began to use alcohol and cocaine as courage builders to attract and seduce women, and became the life of the party. Thanks to his well-tuned body and his BMW in the parking lot, he rarely slept alone, and his nonwork time was spent in a fantasyland of excess. The betrayal by his first girlfriend, as well as observing his parents' comatose marriage, inhibited any nonsexual intimacy. He indulged in pleasure but avoided emotion. "I'll have my fun, but I'll stay in control. If that means I'll be alone, so be it. I will not be hurt again."

Beyond his electronics fiefdom, Fletcher became a shrewd deal maker, especially in real estate. He had an eye for the potential of a property. He'd fix up dilapidated apartments and small office buildings, making them cash positive within six months to a year. By his late 30s he oversaw a multimillion-dollar real estate empire yielding as much cash flow as his service business.

For 38 years the pace of Fletcher's life allowed little time for self-reflection. He focused on maintaining control, gaining independence, achieving financial security (over $1 million in annual income), and experiencing every pleasure. He had achieved all of these, and he had achieved them all alone.

He joined small groups of senior executives that met monthly to talk about both business and personal issues in a confidential setting. He felt disdain for the weaker participants, especially the silver-spoon, second-generation family business members who were still subservient to the family patriarch, usually their father. He was equally irked by whining entrepreneurs who moaned about financial problems, competitive pressures, or difficult employees.

On the flip side, he felt ignorant, weak, and inferior around big-school-MBA CEOs who were running successful multitiered businesses. He felt shame about having only a high school education and being unable to go toe-to-toe with them on corporate-level marketing, financial, or consolidation strategies. He was just a blue-collar stiff, working his ass off and running a low-tech, nice-cash-flow, nothing-fancy business. The shame occasionally leaked out as scalding disdain for his peers when they couldn't make "simple decisions" in their relationships: "If your wife is hounding you, tell her to shut up, or dump the bitch." Compassion and compromise eluded his vocabulary, and his brusque nature didn't get him invited to many black-tie dinner parties. So he gravitated back to his old carousing pals for company.

His combined anger and insecurity around these potential peers inhibited more-than-social friendships. He'd had no mentors or advisors since his first boss in the electronics store, the wise old-country retailer who had seen his potential for greatness. And he had no one with whom to share his growing angst about relational emptiness and loneliness, his longing to be in a loving relationship, or his fear of betrayal. A small voice inside of him hinted that, at 38, he was approaching middle age, and his life was spinning out of control. The alcohol, the women, the money, the toys—what did they all mean? He had no tethers in his life, no accountability, no one to tell him he was headed toward a train wreck, toward a Scrooge-like life of selfishness and loneliness.

7

The SMALL
COMPANY PARTNER

L arry was a natural leader, organizer, and mediator. He loved being out front, being seen, as the altar boy at funerals and the captain for sandlot pickup games. His mother anchored the home front while his father labored long hours in a start-up company. They were there, yet not there, in Larry's life—papier-mâché presences. The only real direction he received was from the steely-eyed nun and her metal-ruler-across-the-knuckles discipline, and Father O'Reilly's in-your-face, boot-camp respect. No compromise, no finesse, just the straight truth. Larry hated it, but he also longed for rocks in his life that he could rely on and cling to, beyond the syrup and spinelessness at home.

Sports and leadership became the twin anchors in his life. He excelled in all team sports, but gravitated most to football. He was the initiator, the organizer, the figure-it-out, take-charge guy, and was elected class president three consecutive years during high school. Academics were a necessary nuisance, and he had no qualms about cheating his way through several classes.

Larry released his continuous sexual drive through masturbation to pornography. He lost his virginity during his junior year in a sleazy motel room with the knock-out cheerleader he coveted. He was determined to have her and applied all the tenacity he normally put into sports or student leadership into her conquest. Once he got the taste, he knew he wanted more of this. But blanketing his sexual longings was a smothering humiliation around his actions. His sexuality became a duality of ecstatic encounters and buried shame, bottled within him, shared with no one.

Though a capable all-conference athlete during high school, he was not Division I college caliber. Nevertheless, he tried out for the state university football squad, and by sheer determination made the team. Although only a tackling dummy on the taxi squad, he poured his life into the sport. For two years it was his college identity. Now a small fish in a big pond, instead of the athlete kingpin he'd been in high school, he observed the dynamics of big-time collegiate sports. He noted the racial tensions, the favoritism given to the stars, the recruiting violations, and how the coaches manipulated the players like cattle. When he became a bag boy for one of the assistant coaches during a blue-chip high school athlete's recruiting trip, he quit. No outward rancor, no fist-on-the-desk demands, just a quiet departure and the end of his athletic dream.

Competent but not particularly gifted in mathematics, he limped through engineering school by a combination of cheating and all-nighters. He was three-year president of the elite fraternity, and its best athlete. Again he reveled in being the leader, the big fish in a small pond. He recruited and encouraged his fraternity brothers to participate in intramural sports, and found sharing the limelight more rewarding than being the lone star. While he still sought recognition for himself, he found deep fulfillment in helping the underdog and figuring out how to get 100 percent participation. His classmates came to him for counsel on whole-life issues, and he embraced the role of teacher and advisor. He strove to be nondiscriminatory and was touched by the plight of outcasts and misfits, whom he would befriend and mentor—though never in public.

Larry met Beth in a bar during his junior year. Her dad had died when she was a toddler, and to survive financially her mother had then married a harsh, control-oriented disciplinarian. While caring toward Beth and her brother, Beth's mother carried deep resentment for the cruel blows fate had dealt her.

Beth and Larry had a natural attraction, an electric connection that was deeper than physical, and unlike any of his other conquests. He felt they were made for each other, and the sexual connection, six months into the relationship, enhanced their natural chemistry. They became engaged midway through his senior year, after a 12-month courtship.

In one of those pivotal life encounters between father and son, Larry sought his father's approval and blessing for the marriage. Instead, he received financial counsel and the tepid admonition, "Why make a decision this important now? Take some time first; get settled into a job." Inwardly enraged and saddened, Larry expressed no emotion to his father, but resolved to take full control of his life. Though he maintained an outwardly cordial relationship with his parents, he removed them from the critical path of his life's decisions.

Larry and Beth married shortly after his graduation, and she quit school to be a full-time wife. Weary of academia and yearning for a taste of "real life," Larry prepared to enter the work world, proud, confident, determined, happy—and scared.

He took an entry-level programming job in the bowels of a large government contractor. He immersed himself in on-the-job training, recovering from the cut classes and squandered learning opportunities in college. He now had two important things in life: his work and Beth. Yet Beth quickly became a distant second. When she spoke of separation shortly after their first year of marriage, he was repentant and promised to change. She relented, but Larry never really changed, still immersing himself in the intriguing competition of the work world. Resigned to be the dutiful spouse, Beth found relational and physical solace at the local health club.

After a year of grunt-level programming on meaningless government projects, Larry needed a change. A sports connection led him to a real estate management firm that had just lost its information technology director. Though the job's responsibilities were way beyond his experience, the company was desperate and Larry was hired. With the grit and determination he had used to make the college football team, he immersed himself in the back-office chores of financing and managing properties. In a short time he mastered his job, and learned about "being in a *real* business."

The company principals knew they had a loyal soldier and piled the work on Larry. They kept deferring his requests for increased compensation and scoffed at giving him a piece of the action. He quit in a huff after three years, threatening to open his own competing firm. Their derision triggered an unslakable "I'll show them" attitude as he resolved to build his own business.

But all he knew was the back office; he needed a wheeler-dealer partner to get them some business. Concurrent with Larry's displeasure, a junior partner in his old firm had also become disgruntled. They wrote up a sketchy partnership agreement, scratched together $25,000 in seed capital, and opened their doors. They rented space from Larry's dad, who was also in real estate. His father's good name gave them a foot in the door to a handful of small accounts, which they nurtured into stellar references.

For the next three years they worked 80-hour weeks, growing the business to $5 million in managed properties. Still childless, Beth worked part-time at the local mall and escalated her body sculpting at the health club. Larry transitioned totally from the back office to sales and marketing. He loved selling, and landing a new account was as good as sex. With a minnow-eating-the-whale maneuver, they bought another agency four times their size, using future earnings. The stodgy sellers liked "the aggressive young guys." The partnership now had the critical mass to land million-dollar accounts, which it did. Larry's aggression from the football field, blended with his interpersonal gifts honed in the fraternity, pushed the company to $90 million in annual billings.

The two-man partnership evolved into a multitiered regional company begging for professional management. Larry's role underwent another transition, this time from chief deal maker to in-house shrink. His new job was to rally the troops, keep them happy, solve their problems. As in the fraternity, he liked being sought out for help, smoothing over problems, mediating, getting employee buy-in to his ideas and company vision.

Meanwhile, storm clouds were brewing. His partner, the original creative brains of the partnership, had become an impediment to their growth. Larry convinced him they needed a third partner to fill both the creative and professional management holes in the company. In time, Larry would deeply regret this move.

After 18 years in the partnership, and now in his mid-40s, Larry's fire for the business had been reduced to embers. He had tried different bellows, but nothing would reignite the flame. When he lashed out at a customer one day, he knew the situation was serious, unhealthy for him and for the business. He needed to leave the business and find a new passion elsewhere.

Larry and his partner had never taken lavish salaries, preferring to build equity and anticipating a big payoff when they sold. Almost all of his net worth was tied up in the business, and now it was harvest time. But, sensing Larry's burnout, the new partner delayed and nitpicked Larry's proposed buyout. His original partner rebuffed his plea for reconciliation and a quick resolution, and sided with the new tyrant, saying, "I've got to look out for the best interests of the company and myself." These partner rumblings were taking their toll on both Larry's health and the morale of the employees. So Larry finally gave in, rationalizing, "It's only assets and money." But inside, he seethed with anger over the betrayal by his partner.

With a $300,000 annual family cash burn rate and a settlement that left him far from financial independence, Larry still needed to work. While at one time he had loved the swashbuckling nature of an entrepreneurship, at 46 he had neither the stamina nor the desire to invest 80-hour weeks growing a neophyte business, especially when he didn't have the investment cash to demand a majority ownership. But an intrapreneurship with the corporate trappings and cushy salary of an industry conglomerate—that had appeal! So he joined a large public company running a specialty spin-off.

The first few months were invigorating and he felt like an entrepreneur, running his specialty-marketing group. But then, in a classic case of big-company politics and face-saving, a failing long-term executive, whom no one had the courage to fire, became Larry's boss. Before long this buffoon had disassembled Larry's organization, and Larry found himself to be a well-paid yet powerless staffer, a mercenary.

Meanwhile, the already potent sexual drive of Larry's adolescence had increased through his adult years. Very privately throughout most of his married life, Larry engaged in telephone sex, pornography, and affairs. He rationalized, "Healthy males just like to have a lot of sex." He still loved Beth, and they now had two sons whom he adored. Yet the power of his sexual drive propelled him into repeated serial relationships—for sex, nothing more. Now, nearing 50, with young teen sons, a wife he loved, a holding-pattern job, and *still* in a clandestine relationship, he knew he needed a major life change.

8

The MINISTER

Growing up, Marty was the tagalong fat kid that everyone teased and tolerated. Born in a dot-on-the-map town in rural Kansas, he lived most of his childhood in his brother's shadow. Though overweight, "Marty the Marshmallow" was a good athlete, but never as good as his brother. His father, a kind man with natural artistic talent, put bread on the table working the incongruous duet of salesman and musician. Eventually he moved the family to Wichita, where he played in the symphony at night and peddled annuities by day.

While Dad was the iconoclast dreamer, his mom was the family glue, working her own full-time job and helping the boys with their schoolwork. She had escaped an abusive home and met Marty's father, her knight in shining armor, when she was 20. Enamored with his musical skills and ability to weave a dream for their future, she married him. But when they moved to the city and needed two incomes to survive, her dreams of a comfortable, secure life crumbled as she labored at an unfulfilling job to help support the family. Though dedicated to her husband and children, she became emotionally closed. Her bitterness and caustic humor kept her sons on edge; they never really knew where they stood with Mom. So Marty, seeking to earn her favor, became the family peacekeeper, cleaning the house, mowing the lawn, being "nice."

With a tormenting brother and his father never around, Marty became the class clown to compensate for his low self-esteem. Occasionally his stuffed frustration would erupt, and he became feared in the schoolyard as the jokester bully. He led a dual life of aspiring athlete and juvenile delinquent—he and his friends would shoplift and vandalize, yet they never got caught. Unbeknownst to his friends, he also had gifts in the fine arts, painting, and sculpting, inherited from his father. With virtually no formal training, he became quite accomplished as an artist, but never saw this as a primary gift.

Marty had become a rudderless teenager when a Christian youth group leader befriended him after football practice. Other than his Little League coach, this was the first time an adult had taken any interest in him as a person with potential. They met weekly, and he accepted Christ as his savior after three months of intense discipleship. He became the leader's "I did it—you can, too" poster boy for the youth group, accompanying the leader as he met with other down-and-out kids around the area.

While his new Christian identity gave him occasional flashes of worthiness, he still felt trapped in the darkness of low self-esteem. He retained his hair-trigger temper, and his humor had been honed into a biting sarcasm targeted toward weaker classmates who crossed his path.

He entered a large state university as a "zealot for Christ," but his spiritual roots ran shallow. Seeking peer approval, he joined a fraternity and drank heavily. His "brothers" would get him into fights at parties so they could watch Marty, the junkyard dog, ravage another boy. Meanwhile he hid from his Christian friends, ashamed of his double life.

Toward the end of his freshman year he was befriended by a youth-group peer, who looked up to Marty as an athlete and protector, yet also mentored Marty with his patience and quiet maturity. Marty accompanied the boy back to his hometown that summer and worked in the local factory. For the first time he experienced a true family environment with nurturing parents. He reflected back on his misspent freshman year, felt disgusted for what he had been doing, and, with a reawakened conscience, vowed to change. He became "reborn" spiritually and returned to the "God squad" at college.

During the next school year he became a youth group leader and befriended boys in nearby high schools, as he had been befriended. His life started to matter, and as others began to look up to him, he reveled in his new identity as leader rather than sidekick or stooge. He changed his major from the fine arts to English, aspiring to teach after graduation.

But a local youth group donor encouraged him to solidify his faith walk and prepare for a life of ministry. It was 1970, and given the alternative of military service in Vietnam or Cambodia, he enrolled in a California seminary.

The seminary itself was sterile and academic. Most of his fellow seminarians were straight-A students in undergraduate school, and his 2.3 grade point average granted him only probationary admission. Still, California was the fresh start he needed. No one questioned him about his past. Gregarious and a good athlete, he was accepted immediately. For once he was around solid, grounded people, and he was the center of attention! Mirroring the pattern with his childhood friends, he bonded with the renegade seminarians—"Heaven's back row"—who became his first real community. He treasured the affirmation and returned to the Midwest tanned, fit, confident, and ready to save souls as a sponsored leader in the university youth group ministry.

Coming from a poor background, he had been a misfit in the college Greek life. The affluent, suburbanite sorority girls would use him and dump him. In high school his only sexual release had been through masturbation to pornography. In the fraternity he became a voyeur at "Super Eight night"—three hours of pornography followed by strippers and prostitutes. He became a foreplay expert but avoided intercourse. He talked a good game with the fraternity brothers, aspired to "get lucky" some nights, and actually had lots of chances, but always got scared at the critical moment and backed off. When he was set up with the sorority girl who had "done" everyone else in the fraternity, she declined to have sex with him, saying, "There's something different about you. I don't want to do it with you." Later, he felt that God was protecting him, and he maintained his virginity until his wedding night.

Single and 23 after seminary, he began to experience the loneliness of youth group ministry. As a leader, he always needed to be "on" and upbeat among his high school and early college disciples. Yet in the evenings, out of confusion and loneliness, he would unravel in his apartment, begging God for a partner, someone to share his life.

Sarah, a hometown girl and sophomore at the university, was a youth group volunteer assigned to Marty's ministry. As they worked together for a year, he quietly fell in love with her. First attracted by her great body and flirtatious manner, he watched her devoted ministering to disoriented high school students and fell in love with her heart. Naive in courtship, he found himself sulking around her, unable to express his feelings and deeply hurt as she ignored him. Marty's supervisor, assessing the situation, orchestrated a meeting between Marty and Sarah. Stammering for half an hour, Marty eventually poured out his feelings in the most vulnerable moment of his life. The two were inseparable for the next few weeks, became engaged, and married after four months.

Marty's sponsors gave him the down payment for a small house near the youth group headquarters. Affluent, visible men in the local community befriended and groomed Marty as their project, selecting his clothes and eyewear and helping him smooth his brusque manners. They saw Marty's potential in the ministry and they invested in him, helped him, sanitized him. They were upward-and-outward movers and shakers, image makers with little knowledge of their own souls and zero knowledge of Marty's.

While his outward identity and purpose were clear—an evangelist, teacher, and friend in service to Christ—his personal identity remained a mystery. Nobody knew the man behind the charismatic exterior, the man who twice daily disgorged his meals in a well-hidden, 10-year bout with bulimia.

Youth ministry is like most other organizations, with a ladder to climb, only a few coveted positions in management, and little upward mobility. After Marty had served three years, the regional director position became open. Marty expected a coronation ceremony when he was invited to lunch by the divisional vice president, who instead told him he was simply the local stalking-horse candidate. The person they *really* wanted was a protégé of the VP's from out of state. Would Marty be the dutiful foil and go along with the plan? Devastated, but ever the team player, he agreed.

Within a year, the new director had an affair with a subordinate and was ousted. Expecting a rubber-stamp promotion, Marty again had ice water poured on his psyche as the VP pummeled him with the litany of reasons he was not chosen. Stunned by this man's frankness, he told Sarah the story that evening, expecting her sympathy. Instead she confirmed his blind spots: off-putting humor, arrogance, and misplaced ambition. They considered him unteachable. He sought second opinions from the local elders and image makers, but they confirmed the VP's assessment.

Numbed and angered by their directness, he eventually came to see his own shortcomings. The new regional director, a gifted mentor, nurtured him and taught him the meaning of true community. Marty stayed. Ten years passed as he ran weekly youth group meetings, oversaw summer camps, and related one-on-one with high school kids.

Ultimately Marty was promoted to director of the southern region of the ministry. At 36 years old he finally felt rewarded for his dedication. Sarah, though, became deeply depressed. For the first time, at age 32, she would be leaving the lifeline of her hometown and entering a new environment with two children and a husband who would now live on airplanes. But they moved. It was his big opportunity—and her duty.

Marty discovered that his new role was more about fund-raising and administration than ministry. He rarely had the chance to use his relational and creative gifts with young people, and he had no local community. He'd finally gotten what he had coveted for so long, and he did everything right, yet he felt empty. Then, as funds got tight nationally, a regional consolidation left Marty without a job. He could stay, in a demoted role, finding his own donors, or take a three-month severance package as a tribute to his nearly two decades of service. At 38 and 34, Marty and Sarah moved back to her hometown, with no job, little money, two adolescents, and no plan.

He went into career counseling, and for several months they lived in the guest house of friends. Though bridling from the betrayal of the youth group ministry, he still felt called to God's service. Outplacement testing confirmed this calling. As he forgave the betrayal, he began to feel the exhilaration of a clean slate to start from after 18 years of service within the ministry. To get a job, he was wisely coached: "Find a need and convince them you can fill it."

A logical move would be either a staff or associate pastor position in a local church—a common transition for burned-out or aging youth group leaders. Having been a Green Beret in youth ministry, he abhorred the thought of kitchen patrol inside the organized church. But he and Sarah needed the money, and he needed a foothold. So again they moved, this time to a larger city, where he convinced the suburban megachurch leaders that they needed a small-group ministry—someone to connect the lay people—and that he was the champion to launch it.

Within a year he became an expert on small groups, with a national reputation, regular speaking engagements, and a thriving local ministry. He liked spearheading the new program, and Sarah liked the regular paycheck. He launched a Saturday evening contemporary service and became very popular with the congregation. Concurrently, he was gradually alienating himself from the church elders. They wanted him to keep his head down and manage his current turf; he wanted to set the vision, take risks, shake up the status quo. He wanted to build the church from the inside out, staffing it with people who loved each other. They wanted a professionally managed organization with nonintegrated professionals who did their jobs.

The church elders viewed him as a disloyal renegade when he proposed starting a new church and sought their blessing. Their answer: "You don't have what it takes to start a new church." Fearing a church schism, and needing his salary, he hunkered down and went back to his lay ministry. But deep within him seethed a frustration at once more being passed over for the role he sensed was his destiny.

II

MIDLIFE
MELTDOWNS

9

COMMITMENT, FOCUS, SUCCESS

The Tragedy of the Tower

The young man building his tower can't laugh. Equally tragic, he can't cry. He can't feel the pain of the world because he's too serious. He has to do what he has to do to get saved, to become holy, to be correct. There is neither time to smell the flowers or laugh at himself, nor to cry over the pain of the world. He is busy on the tower, trapped in an excess of spirit and lack of soul.

—*Richard Rohr*[1]

Commitment

Each of us navigates periods of life characterized by definition, action, and zeal, when we hone our energies, set boundaries, assume responsibilities, and get things done. They are times of focused, achievement-oriented thinking that takes place in rule-based realms. Childhood laziness, indifference, or laissez-faire approaches to life give way to responsibility and duty, a growing up that propels us in a zealous, undeterred pursuit of goals. Commitment is high, and loyalty—to a person, an entity, a goal, or an ideology—is unquestioned. Performance leads naturally to recognition and advancement.

Richard Rohr likens the commitment stage to building our personal monument, a tower that we try to make bigger than, taller than, stronger than the towers of others.[2] It is a time of growth, recognition, and making our mark on the world.

The peak experience of achieving excellence in the commitment stage can be described as "being in the zone"—when our giftedness and energies are focused on achieving a singular goal. In our riveted concentration, all other pursuits diminish or evaporate in importance. The zone metaphor is often applied in competitive sports when an athlete or team excels beyond previous standards. It applies equally in business, professional, or ministry life when a sterling performance—a presentation to investors, a delicate surgery, a shredding cross-examination, an impassioned sermon—rewards diligent preparation.

The educational system introduces the child to the culture of the commitment stage—completing assignments, taking tests, striving for mastery of skills, and earning the best possible grades. Similarly, the military stresses duty and proficiency, where conformity, consistency, and mastery accelerate promotions. Young adults entering the workforce after their formal education continue in this make-my-mark stage, learning vocation-related skills, adhering to the system, and being rewarded for the realization of goals. Some altruistic young adults embrace causes beyond themselves, playing their part in the effort to achieve such aims as eliminating hunger, humanizing government, protecting the environment, or saving the "lost." The student, the soldier, the worker, and the activist are all warriors either in preparation for action or in execution of assigned tasks.

Vocationally, the commitment stage often begins with our first job, where we have at least a chance of controlling our own destiny or managing our own success. The business world has several further levels of the commitment stage, almost always marked by a new challenge, opportunity, or reward. In conventional business hierarchies, employees strive to climb the ladder through the rungs of individual contribution, supervision, middle management, executive-level or strategic-level management, and perhaps running their own division. They are loyal to the company flag, and their rewards are greater levels of personal recognition, higher pay, more perks—and more power.

For a physician, the invitation to enter an established private practice after 10 years of medical school, internships, and residencies signals the start of "the real game." The pressure and competition of law school ratchets even higher for the pledge-level attorney working endless hours in a prestigious law firm on the 7- to 15-year track toward partner and its implied promise of recognition and wealth. To achieve these goals, the practice or firm must come first.

In most religions, the commitment stage is characterized by high dedication and unswerving obedience to the law (teachings, heritage, doctrine). Boundaries are rigid and performance (Bible reading, devotions, church attendance, fasting, meditation, evangelism) is expected and praised. This stage often follows a conversion experience where a new believer, bold in his faith, zealously presents his beliefs to others, becoming a "Warrior for God."

For people in ministry the real commitment stage begins when they get their own flock, a collection of souls under their care to befriend, love, teach, shepherd—and grow. This flock may be a remote missionary outpost, an assigned high school for youth ministry, or a new church start-up. Regardless of size, the shepherd is focused on and devoted to the care and growth of his flock, and thereby his own advancement.

Consider the following axiom of the commitment stage: Anyone with the title of president, CEO, senior pastor, general partner, or senior partner has established his enterprise (church, medical practice, law firm, company) as the top priority in his life. While most *claim* that God or their families come first, their actions speak otherwise—especially if they are committed to a healthy (growing, profitable, vibrant), successful enterprise. In my work with over 500 leaders of these organizations, most have devoted their lives—and often sold their souls—pursuing the success of their organizations and the attendant rewards and recognition for themselves.

The commitment stage is defined across six categories:

1. Identity/success.
2. Destiny/purpose.
3. Materialism/money.
4. Family relationships.
5. Other relationships.
6. Spiritual life.

Identity/Success

Our culture rewards individual significance. Even those who make a spoken covenant to "serve society" are usually masking an unspoken hunger to be "seen"—to have others recognize that "I am a wealthy/independent/successful/secure/powerful/dedicated *somebody*." Our identity hinges on what we achieve.

"Success" is euphemistically defined as "somebody else's definition of a good thing." Once you have enough—money, equity holdings, subordinates, properties, clients, vacation accrual, billable hours, fill-in-the-blank—you'll be "successful," you'll have "made it." We are challenged to do whatever it takes to achieve our goals. But then, having achieved them, we must not stagnate; we must set higher goals. The more goals we reach, the more control we'll have, and the more we'll be wanted, valued, respected—and seen.

We often couch this desire to be seen in less selfish terms like wanting to "serve others," "grow the company," or "achieve financial security." Our society applauds the achievement of these goals as the noble hallmarks of success. And while they may indeed be commendable, a gray area remains between commitment to the world I serve and building my tower—that is, obsession with self.

The telltale signs of obsession overshadowing commitment include:

➤ A constant need to compare—to be better, faster, bigger, younger, healthier, wealthier than others.

➤ Ignoring or diminishing the derailments and train wrecks of peers: "They simply weren't prepared like I am."

➤ A fear of being ordinary or unseen; not necessarily a need to be the best or to live in the limelight, but a belief that unless I am a cut above others, I have failed.

➤ Constant restlessness; a need to be busy.

➤ A belief that "I can think my way through anything." Intellect is god.

➤ Investing more time wallowing in failures than in celebrating successes.

➤ Thinking that nothing is ever good enough. No matter how laudable the achievement or lavish the praise, *something* was not right. I could have done better.

➤ A take-no-prisoners competitive drive, essentially saying, "I will win no matter what the cost." To paraphrase Vince Lombardi, winning becomes the only thing.

➤ A lead-by-example compulsion that demands working more hours, flying more miles, making more sales calls, more, more, more than anyone else. The leader must model devotion to "the Cause" over all.

➤ A vicious compulsion to seek revenge when wronged by others in pursuit of the Cause. Anyone who blocks my path or impedes my progress must pay.

➤ Reticence to delegate control or responsibility to others who might delay or weaken the erection of the tower.

During this commitment stage of life we prefer a black-and-white, rules-based world: succeed or fail; win or lose; face problems, fix them, and move on. We eschew ambiguity, paradox, and mystery. We serve our world by single-mindedly building our tower.

Destiny/Purpose

Chapter 22 explores the elements of our true calling, which always manifests as some form of service to others. Absent this underlying call to serve, the life purpose of driven people languishes in the future, perhaps vaguely defined as the pursuit of some ephemeral happiness. Their stated purpose is often "to be financially independent, to be happy and to love my family," which seems noble and inarguable until we see that the motives are usually egoistic. Sometimes our life purpose is brandished in even more exalted terms, like "building a successful company (practice, ministry) that will live on after I am gone." Often, however, this motive has the unspoken clause, "so my legacy will live on and others will venerate me as a great leader."

When in our true calling, which we will later define as our "genius," we deploy our talents freely in service to others without expectation of recognition, measurement of successes, or dwelling on failures. While the tower-building commitment stage often begins with sincere altruism—that my life work will make a difference in the world—over time, an escalating rhythm of achievement can replace youthful exuberance for the Cause with aggrandizement of the self. Obsession with self then corrupts service into narcissism, and shackles us to the expectations and exaltation of others.

Materialism/Money

During tower construction, money and materialism are typically not prime drivers but simply a metric for success. On the hazy fringes of life's horizon, beyond the scope of the early-stage tower, is a number that, when reached, will eliminate money worries forever. During the commitment stage, personal needs are often modest and profits or earnings are either reinvested in the company, practice, or ministry, or used to reduce debt. The exhilaration of tower construction overshadows the eventual rewards.

For successful professionals, entrepreneurs, executives, and ministry leaders (at least those who have not taken a vow of poverty), personal wealth inevitably begins to accrue, and the number becomes not only achievable but a virtual certainty. The role of money then shifts from measuring stick to Holy Grail. The definition of commitment mutates from making a difference to accumulating and protecting wealth.

This shift to accumulation and protection typically occurs in midlife, with the move to the larger home in the right neighborhood, looming college expenses, and anxieties over the fail-safe retirement portfolio. Preoccupation with security, comfort, and lifestyle replaces our earlier hope of making a difference with our lives. For many, especially those at the high end of the income scale for whom no amount of money guarantees financial independence, this commitment to security becomes an obsession that keeps them living perpetually in the future, unable to experience the present.

Family Relationships

Most vocationally driven people somehow find time to marry before or during the early part of their careers. The early infatuation and romance years of the marriage are often enhanced as both husband and wife move forward in their careers, and the passion for their vocations amplifies passion in the bedroom.

Eventually, by either joint decision or a "surprise" announcement, the couple become parents, and one partner, usually the woman, becomes the primary parent to the child and support person to the other partner. Often both partners continue to work, building their respective towers, with the added zeal of providing for their emerging family. In these dual-income, dual-career homes, the partners generally remain committed to both their work and the children. But their commitment to each other—to growing their relationship and nonsexual intimacy—is sacrificed to support "the good of the career and family."

This relational sacrifice unfolds more slowly when one spouse gives up her work to raise the children and uphold her partner. The wonder of and commitment to the new child allow her to encourage her husband as he pursues, and often escalates, his career goals. Her support means understanding and accepting his emergency road trips and late nights at the office, entertaining boorish clients and prospective employees, attending industry functions and nonprofit fund-raisers, and being available when he craves affection and lovemaking.

With time at a premium, the breadwinner schedules "quality time" with the kids, and their key events are videotaped so he can enjoy them later. Meanwhile, he placates his wife with gifts, domestic help, and the rare weekend away for the two of them. In essence he is buying connection.

For several years, often until the children reach adolescence, this marriage relationship works. He focuses on building his career so they can eventually "enjoy life." She supports his quest, nurtures the children, and regulates family routines, hoping that someday she'll reclaim her own life.

Other Relationships

Relationships with friends often remain strong for the first few years of the career commitment stage. College and sports buddies are welcome respites from the intensity of vocational ladder climbing. The strongest and most enduring relationships are those forged in the furnace of crisis, where the support encompasses the depths of emotion and selfless service between the friends.

As vocational focus intensifies, so does the loneliness that so often accompanies leadership. Social friendships are superseded by mentoring, which may come from the head of surgery, senior partner, senior pastor, family patriarch, or boss's boss—almost always someone "in the business." Young Presidents' Organization, The Executive Committee, and various professional associations offer peer-level networking, but even these focus primarily on business or professional development, and infrequently provide the confidentiality and honesty required for mentoring on deep personal issues.

Immersed in his commitment to vocational excellence, the tower builder is often oblivious to the gradual erosion in his family and outside relationships. Only when the disillusionment and breakdowns begin to arrive does he realize that the cords of his interpersonal safety net have become either threadbare or broken.

Spiritual Life

During the years of achievement, recognition, and growth, a relationship or communion with a Higher Power often becomes either a check-the-box-on-the-Sabbath duty or a "C" item on the whole-life to-do list. Spiritual connection becomes a "good idea" to be revisited at a later date—"once I get my life under control."

For many tower builders, especially those from doctrine-based religious backgrounds, spiritual commitment parallels vocational commitment. They study about and serve a CEO-like God who expects them to learn and labor their way into heaven. They attend religious services or study groups out of obligation, rather than as an act of worship and joy. They live a play-by-the-rules-and-get-my-reward faith, often devoid of connection or exultation.

Many leaders of growing organizations (businesses, professional practices, ministries) espouse the transcendent values of truth, love, respect, and service to their constituencies—clients, employees, vendors, congregations—yet their actions reflect a rationalization reeking of self-interest and self-protection. As their personal tower grows in height, "truth" morphs from "what is" to "whatever can be rationalized so my needs are met."

The commitment stage for people in ministry is usually marked by fervor for their chosen religious tradition and a devotedness to "saving souls." Often fed by their own conversion experience, these well-meaning champions become dedicated to God's work in the world. Their flock comes first; family, if any, comes next; and their own needs are well down the list.

The purity of the service or ministry professional's early vision and commitment to the Cause is genuine and potent. Their words and actions make a difference in the lives of others. Gradually, however, as with business and professional tower builders, these dedicated emissaries become prone to materialism, comparison, and competition. They often begin their ministry careers living simple lives of integrity and innocence, just "showing up and waiting to see what God does." Flush with their early successes of grateful converts, a thriving ministry, or a successful building campaign, they often succumb to the myth that more is better, seeking to expand their outreach, grow their congregations, secure more and wealthier donors—all with the admirable goal of touching *more* lives or saving *more* souls. Although they are dedicated to the Cause, the comparative pressures of hierarchical ministries, just like the growth pressures of secular hierarchies, suck them into a world oriented more toward measurement than connection.

Stories about Commitment, Focus, and Success

Through my teens, 20s, and 30s I arranged my life so I could be the big fish in modest-sized ponds. The goal was not so much to be extraordinary but rather to avoid, at all costs, being ordinary. When the competition stiffened or the stakes were raised, I moved to another pond, another place where I could be "big." In high school and college my pond was sports: class-B tennis champion, top intramural athlete. When the competition got too stiff, I got out.

My stints as an athlete and programmer were dress rehearsals for the main attraction, the formation and growth of my company. The competitive juices I had invested in academics and racquet sports were now channeled into the vast, multidimensional, win-lose playground of business.

At 30 years old I had never had a significant failing in my life, I still felt physically immortal, and I was cocky. Though laughingly naive in the protocol of selling, finance, and planning, I was a quick study. I relied on a handful of business mentors and invested every waking moment, and most dream time, in growing our fledgling company. I was an entrepreneur and loved it.

A whatever-it-takes teamwork bred an unspoken intimacy among the cofounders as we worked night and day to nurture the fragile embryo of a company into a stable organism and eventually a thriving body. My other identities of athlete, technologist, even husband and father receded as I evolved into the hold-it-all-together, benevolent patriarch of a growing, profitable enterprise. Benevolence and affirmation were easy during the growth years; the market makers loved us, and my paper equity was soon valued in the millions. It was easy to care for others when life was going my way.

In the early days every new sale was cause for celebration. Within two years, especially after the venture capital injection, growth had become an obsession. I felt compelled to lead by example: the most hours worked, air miles flown, sales calls made. Success was measured against a set of ever-escalating metrics. The celebration, even joy, accorded early victories dwindled to "attaboy" voice mails and the inexorable raising of the bar. Win the account. Harvest the account. Make the numbers. Beat the deadlines. Grow or die.

During these "zone" years, I would sometimes feel almost otherworldly in my ability to captivate or motivate others during sales presentations, strategic planning sessions, industry interviews, or quarterly all-company meetings. When "in the zone" I merged the farsightedness of the chess master and the focus of the poker player to sift through alternatives, choose "the right play," and then guide my management team out of times of distress or chaos. But the "zone" times became less frequent as competition intensified, sales plateaued, and more dry holes were drilled. Extensive research studies and office-of-the-president leadership replaced cunning, intuition, and connection. My leadership style and commitment shifted from innovate and attack to insulate and defend.

The success of the first seven years of my business barely changed my family's lifestyle, and I considered money primarily a way of measuring progress. However, though I gave it little thought, I knew I was accumulating my nest egg. Despite supposedly having an abundance mentality, I rarely gave to charity, rationalizing that once I cashed out, once I was rich, then I would be magnanimous and philanthropic. But now was the time to invest, not to give.

Our first child was an infant when I formed the company. My wife was an integral part of the firm for many years as bookkeeper and board member. We had two other children during the growth years, and her vocational identity shifted to full-time mom, fill-in worker, and the president's wife. The serendipity of our pre-kids, pre-business years was gradually shunted down to two roles for Judy: manage the family and support me.

As my work became all-consuming, she arranged her own life and our children's lives to be available on my schedule. My intensity had so narrowed that I became oblivious to her needs while relying on her availability to fill mine. Our life revolved around measurement and deadlines, and we allowed ourselves little time to savor and celebrate our progress and accomplishments.

My toddler children's innocence and indifference to materialism offered an escape into the peace and fantasy of their world, and occasional glimpses of joy. But I have only dim recollections of the years of my children before age five. And with each new birth, the slice of time available to each child grew narrower.

Almost all of my outside relationships had some link back to the business. My board of directors mentored me with their business acumen, but only a single college friend and my wife were whole-life mentors. All our entertaining had either an overt or a hidden agenda of strengthening or growing the business. With our singular focus there was simply no time to seed and nurture personal relationships.

During these years of commitment I embraced the gospel according to Stephen Covey,[3] studying and adopting habits of effectiveness to be more organized, more time-conscious, and more effective in my work life. I used reflection time and "sharpening the saw" to prepare for the next business challenge. God remained a footnote in my life—acknowledged, but not a priority. I returned to church on Saturday evenings (so I could work on Sundays) primarily to raise the children with some religion. In my sporadic prayer life, which flourished only during times of duress, I implored God to "get me through this tough time," after which my gratitude was, "Thanks, God, I'll call you again when I need you." All resources, including my "divine connection," were oriented toward maintaining success and achieving security.

A quiet narcissism marked these years of tower building. The blur of the action, the constant intellectual challenge, the pressure of the competition, and the accumulation of wealth defined my identity. While it's easy to look back now, on the other side of 50, and chastise myself for missing the warning signals of impending problems, for not taking more time for reflection and relationships, at that time my life was working "just fine, thank you." In a little while I might relax and reflect, pray, connect, give back, but now was the time to make my mark, and I would not allow myself to fail.

The tower-building years for Stan, the breakaway entrepreneur, occurred when he was growing his custom software company. He and his partner believed in their approach and were rewarded both in the marketplace and by employee loyalty. They were totally committed to expanding the business, with no peripheral vision for other parts of life. Stan's focused aggression in sports and dedication to academics were being rewarded.

Stan had no specific sense of a higher calling; he was just doing what he loved better than any competitors. Though the company made a lot of money, he maintained a simple lifestyle as they plowed profits back into the business. His unstable home life further encouraged him to focus on the business—he had nowhere else to go. The company became his *real* family where he was revered. He lived out his father's values of hard work, honesty, and care for people every day at the office. His work was his spiritual fuel.

Fletcher's "zone" blended a lust for business with a lust for pleasure. Where Stan's encouraging management style motivated his employees, Fletcher managed by pacesetting. "My solid players ate it up. The mediocre ones performed out of fear they'd be exposed. My intensity scared people, but they still gravitated to me. I got their blood going."

Fletcher led by example and knew every phase of his business completely. He poked, prodded, and praised his employees, mostly blue-collar technicians, to excel in their work. At night, he'd use either whiskey or cocaine to go into another zone, and then whore around town, often until dawn. Most mornings he'd be the first one back at the office, and the cycle would be repeated. Whether expanding his service empire or pursuing pleasure, Fletcher was obsessed with being the best.

Unmarried and with only pleasure-seeking friends, Fletcher, the maverick, had few outside constraints on his time. His life focused around his work and satisfying his immediate desires. He bought ostentatious cars and multiple airplanes, indulging his every whim. Lacking any outside accountability or mentoring, he did what he wanted, when he wanted. Yet other than the women whom he used, he still carried a value of "treating people right," including customers, employees, and vendors. While he certainly looked out for himself first, he was also wise enough to protect these human assets who were the ticket to his wealth.

Peter, the family business heir, never aspired to construct his own tower. Instead, he inherited a fourth-generation, rickety tower on the verge of collapse and accepted the challenge to fix it. This was exactly the kind of crisis Peter needed to give him a sense of identity and purpose for his life. When he was driven by the terror of failure, he invariably marshaled his talents to solve any problem. Commitment for him meant "perform or die," and he knew how to prepare and perform. He relished the research for and delivery of stirring presentations to new customers. He leveraged his Toastmasters training to motivate listless employees and galvanize his operations team—but only during times of outside pressure or crisis. Without a dragon to slay, he felt embarrassed and unworthy of his accomplishments.

Peter never had a sense of purpose beyond the present moment, doing whatever job was set before him. Though he occasionally mused about a vocation in teaching, he also liked being the company spokesman. But regardless of his musings and preferences, his destiny was to serve the company his great-grandfather had founded.

Even this wobbly tower had financial value, and Peter always felt financially secure. As the company grew, his personal net worth increased to over $30 million. He joined a couple of country clubs and skied the Rockies every year with his family, but didn't otherwise flaunt his wealth. Even as the company expanded under his leadership, he rarely derived satisfaction from his accomplishments and often felt unworthy of his success.

Jennifer, on the other hand, brimmed with self-confidence. Her healthy, accepting ego buoyed her man during his bouts with guilt and unworthiness. But their first child and only son was born with Down's syndrome. He would never follow Peter into the business, nor would Peter ever teach his son lacrosse or golf, help him with homework, or attend his wedding. Peter and Jennifer loved their son, but Peter struggled in tending to the boy's basic needs, and dreaded the day when he would require full-time institutional care.

While he grew close to his immediate family, Peter became detached from his uncle and cousins still in the business. He had little in common with his extended family outside of the operations, and he intentionally phased them out of his life. His carousing friends faded away soon after his marriage. He enjoyed jocular times with the buddies at the country club, but shared his problems only with his wife.

Other than his father and uncle, Peter had no mentors in his life. He visited a therapist twice monthly for 10 years but rarely delved into his bottled emotions. He joined The Executive Committee (TEC) and participated in a small group of men who met monthly in a confidential setting to discuss their business and personal issues. Again, while he developed some camaraderie with these men and spoke of the tensions within the family business, he never expressed his emotions or shared the deep issues of his personal life.

Peter kept alive the spark of spirituality from his childhood through regular Mass attendance and daily devotionals. He enjoyed the rituals and traditions of Catholicism and prayed daily. While he longed to connect with God, he felt riddled with guilt and shame, perpetually unworthy of a relationship with the divine.

Larry enjoyed tackling seemingly insurmountable problems. Whether as a college football walk-on, a real estate neophyte, or a partner in an underfunded start-up, Larry immersed himself in the challenge of the moment and, through tenacity and grit, invariably found a way to win. He thrived on competition and adversity, and he loved to sell. As with Stan, he channeled his sports aggression into business.

Larry prospered by doing whatever it took—research, persuasion, manipulation—to achieve the desired outcome. The company became his identity as he and his partner devoted seven years to building their real estate management firm. Driven to achieve their goal of $75 million in annual billings, they eventually exceeded $90 million. Larry paid little heed to the growth of his net worth, confident that someday they'd cash out and he'd have financial independence.

Thad's vocational zenith was as chief operating officer (COO) of the insurance firm. Though only a hired hand, he sought to mold the company as his own creation. He motivated the troops and manipulated the owners. He leveraged his legal and business cunning to achieve phenomenal growth and profits, while connecting at the gut level with frontline workers. He was the adopted prince aspiring to be king. The business was his stage, and he performed with panache and purpose.

Prior to his betrayal, Thad's position and responsibilities bespoke the power he had yearned to wield since childhood. His commitment to his career paralleled the fulfillment he had received from leading the Jewish youth group, with a hundred times more visibility. He had no excuses or any need to "play small." His walk became a swagger, and he forgot that he was only the adopted prince—that the true heirs to the throne were pouting in the wings as he strutted before the footlights.

His marriage with Rachael remained vibrant during these dual-income, no-kids years. Earning nearly $1 million a year in salary and bonuses, he gave little thought to wealth accumulation or material possessions. As in his youth, the money just came naturally, only now in much greater quantities. Though not particularly religious, he retained a connection with God and believed that his success was somehow aligned with "God's will."

From the time of his commitment to Christ in high school, Marty always felt alive in his ministry work. He was most engaged as director of the summer youth camp, managing a hundred staff and volunteers and ministering to hundreds of teenage seekers. He relished the evening preaching sessions, sharing the gospel—and himself—with an energetic, emotional audience who embraced his message. Afterward, he just hung out with the kids, hearing their stories, telling his own, guiding them toward both a deeper connection with God and a new belief in themselves.

While his gifts lay in teaching and preaching, most of his time during the school year went to management and travel, one level removed from the evangelism and discipleship he loved. He endured the bureaucracy out of commitment to the goals of the ministry and devotion to the thirsting teens. Donor solicitation became an unpleasant but necessary part of the job, and when he didn't dwell on it, the money somehow always appeared.

Overall, Marty liked the work but, while monetary reward was irrelevant, he wanted recognition. He knew that few frontline ministers became regional directors, and he coveted the title, visibility, and span of control.

Ministry was his life and his purpose. The summer camp staff became Marty's surrogate family, and he enjoyed the Bible study and camaraderie with his fellow youth group leaders. Since the leaders' tenure was often short, they rarely shared their personal issues, and he never developed an intimate community of friends.

Susan's medical practice was the oasis in her life. She arrived before dawn, answered the phone, paid every bill, and learned how everything worked. Committed to education, she attended cutting-edge workshops, served on national boards, and taught at the local university. Her reputation soon extended to the neighboring states as she incorporated state-of-the-art technologies into her practice. And the tender human interaction with frightened patients, followed by their tearful gratitude for her healing, was priceless to her.

Besides her dedication to her practice, her sense of life purpose also encompassed the raising of her children, the bond with her husband, and her connection with God. Even with the tension in John's business, she deployed her time and talents to nourish her multiple constituencies. When her practice was thriving and she had a little solo time at the piano, she was invincible.

Money and materiality mattered little to Susan. Her work was one of her joys, and the money would naturally follow. She would prove to her in-laws that she could earn her own way, but the actual amount of wealth was irrelevant. John managed all the family financials. If she became involved with the books, she'd fret over the money they could have saved. Why be miserable?

Their marriage remained stable while she grew her practice and bore their children. Her earnings were essential to undergird the family financially during John's legal bouts with his brothers and ex-partner. Resolving to ride out the roller coaster of her employee's embezzlement, John's lawsuits, and her overbearing in-laws, she remained steadfastly committed to her marriage. Susan was a survivor.

Other than her parents and a physician mentor during her residency, Susan had few friends. The pluck and character of her lineage fostered a resolve that welcomed friendships but persisted without them. But she clung to her relationship with God. Four generations in her family had embraced the Presbyterian faith. Since childhood she had experienced a personal connection with the triune God—Father, Son and Holy Spirit—that honored and transcended the structure and ceremony of her religion. Her faith anchored her commitments to medicine and her family. Yet while she believed God loved and supported her, He wasn't her "answer man." He might nudge her in certain directions, but her life issues were her responsibility to solve.

Having built their towers, many midlife leaders find the view from the penthouse isn't as dramatic or fulfilling as they had imagined during construction. Fissures appear in the foundation in the forms of questioned identity, marital tension, waning passion, money worries, spiritual emptiness, and shallow relationships. A mist of unfulfillment dampens the zest of achievement, and they begin to wonder, "What is all this for?"

The following chapters explore the murky terrain of midlife disillusionment—how leaders deny, compensate for, or escape from their discontent—and the inevitable choice point between the quest for deeper meaning and a life of security, significance—and numbness. We'll see that finding our true purpose and a feeling of aliveness involves descending from, dismantling, or, more drastically, leaping from our tower of success.

10

DISILLUSIONMENT and BREAKDOWNS

Life's Scoreboard

When we start being too impressed by the results of our work, we slowly come to the erroneous conviction that life is one large scoreboard where someone is listing the points to measure our worth. And before we are fully aware of it, we have sold our soul to the many grade-givers.

—*Henri Nouwen*[1]

The commitment stage described in Chapter 9 often lasts years or even decades. The upward-and-outward focus and the blur of constant growth distract or blind the earnest tower builder from life's warning signals that all is not well. At some point, though, whether by a small inner voice of discontent or a jolting personal train wreck, these successful leaders face the mild or blunt realization that parts or perhaps all of their lives are in disarray.

The transition from commitment to disillusionment may be sudden, as in the death of a parent, a debilitating illness, unexpected divorce proceedings, or some other jarring event. Sometimes the jolt hits during a rite of passage, like turning 40, sending the eldest child off to college, marrying off a daughter, or baptizing a grandchild. Most often, however, the realization of a burdened, out-of-whack life evolves slowly as energy-sapping straws are added to the load of uneasiness, weighing down the shoulders of zeal and commitment. If we're lucky, we have friends or loved ones who have the courage to name our blind spots and perhaps intervene around our addictions.

77

Often the first symptoms of midlife malaise begin in our bodies. The taken-for-granted fitness and vibrance of our 20s and 30s gradually regress into a constant battle to maintain our weight and overall health. We reproach our friends who have gone to seed, then realize with disgust that we, too, are 20 pounds heavier. A perpetual weariness siphons away our formerly boundless energy. We get sick. Muscles ache, joints swell, and backs go out. Injuries are more common and heal more slowly.

Beyond these physical symptoms, long-suppressed emotions, especially fear and anger, make more frequent visits to the surface, often at the least opportune time. This agitation, normally occurring at midlife, is different from the gut checks and strategic questioning that occur in everyday life. For perhaps the first time, we can't think our way out or bull our way through the questions and fears. Through our body and emotions, our soul is telling us to pay attention, to wake up.

During the commitment stage we seem to skip across the waves of life, deftly navigating or ignoring the swells of minor setbacks or even outright failures. But when zeal turns to duty, and then to drudgery, we begin to question everything, floundering in the chop of nagging details or petty frustrations. In the trough of these swells clear answers are rare and we become easily discouraged. Fear and lethargy, triggered by an increasing fog of questioning and uncertainty, replace the decisiveness and direction possible earlier in calmer waters and under clearer skies.

What were previously minor disappointments—a lost deal, an unhappy client, missed targets, key people leaving our organization—become painful betrayals that cut deeper and last longer. Where we previously welcomed the candor and encouragement of peers, their honesty now feels like stabbing criticism or damning indictments.

Laughter is infrequent and often forced. Our children, who used to be our link to serendipity and innocence, seem annoying, careless, or belligerent. Asset protection replaces wonder and celebration. Life is approached with a set jaw and steely conviction, a wariness of ubiquitous attackers. Grumbling and pouting replace identifying and fixing.

Besides our own derailments, the wrecks of our friends and peers can be most unsettling. Seeing our once-bulletproof friends navigate an ugly divorce or a bankruptcy, battle cancer, or face a teen pregnancy shakes us up. If it can happen to them, we're likely not far behind.

These potential woes were always there, shrouded by the seductiveness of tower building. Our friends—if we have any, if they are truthful, and if we will listen to them—can typically see and point out our problems long before we see them ourselves. But usually we ignore warning signals, trusting that, as always, we'll reason a solution, or at least a temporary fix. Figure 10.1 shows this commitment-disillusionment cycle.

Identity/Life Purpose

While building our tower, as we pare back outside interests and relationships, our identity and self-worth become more interwoven with our work. Whereas setbacks and even outright failures in our 20s were simply blips on the self-worth radar screen—here today, forgotten tomorrow—they become bone-crushing hits on our ego without the shock absorbers of diversified interests, intimate friendships, and a spiritual connection.

During the commitment years our work is our passion, our sandbox, our sport, our joy. We typically evolve through increasing levels of competence toward local, regional, national, and sometimes world-class levels of excellence. With this excellence come "better than the others" comparisons and recognition as being successful, a difference maker, a player. But when the self-worth roots outside of our vocation are shallow, they are often yanked from the soil of our identity to become insignificant elements of support to our new persona of successful businessperson, professional, or minister. Then, as the bloom begins to come off our work life, when the passion fades and the many grade givers keep setting the bar of approval higher and higher, when the uprooted connections with family, friends,

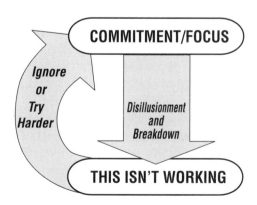

Figure 10.1　The Commitment-Disillusionment Cycle.

self, and God have withered, we desperately seek an identity from any available source.

Success, approval, and recognition are at first an enticing garden, drawing us in, rewarding our endeavors with beauty and abundance, and inspiring us toward greater achievement and accumulation. The deeper we go, the more we become entangled in the vines of others' approval and the outside world's measures of success. Slowly the jungle of "more" envelops us, wrapping its thorny tendrils in a choking grip around our weakening identity.

Western culture self-worth is fabricated on comparison. Once our children start going to school, playing peewee soccer, joining Scouts, or playing an instrument, we begin to *measure* their worth, sometimes consciously, usually unconsciously, by how they compare with others. Sadly, the "I love you just the way you are" relationship between parent and child shifts into praise for performance—the unspoken but clearly communicated "I love you if . . ." of adolescence and early adulthood.

The material world sanctions the "I love you if . . ." approach. When we enter the tower-building years, the tender inner voice that said "I love you as you are" is overwhelmed by the booming tone of our success-oriented culture, which resonates, "I love winners. Be big, be somebody, be great, become independent, be in control." Early wins during the commitment stage further muffle the tender voice, amplify the "winner" voice, and propel us toward bigger accomplishments, higher recognition, and greater wealth.

The make-a-difference-with-your-life mantra can work when it's backed by a foundation of self-esteem that confirms and grounds a spiritual-level worthiness and goodness, even in the midst of abject failure. But by the time failure or disillusionment hit, the obsession toward success has hidden the cushion of supportive love, and we fall prey to the converse of "Be big, be somebody, be great," which is "You're nobody, you're a loser, you're worthless." We wander around the jungle floor, desperately seeking any path into the light.

My retreat work corroborates this sense of personal unease. Nearly two in five CEOs at the retreats lament the absence of peace in their lives. Forty percent report that their career has become their identity. More than 40 percent of successful executives and professionals confess to shallow or selfish life goals. While 29 percent of these supposed bulwarks of industry *admit* to low self-confidence, my experience tells me that at least that many *more* question their abilities and dwell on their weaknesses, but just don't admit it.

Money/Materialism

The early years of the commitment stage focus on accomplishment and growth. Accumulation of wealth is a positive side effect, a gauge of success, and while we might aim toward some hazy dollar number signifying financial independence, it doesn't impact our way of life. If it all goes away tomorrow, we'll just start over. When we don't have much, there's not much to lose.

This all changes when success invades our lives and we begin to count and compare the wealth. We then get serious about financial goals, the "how much is enough" number. Wealth accumulation starts as the prudent path to a secure life, but eventually becomes an obsession. We believe that once we accumulate a certain amount (usually an achievable number), we'll be independent. Then we won't have to worry anymore about money. Over 70 percent of the CEOs interviewed prior to retreats feel *driven* to achieve financial independence.

As annual income rises so does our cash burn rate, the amount we spend on an annual basis. The "enough" number set in our 30s is not nearly "enough" now to support our lifestyle, secure us against unforeseen catastrophes, and fund our retirement. Financial gains, even windfalls, begin to be taken for granted, while financial losses, any cuts into our hard-earned net worth, shatter our self-esteem.

Many executives in midlife long for the simplicity and carefree nature of the years before they made it. They bemoan the complexity of their lives, yet refuse to ratchet back their lifestyles. They rationalize all their stuff (multiple homes, cars, pleasure craft, club memberships, home staff, retained legal and accounting professionals) as being "necessary" to live a "happy" life.

Where 70 percent of the interviewed CEOs felt driven to make their piles, nearly 40 percent expressed fear of losing their wealth. Having made their money and become financially independent, they take great pains to protect their assets, and then bequeath them to their children so the next generation won't have any financial worries. They invest time and energy insulating and hedging rather than dispersing and enjoying. They create a labyrinth of diversified portfolios, prenuptial agreements, offshore accounts, and other legal blockades to ensure that "Even if everything else goes away, I'll still have my money."

Many financially independent people live despondent lives. They can have anything they want, go anywhere they want, do anything they want.

Beyond money, they have the added blessing of free time. Our culture would say they have won the game. In their youth they heard the maxim that money doesn't buy happiness, that money will make you miserable, but they figured, "It will be different for me." It isn't.

So, if having money is so debilitating, why not just give it away and return to simpler times? Two primary reasons: First is the anticipated ridicule and alienation of friends ("You're going to do *what?!* Are you nuts?"); second is fear of a return to dependence, either on others for support or on a job to provide ongoing income. In our material culture, control and self-sufficiency are prized, while dependence on others signifies weakness and failure. Once you've achieved your level of independence, you can become service-oriented, philanthropic, even magnanimous—*but not until you've made your own money and established your financial self-sufficiency.*

The accumulation of wealth creates a dilemma. Wealth leads to complexity, which breeds discomfort. Simplicity may lead to greater peace but it implies dependence and loss of control. The disillusionment stage of midlife magnifies the quandary: complexity and control versus peace and dependence.

Balance/Boundaries/Responsibilities

In our 20s, single, independent, and embarking on the erection of our tower, we support only ourselves. We have few entanglements or responsibilities other than pursuing our goals. With marriage and vocational success we begin to shoulder responsibilities. Before long, our family expects our monthly income, employees count on a regular paycheck, customers demand timely delivery. Church committees and nonprofit boards seek our wisdom. Our children want our presence, and their teams need coaches. Our spouse seeks intimacy and a listening ear.

Clean boundary definition requires the ability to say no to some of the requests of others. A third of the interviewed executives admitted they struggle with saying no, and their lives have become overextended. Twenty-eight percent said their lives are a blur of issues. Over 40 percent confessed that their lives are being run on a treadmill.

The dilemma is that almost all of the requests of others, ranging from desperate pleas to threatening demands, can be rationalized as valid and good. A tower builder seeking the support and approval of others concedes to the rationalizations—"Well, I guess I can find the time. Sure, I'll do it"— further complicating his life and blurring his priorities. By our peak earning and tower-building years, these multiple constituencies clamor relentlessly for our time. Midlife leaders and spouses seek an elixir for balance: "Just tell me how to hold it all together."

Here's the bad news. Balance is a myth. No elixir exists. Someone or some group will be shortchanged, either intentionally or subconsciously. When addressed consciously, normally the squeakiest wheel gets oiled. When we try to grease all wheels, they *all* keep squeaking, with greater and greater amplitude.

In the midst of tower construction, and finding themselves forced to jettison one or more responsibilities, most leaders choose to defer or ignore either their personal needs or the needs of their family. With rare exceptions, all the clichés about "My family comes first" are simply platitudes; they mock reality. Delaying family needs, especially the husband-wife relationship, is the easiest to rationalize. Yet each rationalization, each late-night meeting, crisis at the office, or unexpected out-of-town trip, withdraws hard-earned funds from the interpersonal bank account of our loved ones—emotional and connection funds that are very expensive to replace at a later date. For corroboration, ask the executive fathers of adolescents, who now seek a relationship with their teens after years of absence while they built their towers. The currency of the interpersonal bank account is not money but time and tenderness, rare commodities for most midlife fathers who yearn to connect.

Often, we somehow meet family and vocational needs, but sacrifice our personal needs. We postpone fitness, recreation, solitude, prayer, or reflection time—what Stephen Covey labels "sharpening the saw"—until life calms down. But life never calms down. There is always just one more hill to climb, one more deal to close, one more quarter to make. David Deida proclaims this eloquently in *The Way of the Superior Man*:

> Most men make the error of thinking that one day it will be done. They think, "If I can work enough, then one day I could rest." Or, "One day my woman will understand something and then she will stop complaining." Or, "I'm only doing this now so that one day I can do what I really want with my life." The masculine error is to think that eventually things will be different in some fundamental way. They won't. It never ends.[2]

Without examining our life game plan and consciously choosing what we will pare from our lives, we remain trapped on an accelerating treadmill of fulfilling our multiple responsibilities.

Midlife leaders in the disillusionment stage experience gradual erosion of their physical, emotional, and spiritual health as they find themselves caught in a double bind. They feel compelled to place others' needs ahead of their own, partly because the affirmation of others is essential to the precarious foundation of their own self-worth. They presume that if they take care of themselves, they'll be viewed as selfish, letting down their family, their company, their partners, their church, their world, and possibly losing the few fragile relationships they have. But if they continue to try to fulfill all the demands on them, seeking an elusive balance, the mounting burden will crush them.

As they dutifully shoulder their ever-mounting responsibilities, caring evolves into a quiet loathing, an anger that either leaks out sideways, usually at loved ones, or erodes the soul—and the body—as depression. By perpetually saying yes to the needs of others, they are thrust to the edge of their physical and emotional health, and, occasionally, to the edge of their sanity.

Marriage and Family

Marital disillusionment has a variety of symptoms. In the two-career family, the ships pass in the night, with an occasional conjugal connection— kind of a sexual refueling. Communication consists of factual calendar-matching, oriented toward family problem-solving. With or without children, the relationship becomes a shadow of the excitement and wonder of the courtship years. Nearly 40 percent of the interviewed executives felt their marriage was bereft of the romance and sexual passion of their courtship.

In homes where one partner builds a vocational tower and the other minds the home and family, *support* ("Oh, honey, it's okay that you have to stay late to prepare the client presentation. Just wake me when you get home") turns to *tolerance* ("Put out the garbage when you get home, and don't wake me up!"), then to *animosity* ("This is the third time this month. You owe me!"). Pent-up anger erupts over seemingly trivial issues, which are simply the signals of long-stuffed frustrations. The cute nuances of courtship become annoying idiosyncrasies, then vile habits.

At least anger keeps the communication going. Worse is the ambivalent cold war where neither party shares anything that might show vulnerability, wary of cynical one-liners or other displays of animosity or indifference. Beyond the romantic and sexual decline, a third of the executives report that their marriages have become listless. They live as room-mates, managing their domicile, occasionally satisfying physical needs, and devoting their connection time to their children.

As new parents, both partners derive solace and pleasure from time with young children. Later, tensions escalate as Mom and Dad contrive a united front to testing teens, who are seeking their own independence just when Dad would like more bonding time.

Sex becomes the one form of communication both parties seek, though rarely on the same schedule. In the best case, both of them shelve their differences and seek to please each other while receiving the physical gift of their partner. More often, denial of sex or a let's-get-this-over-with manner are not-so-subtle ways of expressing anger toward the partner. Without open, verbal communication about family frustrations and sexual tensions, lovemaking becomes so strained or unpleasant that both parties avoid the dance—or seek satisfaction elsewhere.

The bodily changes of midlife exacerbate sexual issues. One or both partners' physical drive diminishes from the thrice-nightly ecstasy of the early marriage years to the once-monthly obligation. Dysfunction or problems around sexual performance often breed an unspoken shame that manifests in either depression or anger.

Romance and sex were the language of intimacy that launched and carried the relationship for perhaps a decade or more. Yet few couples learn a verbal or other nonsexual intimacy to bond them when either tensions escalate or their sexual drive lessens. They never learn the touching, caressing, listening, and serving forms of intimacy that can be even more connecting and fulfilling once sexual drive wanes.

The stay-at-home spouse dutifully manages the home and supports the breadwinner during the tower-building years. Without occasional respites and regular affirmation, the joy of child-rearing becomes duty, then responsibility, and often incarceration. He has a life through his profession; she is a minion. Her quiet support switches, seemingly overnight, into the demand, "What about *me*?! It's *my* turn. I want *my* life." This usually happens when the breadwinner is at a crucial stage of tower construction. He often fails to recognize the gravity of her needs, tries token amelioration (gifts, trips, home support staff), and is generally naive about what to do. His supposed base of stability, the home, has become yet another squeaky wheel to be greased.

As the marriage languishes and career pressures escalate, the beleaguered tower builder seeks connection with his children. They remain the one oasis of safety and innocence, especially when they are young. Over a third of the interviewed executives confirmed that, once the marriage begins to suffer, their home lives revolve around the children.

Yet the glow of the parent-child relationship fades as tower crises draw the parent back into the fray of work. Meanwhile, both peer pressures and the entertainment media lure the children into comparison and materialism, and tag-team to label parents as out-of-it oafs who "don't understand and never will." As adolescents step into their own lives, executive parents often find themselves truly alone.

Another depressing complication and wrenching obligation at midlife is the care of aging parents. As they become incapacitated or approach death, the desire for emotional closure overlays agonizing decisions around "Grandma and Grandpa coming to live with us," independent assisted-living arrangements, nursing homes, and, eventually, hospice. The death of one or both parents anoints the midlife professional as the new family patriarch or matriarch, and punctuates his or her own aging and eventual date with death. Questions around life meaning, legacy, and disjointed relationships tumble from the closet of the subconscious, pleading for healing, and shaking the foundation of the successful tower builder.

Relational/Spiritual

By midlife, college, sports, and early marriage friendships have typically dwindled to a few or none. After marriage and children, most of these friendships wane to annual holiday cards—handwritten at first, then deteriorating to an embossed, signatureless message with a peel-off address label on the envelope. Eventually these blood-brothers-forever friendships die from want of the time required to keep them alive and honest. Net worth disparities and unspoken comparisons further hobble, and eventually cripple, long-standing relationships. The competitive pressures, financial jockeying, mountain home planning, and kids' boarding school issues of the successful multimillionaire tower executive are incongruous compared with his working-stiff college roommate's month-to-month alimony and mortgage payments. Truthful, transparent relationships demand time and aren't "important" enough to make the tower builder's radar screen. While contact is maintained at the occasional dinner parties, church socials, high school reunions, and fundraiser galas, these friendships are unsafe for sharing the fear, grief, anger, and loneliness of midlife malaise. The loneliness increases and, when unexpressed, leads to depression.

Midlife leaders long for a safe haven where they can expose their entire lives, wheat and chaff alike, without being judged or shamed. They yearn for unconditional love and honesty, perhaps not experienced since early childhood, if at all. They seek connection and belonging. In a spiritual sense it feels like God is calling to them across the abyss of a misspent life, inviting them into a relationship with Himself.

Thirty-seven percent of the interviewed executives admit their yearning to know God better. My intuition is that an even higher percentage feel blocked from any spiritual connection, either by shame for past sins or fear of a repeated betrayal by a religious person. But who is this "God"? Various religions offer bridges across the abyss, but which one should they choose? Each claims to be the "right," the "one and only" bridge. But the recent spate of fallen or duplicitous religious leaders, coupled with indifferent or even deviant religious experiences from their youth, further fog the path across the abyss.

After 20 years of tower building they have learned to create their own security. They lead cautious, deliberate lives of golden parachutes, estate tax insurance, private schools for the kids, and semiannual physicals at the Mayo Clinic. Ambiguity, mystery, and paradox are not in their lexicons. Their subtle spiritual urgings hint at a surrender of possessions, attachments, and, hardest of all, control. Yet 3 in 10 express a deep fear of being ordinary, and the desire for a simpler life strains against their appetites for recognition and affluence.

Midlife leaders seek a nonjudgmental place to explore these issues, without being either derided as having "got religion" or evangelized by a fervent sentry on one of the bridges. They long for friends, elders, and guides who will listen to their stories, mirror their angst, lovingly point out their blind spots, and, every once in a while, suggest some direction.

Our culture of success has mostly lost this art of listening to and holding other human beings. We've become well-honed, cut-to-the-chase solution providers who stomp through the emotional mush and impose formulaic solutions. This approach leads to a Band-Aid quick fix, like a spiritual field dressing, but rarely touches or heals the soul. When a tower builder's attempts to be vulnerable are met with such triage, his tender soul recalls past betrayals and retreats again to the dark recesses of the abyss.

As a result, most people in midlife deal with their spiritual longings and their personal "dirty laundry" alone. They may read self-help and spiritual books, listen to positive mental attitude tape sets, and attend conclaves with inspirational speakers. Yet few meet in a safe place—a sanctuary— with other wounded pilgrims to share their dis-ease and their longings in open fellowship. Over a third of the captains of industry interviewed have *no* sounding boards, no mentors, to hear their stories.

Stories of Disillusionment

> Slip-slidin' away . . .
> Well, the nearer you get to your destination,
> The more you're slip-slidin' away.
> —*Paul Simon*[3]

My own midlife malaise spanned the five years of ages 38 to 42 as my company and psychic health plateaued, then declined. My tower was nearly complete when the company crunch hit and we retrenched to save the business. A lucrative exit became impossible, given our multiple layoffs and spotty profitability. I took the downsizing as a personal failure, the first of any significance in my life.

While I maintained ownership and executive control, my self-confidence plummeted. Without a strategic overhaul, including product line, pricing, distribution channel, and marketing approach, and an injection of outside capital, we would gradually decline into a sleepy, then desperate, third-tier company—what the investment bankers call "the walking dead." My gut knew this, but my leader persona tried to convey enthusiasm and confidence to dubious employees and customers. My ego and greed would not relinquish control to a new chief executive or accept outside financing that would dilute my majority ownership. My planning horizons shrank to making it through the next quarter, hoping that some white knight would materialize to buy us or that my instincts, and my board's insight, were wrong.

I had never been taught how to deal with challenges where hard work wasn't the antidote. Waves of unworthiness, guilt, and anger washed over me, exacerbated by the necessary pretense of appearing calm and upbeat to the troops. The depression became more regular and woke me at night with a whirl of ugly what-if scenarios and the damning voice that it was all my fault. The knots in my stomach rejected food, and I had neither the urge nor the confidence to love my wife. I pouted and whined, and felt both unworthy of love and incapable to love.

Judy experienced the double pressure of nurturing our three young children while bolstering her beleaguered husband. As I spun in the whirlpool of my depression, her challenge was to cheer for me from the rim of the vortex without getting sucked into my despondency. Only years later did she share the pain this caused her and how she had to separate from me emotionally to maintain her own sanity.

I had assumed that my work would eventually result in financial independence. When I'd been worth multiple millions on paper during the early years of tower building, I had focused on the fun and challenges of construction and had taken modest salary and bonuses. When the tough times hit, I continued the ruse of benevolent patriarch within the company, but getting my money out became my top priority. My pledges to uphold company culture and invest in the future faded quickly as company net worth hovered near zero and I saw that the prime years of my tower-building life might be for naught. And I was to blame.

Stan's first bout with betrayal occurred when his father died. How could his best friend and mentor leave him stranded and alone as he entered adulthood? Immersion in his company numbed the pain of his father's death and propelled him into the ranks of the highly successful. His first marriage, to Juliet, was a mistake, but Linda's convenient appearance during its waning days eased that pain. It took three near-concurrent betrayals around his 40th birthday before Stan realized his need for help.

The first deception came from the acquirers when they forced their cutthroat, cover-your-ass culture onto Stan's open-door, team-oriented company, with Stan as the hatchet man. The second betrayal came from his founding partner who jettisoned all loyalty to both Stan and their original employees to maximize his personal earn-out from the merger. When money was on the line, teamwork and loyalty to one another became empty rhetoric.

Even through these business betrayals, Stan remained stalwart and loyal. He knew no other way than to keep plugging, hoping that someday things would work out. The devastating blow emerged from the squalor of his marriage. Linda demanded his time, his money, and his testosterone—all of them, all of the time. She berated him mercilessly, both for his commitment to the company during the merger and for his exploration of new opportunities after the merger. She shopped and purchased capriciously, drawing from what she considered to be Stan's bottomless money supply. She demanded sexual fulfillment on her terms in her time, and he'd better be available to service her.

They could not conceive, and Stan became her scapegoat for a barren womb. Terrified of losing another marriage, Stan fell prey to her regularly played trump card: "If you don't meet my needs, I'm leaving you!" She needed a whipping boy, and he desperately longed to be seen and loved, no matter what the form. They were the textbook codependent couple.

Stan's self-image reeled in the shock waves of these betrayals. "Is it my fault or her fault? Who am I in all this mess?" When his first marriage had turned sour, he had escaped into his growing business. But when his company was sold, "All of 'me' was gone. The one positive place I had in my life disappeared." With the work outlet severed, he must face, head-on, the malaise at home and his own lack of both identity and purpose. He'd built his life around being a rescuer, but the upside of rescuing his marriage looked pretty meager.

After the Juliet fiasco Stan sought to suture together a relationship between Linda and his mother and sister, his only close family. But Linda torpedoed any chance of such connection, delivering the ultimatum "I want nothing to do with them. Choose—them or me." So as long as he stayed with his second wife, he would be estranged from his family.

After the betrayal by his partner, only his small group offered unfettered guidance as he contemplated the emptiness in his life. His prayer life returned as he sought connection with and love from God, the only haven he felt was truly safe.

Wealthy, healthy, and otherwise self-assured, Fletcher feared being in a genuine relationship with a woman. For nearly two decades alcohol and cocaine had transformed him into a playboy around women. Glib and free-spending, knowing when to feign compassion and appear attentive, he navigated his nightly conquest from the restaurant to the upscale dance clubs to the bedroom. Everyone had a good time. Lots of laughs, great sex, ending with "I'll call you soon," backed by the unspoken, yet very clear, "but don't get serious with me."

Fletcher knew his business had outgrown both his skills and interest. He was a swashbuckling developer, and the company needed savvy professional managers. "I was in the way, and I knew it." His real estate moonlighting, coupled with the profit engine of the company, provided him with ample cash. He had nothing to prove to others or himself.

He initiated the process to sell the company and, sure enough, multiple candidate buyers started a bidding war. He would have his pick of offers and financial independence beyond his dreams. He could escalate his real estate investments and still have ample cash to maintain his lifestyle.

The forewarnings about shallow relationships were soon forgotten, and he resumed his nightly carousing pattern. But, for the first time, he found himself waking up the next morning with remorse for his actions: "Damn, I didn't want this to happen again. I didn't want to use her." He wanted to change, but in the moment, *it was fun*, and he couldn't break the pattern. While his carousing buddies and fun-loving lady friends encouraged him to "stay with a good thing," the uneasiness in his soul magnified.

The death of his father anointed Peter as the family patriarch at the nadir of his passion for the business. For 10 years he had labored for his father and the family legacy, and now, paradoxically, he had both the keys to the kingdom and "permission" to leave. The argument to leave was convincing: "I paid my dues tenfold. I gave it more than it deserved, and lots of good things happened on my watch. I did my job. Can I go now?"

But 87 years of legacy and a lifetime of guilt do not release their hold easily. Peter knew it would have broken his dad's heart if he abandoned the business. He'd been entrusted with the helm of a struggling company and had guided it into a premier industry position. How could he desert the realm now, especially with no successor to the throne available?

To take a sabbatical and do whatever he wanted smacked of the dilettante, playboy days before his marriage, for which he still carried deep shame. Perhaps the business was his ongoing penance for those lost years. And maybe he *hadn't* yet paid his dues. Yet every day that he showed up for work sucked more energy and life from both his soul and his relationships, and fed a festering anger—his only remaining emotional attachment to the business. He remained torn between taking some time off to pursue his ill-defined dreams and persisting in his responsibilities and duty to his deceased father and the family business.

In his late 40s and still needing to work, Larry contemplated his holding pattern within the corporate cocoon. He had designed and nearly finished his own entrepreneurial tower, only to be ousted before the final ribbon-cutting ceremony. Now he worked as a well-compensated hireling on someone else's tower. He could stay indefinitely within the structure, just doing his job and pulling down $350,000 a year, and if the market ever turned around, maybe his options would translate into the financial security he'd thought he had in his old business. Meanwhile, he and Beth had just purchased their dream home in upstate New York, and he relished the three-day weekends and their plans of eventual retirement on the lake. A very convincing voice inside him said, "This is easy. The kids' college expenses are coming. Just ride it out."

But his heart called him to teaching, coaching, some way of helping others. Throughout his youth, other kids had come to him with their problems. He had been the de facto peer counselor and champion for the underdog, the kid with great heart but not much talent. He was able to partially leverage these teaching and guidance skills while growing his own business and within the corporate division, but he had much more to give.

Larry faced the trade-off of security versus fulfillment. Over the years Beth's life priorities had collapsed down to her family's happiness, and she would support Larry's decision, whether to stay in the company or to pursue a new destiny.

Beyond this vocation-destiny dilemma, Larry struggled with his sexual needs. He deeply loved his wife and sons, yet continued to engage in clandestine relationships that satisfied his desires. He now began to heap shame on his infidelity. What he previously rationalized as normal, he now recognized as destructive. To stop would be difficult. To come clean with his wife could be potentially devastating, to both of them. Since adolescence, his sexuality had always been very private, nobody else's business, and as an adult no one knew of his secret life except his serial partners. The secrecy was now crushing him. Something had to change.

The working sabbatical within the insurance firm offered Thad time to reflect. He knew this job was interim and that a change was imminent, but to what? He didn't need to be "big," at least for his own ego, but he felt his father's disappointment that he had never "made it." His talents as a writer, director, performer, and counselor languished as he finessed the banks and massaged payables in the corporate turnaround. Thad the Thinker handled these assignments on autopilot, without passion or even satisfaction. He yearned to connect with, love, and teach others as he had in the Jewish youth group. But the business world had typecast him as the savvy negotiator and clever businessman, and his inspiration and motivation skills were discounted or ignored.

Still childless in their late 30s, Thad and Rachael contemplated adoption but held off, feeling it would confirm their failure to conceive. They stopped discussing it and focused instead on their careers. But Thad anguished inside, reflecting on precious times in his grandfather's candy store or listening to his mother's stories of the old country. He grieved that he might never share this intimacy with his own child. He and Rachael began to avoid sex as a futile undertaking, and Thad kept his deep sorrow to himself.

Ever since they had met as coworkers in the ministry, Sarah had supported Marty in his vocation, at least until their move to the struggling southern region. No one had ever succeeded in this region, and Marty immersed himself in the turnaround effort. By force of will, he would make this work. Sarah became homesick, lonely, and bitter. He bristled, "I have the opportunity of a lifetime, and she's raining on my parade."

After seminary Marty had grown close to his father, and grieved deeply his death shortly before the move south. After relocating, Marty lived on planes, motivating frontline staffers, wooing deep-pocket donors—and rarely ministering directly to the young people he loved so dearly. The local staff expressed either hostility or indifference toward his leadership, and his only support came from infrequent phone calls to friends back home. Living in a stress-filled marriage, missing his father, enduring constant travel, courting hesitant donors, encouraging inexperienced staff, and feeling virtually alone, he remained heartened by the knowledge that at least he labored for the Lord, "doing a great thing in a great place"—until the downsizing and the ignominious return to Kansas.

Though he was unemployed, Marty's perseverance yielded some short-term rewards. Back on familiar turf, Sarah emerged from depression and encouraged Marty in his new role as head of lay ministry at the sprawling suburban church. He was ever the team player, especially since they needed the cash, and his mini-ministry flourished. Sarah rejoiced in the security of his position and the time to raise their two children with extended family nearby. Yet Marty thirsted to lead something of his own creation, with his own imprint. His 28-year apprenticeship was over. He wanted his own church.

The church elders rejected his request. As he languished in the penalty box of associate pastor, he experienced a reenactment of a lifelong pattern: authorities stifling his creativity and ambition. While his marriage rebounded, his son struggled in school and experimented with drugs. The boy needed quantity time from Marty, something Marty had never gotten from his own father. Marty faced a watershed decision: Stay put and deliver acclaimed service within a booming church in a secure, supportive community—or launch his dream of a new church, risking his most prized relationships and his reputation. Was he being called to a new church, or was it his ego craving attention?

On the eve of her 40th birthday Susan felt angry and paralyzed, enduring a comatose marriage and torn between three loving children and the demands of a flourishing medical practice. She wallowed in a profound sense of failure and a spiritual deadness. She wondered if the God of her childhood had closed His ears. "What did I do to deserve this pain?"

Far from the wonder of their courtship, she and John could find no common ground and had perfected the fine art of hurting each other. She hovered near a breakdown as the relentless berating of her in-laws and the communication vacuum with John exhausted her resiliency. She had always been the survivor, the rock, but the blur of demands and betrayals drained her soul and ruptured her confidence. She felt a desperate loneliness akin to her first year in college, but with the stakes raised a hundredfold. She literally had no one to support her.

11

DENIAL, DIVERSIONS, ESCAPES, EXPLOSIONS

The early twinges and later pangs of midlife malaise bring the tower builder to the first edge of fear on the journey toward aliveness. The achievement-based modus operandi of multiple decades no longer works, and a small inner voice increases its volume and asks, "What are you going to do about this mess?" The fear emerges from the realization that facing the issues and truthfully confronting ourselves will lead to a drastic life change—and it may not be change for the better. Exploring the truth about ourselves might lead eventually to a personal epiphany and a second half of stewardship and joy, or it may open a labyrinth of shadows, second-guessing, and depression demons that confuse us and suffocate our remaining life.

It seems to be a "damned if you do, damned if you don't" edge. Why undergo a psychological and spiritual root canal with no assurance that the pain will cease? At least a stalemated career and a gridlocked marriage can be managed. Most midlife leaders, especially those with some level of financial security, *don't want to know* that the tower they've been building for 20 or more years rests on shifting sand, that their marriage and kids are not fixable, and that their habitual escape valves have become addictions that they are powerless to control on their own.

Few midlife leaders have the courage and support community to face, head-on, the initial reality of their discontent. Most employ one or more of the coping and defense mechanisms defined in the remainder of this chapter. Figure 11.1 presents the four common ways these executives, professionals, and pastoral leaders avoid facing their disillusionment. Only a handful assemble a support community, face their issues,

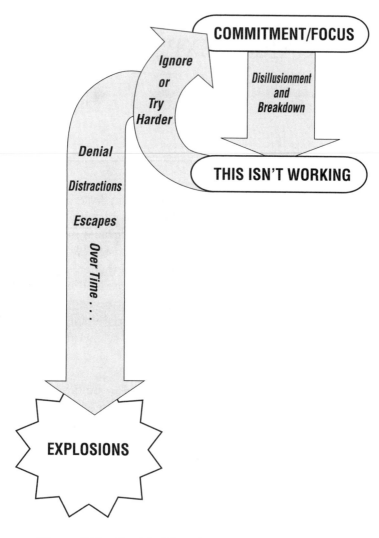

Figure 11.1   Denial, Diversions, Escapes, Explosions.

and break through the edge of fear into a deeper understanding, acceptance, and love of themselves.

Level 1: Denial

Our first-level pain-reduction tactic is to deny that a real problem exists. We view the initial frustrations, even the nagging anxieties or midlife despondency, as just another collection of challenges to be solved by working harder, trying harder, spending more money, or praying more fervently. In the early and middle stages of tower construction, persistence always paid off. Thus, working harder seems the logical antidote to the early pangs of midlife melancholy.

Closely aligned with this tenacity approach is avoidance. Confrontation—which is essential to uncovering the truth—inevitably causes pain, which our culture of comfort abhors. So if the problem is at home, hole up at the office or go on a road trip. If interpersonal problems exist at work, schedule a long vacation, hang around the golf course, or hide behind a network of secretarial gatekeepers. When perseverance isn't yielding results, concentrate on familiar or solvable issues, and hope the ugly problem goes away. The warped rationale: If I don't plunge into this, maybe it will disappear of its own accord.

In the West we thrive on our intellect. American ingenuity is about "figuring things out." Read the manual, do some research, retain an expert consultant. Surround the problem, dissect it, apply resources, eliminate defects, solve it—and move on. First-world countries have embraced this approach and built powerful, affluent nations. Unfortunately, the soul and its shadows can't be analyzed like a lab experiment or healed by research and pro con charts; they defy quantification.

Another common denial tactic is comparison with others. No matter how wretched or scary our situation, *someone* has worse problems. We rationalize:

> ➤ "Yes, our marriage is flat, but at least we're not in an ugly divorce, locked in a venomous custody battle."
> ➤ "I may have no passion for my work, but I make a handsome salary, the board accepts me, and my family lives in a safe, upscale neighborhood."
> ➤ "We no longer have sex, but the antidepressants seem to be working."

➤ "I may be run ragged by commitments, but my boss loves my work, and the company needs me."

Our internal conflict-avoider, backed by our battering-ram intellect, concocts a myriad of rationalizations that justify, even affirm, our midlife plight as normal or merely a phase to be endured. Most friends will commiserate with our whining, affirm our anger at the world, and tell us what we want to hear. We'll identify and sacrifice an appropriate scapegoat (irrational boss, fickle market, fiendish mother-in-law, alcoholic father, duplicitous minister, wrathful God) on the altar of self-vindication. Then, with the blame for our plight placed safely elsewhere, we'll bolster ourselves to endure the pain or try harder. We'll forge an illusory armor, a convoluted logic of excuses and rationalizations, that may protect us for a while, only to be punctured by the next—or the next or the next—arrow to the soul.

The accumulation, harvesting, and stockpiling of wealth also mute the early stages of midlife uneasiness. Carefully crafted security systems and countercyclical hedge funds seem to avert or solve most problems. When in doubt, throw more cash at the problem: boarding schools, his-her-and-their therapists, international experts, management psychologists, and escape havens du jour. Cash solves all other problems; surely it can also be the radiation treatment for soul cancer—the heavier the dose, the quicker the cure.

The positive-mental-attitude, smell-the-flowers approach to midlife unrest has become especially popular since 1980, and has been effective in stemming free-fall depression and injecting hope and wonder into troubled lives. However, while a sense of joy, gratitude, and worthiness must complement and illuminate the route out of midlife malaise, many in our culture use a don't-worry-be-happy, count-your-blessings disposition to mask their sorrow, anger, and anxiety with pap and platitudes. They experience a long-needed rebirth of spirit, but still suffer a paucity of soul.

Besides avoiding the problem, we also avoid emotion. We acknowledge the pleasant emotions (joy, tenderness, excitement) but avoid or deny the painful ones. We pursue joy without embracing grief. We deny the truth about our anger, and thereby never establish clean boundaries. We shroud our fears with masks of serenity and connection. We sprinkle our soul wounds with the holy water of cheap clichés and feigned happiness, but never allow them to ooze repressed grief, to be cleansed with the ointment of truth, and to be dressed with the bandage of community. We tend to inject our souls with painkillers of feel-good rhetoric, and then hastily suture the wounds with the familiar threads of hard work and self-sacrifice. We deaden the pain, temporarily, but the dormant, festering infection will erupt again, usually at the most inopportune time.

Level 2: Bargaining, Deflection, Diversions

When the first-level denial techniques—work harder, avoid the problem, just figure it out, compare with the less fortunate, rationalize, throw cash at the problem, maintain a positive mental attitude—can't quell the sense of malaise, second-level defense mechanisms are engaged to deflect or divert the pain. If the infantry of denial can't do the job, bring in the armor of diversions—activities that prevent introspection and hard truth.

The bargaining approach involves "cutting a deal" with aggrieved parties—including our wounded psyche—usually to buy time. In a fragile marriage where the spouse is saber rattling about divorce proceedings, a common tactic is, "Stay with me a little longer, honey. We're just about to turn the corner. I know it's been rough, but I need your support. When this is over, our marriage is my top priority." Deals with God go something like, "God, if you'll bail me out of this jam, I promise to change my ways and be a big contributor at church." These negotiations position God as a power broker with a ledger book and a long memory, who expects quid pro quo paybacks for answered prayers. Pacts with our psyche usually involve finding refuge in the affirmations of others, like self-worth call girls. All these forms of bargaining are really mental gymnastics designed to veil the real wounds of fear, anger, and unworthiness in our souls.

While psychoanalysis can provide deep insight into the self and the foundation for eventual soul-level healing, it can also become a weekly pity party and bitch session, scapegoating others and avoiding our own culpability for our situations. In such case, whining to the commiserating ear of a "professional friend" may provide momentary relief, but rarely leads to facing and going through fears until the ear is accompanied by a mirror.

Another common palliative for down-and-in malaise is up-and-out action. Any new activity—at work, in our personal lives, or in some form of service—creates a diversion from midlife angst. Fear thrives in idleness, so filling time with activity forestalls the fear demons. In the business world this might take the form of a major change, such as relocating the office, adding new partners, making an acquisition, or raising equity. Each involves taking on more challenge, setting the bar higher, redesigning the tower. These maneuvers demand the full commitment of the instigator and champion, diverting the person's attention away from soul-level probing. Often, this activity *intentionally* adds stress, but it's the familiar tension of comparison, competition, and achievement, which are well-known bedfellows to the midlife leader.

Increased community service and religious organization involvement offer powerful, positive remedies for midlife depression and selfishness. The internal feel-good sensation and external affirmation that come from helping others salves many wounds. However, such service can also become an emotional crutch, a noble detour away from deep conflicts in the home, at work, or in the soul. Our subconscious rationalizes, "If I'm not getting any love at home, and work is a downer, at least I'll get some positive strokes down at the soup kitchen, leading the Bible study, or coaching a Little League team." When the rest of life is in the toilet, *any* chance to do something good relieves pain. But volunteer activities are healthy when performed out of caring and stewardship, and not as a self-validation fix or a distraction from facing hard realities.

Common diversions at home include the major house remodeling, construction or acquisition of a vacation home, purchase of new toys (boats, planes, cars), or immersion in a new hobby. The Internet offers another, potentially addictive diversion for many executives who escape into online investing, games, shopping, or pornography.

Fear of aging and death often triggers a flurry of activity around renewing or regaining health. Resurrecting the 20-year-old body becomes the highly personal cause worth living for, and who can argue against a healthy body and an alert mind? When used as a diversion tactic, though, the healthy habit of using a personal trainer and nutritional supplements evolves into the three-hour-a-day training obsession, regional triathlons, extreme skiing in Canada, and ruthless diet scrutiny. None of these are bad in themselves—unless they are used to divert us from soul unrest.

These diversions repackage old patterns of zeal and commitment from tower building into a shallow or false altruism. The cause is more noble, but the motives—achievement, success, external affirmation—are the same. Activity replaces reflection, and the real wounds of the soul remain undressed.

Level 3: Escapes

Others can see our diversions. Escapes can be less obvious and are often kept carefully hidden. The most common escapes are habits that degenerate into addictions, defined as any behavior with negative pathological consequences. For example, work moves from diversion to addiction when all other aspects of life either disappear or orbit like satellites around the planet of work. Addictions involve a need for immediate and constant gratification. The incessant quest for pleasure offers relief from the depressive weight of a listless, wasted life. Hedonism and selfishness are attempts to find meaning in the material world rather than confront a void in the soul.

Midlife leaders fall prey to the standard, almost sanctioned addictions of our culture: work, power, money, recognition, sex, and alcohol. Our media endorse them as signposts of success or chic. Food, gambling, and narcotics habits are viewed with more disdain and engaged in with more secrecy, but are still prevalent among high-profile leaders seeking escape from their furious lives.

Sexual escape among executives, professionals, and people in ministry often begins with pornography and escalates into prostitution and affairs. Beyond the immediate pleasure, the secrecy of the extramarital affair creates a sanctuary where the parties see and value each other, even if just for an evening. The ego's yearning to connect and be loved—no matter what the source of that love—overrides the rational mind's warning signals about consequences. The feeling that *anyone* accepts me as I am, sees me as being worthy, even for just a night, even for money, casts all prudence to the wind in order to receive this temporary, purchased "love."

Beyond the negative physical and financial side effects of food, sex, alcohol, narcotics, and gambling habits, these addictions require clandestine behavior to keep them hidden from both loved ones and the "proper" world. Maintaining secrecy around these activities takes energy and guile. Though deleterious in the long run, this secrecy energy actually serves the addict by redirecting him from the void in his soul. As with the diversions described earlier, *any* activity that thwarts self-reflection and the likely discovery of a squandered or meaningless existence becomes a valued defense mechanism. The ego says in effect, "Do whatever you need to do, but don't look inside."

Many affluent executives in both pressure-cooker careers and shaky marriages live vicariously through their children. This is especially true when their tower building has gone awry or the marriage is careening toward divorce. They obsess about the right schools, best coaches, and constant recognition for their children, rationalizing, "My life may be in the tank, but my kids are gonna have it great." A shaky or shattered identity seeks healing, and what better way than through the undefiled potential of our children? Little League tryouts are on a par with the Major League draft, disputed calls on the field lead to parental violence, and the "B" on a geography midterm triggers weekend tutoring. When we've failed in constructing our own tower, our children offer us a second chance. We ignorantly inoculate them with low-grade doses of the perform-to-be-loved virus, which incubates through their 20s and 30s, only to flare up in their 40s, contaminating the *next* generation—our grandchildren—with the poison of earned love.

Another type of escape is to adopt a martyr persona. While the whirl of responsibilities and life on a treadmill are prime causes for midlife distress, they are also socially acceptable escape routes from self-reflection and anesthetics for guilt, shame, and unworthiness. We rationalize, "If I'm serving other people, I must be a good person." In this sense, escalating responsibilities and porous boundaries actually serve us: "If I stay busy, I won't have the time to dwell on how much I hurt. And if others like me, it won't matter so much that I don't like myself." Martyrdom becomes noble.

A parallel escape mechanism is the savior mind-set: "I'm the only one who can lead this organization out of the wilderness. They need me." The narcissistic savior outwardly demands courageous efforts and 100 percent commitment from both his followers and himself or the Cause will suffer, maybe die. Visibility is more important than success or failure. He crafts a smothering codependency where all organizational decisions cross his desk. He strips responsibility from others to feed his own self-worth.

The martyr and savior modes sometimes combine in zealous commitment to a movement, such as a nonprofit cause or evangelism for a newfound or reborn belief. Sincere and effective service to religious, altruistic, and philanthropic causes requires a foundation of genuine caring for the cause, indifference to personal recognition, and a grounded sense of self. All too often, however, the escapee's primary motive is a desperate search for significance when he realizes the rest of his life is meaningless. The tower-building obsessions of the material world are simply transferred to the nonprofit or spiritual sector. The subconscious message remains: "See me!" Public accolades, feted dinners, named buildings, weepy new disciples, and over-the-top fund-raising campaigns gorge the deflated ego with importance and ignore the soul. As we'll explore in Part IV, selfless, anonymous service, performed joyfully, with genuine caring for and connection with *all* the people, revives, nourishes, and elevates the soul. The ego needs to be seen; the soul needs to connect. Sadly, our culture begets satiated egos and starving souls.

These last escapes—through our children, devotion or martyrdom to the cause, becoming the savior, service zeal—are common Band-Aids for low self-worth. They gloss over the inner sense that "my life is a shambles and I don't like myself as a person," effectively saying, "so I'll devote myself to an outside cause, hoping that someone out there will see me and love me for my efforts." They deaden the throbbing ego with the balm of short-term wins and outside affirmation.

Level 4: Explosions

The extreme form of escape is the creation of an explosive event that marshals all of our cognitive powers for damage control or, perhaps, survival. An explosion is orchestrated when the fear of facing midlife disillusionment, the soul's malnourishment, and our shadowy selves is so overwhelming that a life crisis is preferred over soul confrontation.

We may ignore obvious health warning signals (weight, blood pressure, history of cancer), or continue to live a life of excess (food, alcohol, unsafe sex, narcotics), thereby accelerating a disastrous event—and soliciting the attention of others (medical triage, sympathy, rage, prosecution). The ego rationalizes that any recognition is better than languishing in obscurity.

In the work environment, when everything is running smoothly and the unfulfilled leader's presence is less needed on a daily basis, he may create a crisis requiring immediate, full-force fire-fighting skills. Financial overextension, a management overhaul, and overhyping the company to investors often lead to crises that demand 100 percent focus to unravel, summon the savior-martyr to take charge, and divert the firefighter from soul-level reflection. The rationale: "When my company is collapsing I don't have time to deal with the rest of my life."

As described earlier, the secrecy shrouding marital infidelity consumes considerable energy and usually suspends soul self-examination. Sometimes the subconscious will have us engage *purposely* in what others perceive as idiotic activities, or *deliberately* leave a trail of clues leading to ignominious discovery. The subconscious *intends* to get caught, preferring high visibility and crisis management over the dull, internal torment of a duplicitous, empty life. For high-profile leaders addicted to the rarefied air of fame, any press, even vilifying press, is better than no press.

These explosives experts choose to live their life at the edge, where mental acuity is king, and emotions and the soul are nuisances. When intellectual gifts and cunning aren't in demand, and inner rumblings begin to echo the emptiness of their lives, they'll orchestrate an event that forces them back to the edge.

Sometimes highly visible achievers tumble from their self-created, lonely edges into the abysses of deep depression, crime, imprisonment, or suicide. In their rise to the pinnacles of their towers, they cultivated no supporting community, no tethers on their lives. Desperate and alone, they either fall or go numb.

Stories of Denial, Diversions, Escapes, and Explosions

The disillusionments and breakdowns presented in Chapter 10 cause pain and invariably breed the specter of more and deeper misery. The avoidance tactics discussed in this chapter are intended to detour us *around* the fear of the pain. Life breakthroughs, presented in the next chapter, require us to go *through* this fear. For most leaders the *fear* of the pain is worse than the pain itself.

As my own business foundered I was haunted by the prospect of squandering the 12 years of my life that I had invested in running the company. All the late nights, long trips, and missed opportunities with my children would be for nothing. While the company losses and downsizing hurt, the gnawing prospect of 12 misspent years in the prime of my life devastated my self-worth.

I abhorred being in the office, and diverted the pain with frequent visits to customers and prospects who either loved or hungered for our products. Sales offered short-term, one-dimensional wins, and masked the reality and complexity of the coming needs of our clients and the looming competition. I got my relational fix from satisfied customers and live-for-today salespeople, and avoided the painful strategic decisions that would reshape the company and my own role.

Vice presidents became the scapegoats sacrificed for company failings. I would then stem my anxiety by taking on their jobs, since working to exhaustion was better than wallowing in the fear of possible failure. Besides, I had to model a fervent work ethic, fostering the illusion that long hours were the antidote for poor strategy.

Stan had lost his safe havens. When his father died he immersed himself in work, walling in the grief of losing his only mentor, the only person who had ever really loved him. After the merger work was completed and he had quit to appease his wife, Linda, he hoped that she would become the new oasis to feed his spirit and, eventually, his soul. Instead she became more vitriolic, possessive, and selfish. He felt truly alone.

Stan battled the desperation in his personal life by dabbling in entrepreneurial endeavors that demanded his time and siphoned his cash. He avoided the harangues at home by working harder and longer, finding some solace in the intellectual challenge and operational fire-fighting of his diverse start-ups.

He also escaped through clandestine, sometimes deviant sexual encounters. He created a surreal world of prostitutes and call girls who gave him perverse pleasure as erotic, secret sex became the outlet for his repressed rage. After this release he would return home empty, and able to endure Linda's tirades, entertaining the remote hope that somehow she would change and his marriage would work out. The pattern was consistent: She exploded; he went numb or escaped. He ameliorated her with sex and with money to feed her obsession for possessions. When her raving became too much, he got his fix with another call girl.

Even as he yearned for a life partner, Fletcher disdained relational intimacy beyond sex. He feared appearing weak, ordinary, or stupid, and being rejected again. He was terrified of sobriety and truth. Cocaine and alcohol gave him the illusion of being in command, offering him wit, confidence, and a drug-induced sense of control—and above all he was addicted to control.

The company sale went smoothly and he entered the four-hours-a-day, baton-pass-to-the-new-owners stage. With work no longer an outlet for his passion, he became a health and fitness fanatic, spending hours at the gym, in the pool, or on the track, training for triathlons. He trained and managed his body the way he monitored his relationships, always maintaining control.

Entrenched in his listless career, Peter accepted the mantle of dutiful martyr, laboring in homage to his deceased father, feeling responsible for the well-being of his extended family. He hated the work, but was trapped in the gravitational pull of a four-generation legacy. He partially diverted the pain by staying active on the parish council, participating in his TEC group meetings, and regularly playing golf. But otherwise, he had no diversions or escapes to mute his loathing for his vocation and the rising sense that his life was slipping away—that he was dying.

Marty never saw himself as the problem. During his hopeless stint as an area director for the ministry, he rationalized, "I'm doing God's work. It's got to be for good," even though his marriage was in the pits and he had no local friends. As the hours increased and the tension of reduced funding rose, he blamed Sarah for her low support: "If only she'd get with the program, we'd be fine." He became a workaholic "in service to the Lord."

Marty suffered from bulimia, beginning in his seminary days. He would binge on food, then vomit, sometimes several times a day. It became his private ritual escape, which he hid from *everyone*.

Susan coped by becoming superwoman. Bred to be a survivor, she rallied with an "I'll show them" reprisal against the ongoing attacks by her in-laws, who now labeled her the family pariah and the cause of her husband's business failures. She unflinchingly embraced every duty, partly as penance for her own sense of foolishness about her fiduciary lapse that had led to her office manager's embezzlement. Amidst it all, she was ever responsible for keeping the family unit together, emotionally and financially. Her only escape was her work.

12

The EDGE, NUMBNESS, and BREAKTHROUGHS

The First Edge of Fear

The recognition and acknowledgment of midlife upheaval brings us to an edge of fear. An inner voice whispers, and sometimes bellows, "Your life isn't working and *you must change.*" The defense mechanisms of denial, diversions, escapes, and explosions repress the fear of change, the fear of self-exploration, and the fear of confronting personal failings. They also mute our sorrow and shame which, if ignored and untreated, fester or morph into guilt and depression.

Over the course of perhaps several years, the midlife pilgrim has multiple glimpses of, and sometimes close encounters with, this edge of fear, which calls him to explore his soul—to plumb the naked truth about himself. The terror of this encounter, especially without friends, elders, or guides to encourage him and light the path, causes the pilgrim to retreat into denial, diversions, and escapes.

Joseph Campbell says that the pilgrim at the edge is being called to the Hero's Journey, to understand and find himself, independent of the "false calls" and lures of the material world.[1] The remainder of this book will consider the step across the edge of fear—the exploration, nourishment, and transformation of the soul—and the return to the material world, open, cleansed, grateful, surrendered, prepared to live fully and serve unselfishly.

Many midlife navigators assess this call across the edge as too terrifying, the rewards too ephemeral, the guides either nonexistent or inexperienced. At different times they confront this inner voice that is calling them to the edge, refusing the call with some variation of:

- ➤ "I know my life isn't working. But I don't know any other way."
- ➤ "The risk of change is too great."
- ➤ "I can't handle the pain of the truth. I know I'm pretending, but I choose to continue with this life of pretense; it's a pain I know and can deal with."
- ➤ "I know it's a sham, but it's safe."

As these would-be journeyers age into their 50s and 60s, especially without any mentors or guides, the denials and defenses squelch and finally mute the inner call of the soul. A subconscious helplessness sets in and, emotionally, they go numb.

Numbness

Subconsciously, many people in midlife pain erect an impenetrable, unscalable barricade a safe distance from their edge. By so doing they can renounce the very existence of the edge of fear. The denial, diversion, and escape tactics continue, but more as a way of life than avoidance of the fear. The ego forgoes wonder, spontaneity, playfulness, reflection, even celebration and joy, to refocus on achievement or the pursuit of pleasure. With the inner world barricaded off, the only alternative for supposed "life" is in the outer world of triumphs and indulgence, or in service or philanthropy that feeds the ego. Since emotions lure the heart back to the edge, the ego shunts grief, anger, and anxiety into cynicism and blame. We scapegoat others; it's never about us.

Absent a sense of wonder and introspection, soul numbness is manifested in one of two extremes: deflated and inflated. The deflated person suffers a monochromatic life, shunning intimacy and avoiding connection with others and with God. He becomes a curmudgeon, whining that nothing is ever quite right or good enough.

Inflated numbness also sidesteps the fearful edge of change, but is bent on bloating and brandishing the ego. Without a soul-level sense of self, the inflated person becomes an arrogant manipulator who maintains a condescending air of aloofness, while constantly guarding against betrayal. He deploys humor and knowledge as either weapons or diversions, and has few, if any, friends who really know him.

Whether deflated or inflated, the numb person squelches his real feelings and quarantines his inner world. He doesn't know himself, and he doesn't *want* to. His options are to get small (deflated) or get big (inflated), but never to get *real*.

The visual media (movies, TV, tabloids) become places of ritual escape for numb people, who become aliveness *observers*, witnessing the suffering, eroticism, anger, and joy of others, but never tasting truth, pain, and love for themselves—the risks are too great. Ease displaces engagement; security supplants exploration.

The numb person may view the spiritual world as either a duplicitous sham, an amusing carnival, or a baffling mystery. He equates spirituality with religion, to be shunned completely or perhaps tolerated a few times a year at the high holidays, weddings, and funerals. The ceremony and pageantry are interesting, and "It's the right thing to do for the children," but religion lacks meaning. "Weaker, more desperate people may find solace within religion, but the thinking man finds it a bore."

On the other hand, when religious people deny their fears, their numbness often manifests in platitudes and constant reference to sacred scripture or great teachers. They pontificate or evangelize, but don't walk their talk. As modern-day Pharisees, they offer lip-service surrender to both God and spirit, experiencing neither.

In Western culture the soul has become like a dying tooth, desensitized with work and pleasure, and capped with the shiny porcelain crown of pretense. We'll do anything to avoid the root canal that cleans out the infection and fills the empty cavity. We end up with a mouth full of glistening porcelain caps concealing decayed, dying teeth.

Breakthroughs

But our soul never really dies. Even though numbed by addictions and diversions, and seemingly in a coma, the soul—our gifts, wounds, shadows, genius, and aliveness—still seeks expression. The presence of God inside us longs to connect.

Our body knows, at the cellular level, that we are muting the song of our soul. The symptoms would be obvious if we were awake; many of our illnesses (cancer, heart disease, back problems) may be indicative of soul dis-ease. We've just conditioned ourselves to ignore these signals.

Our subconscious warns us of the risks of exploring soul wounds. As we open ourselves to others we risk further betrayal. We may do deep emotional excavation, face our demons, and achieve momentary enlightenment—yet nothing really changes in our lives; it may not work at all. Or we might totally lose control and be overwhelmed by the waves of guilt, sadness, anger, or unworthiness. Perhaps the biggest risk in exploring our soul is that we may find our true self and, with it, the call to a totally different way of life. We'll have to take responsibility for our lives, with no more excuses or rationalizations.

Yet even with these risks, breakthroughs into soul aliveness do happen. The midlife navigator reaches the point where he can't think, talk, work, buy, or pray his way out of the angst. Finally overwhelmed by the "blessing" of a bankruptcy, a serious illness or injury, or an intervention for an addiction, he trembles at the frightening edge of powerlessness, and, for perhaps the first time in his life, is ready to explore the inner reaches of his soul.

The breakthrough may begin as the simple recognition that "my life isn't working, and I'm open to exploring why." It's not a commitment to *do* anything yet—just to *understand* the malaise, to pursue the inner mystery, to explore paradoxical issues. In the recovery movements' Twelve-Step programs,[2] this is step one: I'm powerless to resolve my issues on my own, and my life has become unmanageable.

In the Hero's Journey, when the pilgrim accepts the call to explore the unknown, a guide comes on the scene: "When the student is ready, the teacher appears." Downward and inward exploration requires a guide—a coach, counselor, therapist, or any friend who listens and cares without judgment or pat solutions. The task of understanding described in the following chapters may start as a solo endeavor, but the real work of the soul is done in *both* solitude and community. Perhaps that's why the recovery movements always meet in small groups and advocate a sponsor for the wounded, recovering person.

The first movement off the edge toward the abyss may be a tentative step; it doesn't have to begin with an all-or-nothing leap. The soul-explorer may still feel in control of his quest and simply want knowledge about his malaise, understanding the "why." Staying "in the head" is a safe place to start. Movement through the emotions and into the soul may evolve slowly, depending on the depth of past betrayals, the openness of the support community, and the experience and presence of the guide(s). Growth begins with minor movements. The heavy grate covering our soul is nudged back just a few inches, and we peek inside. The life-changing epiphanies usually come later.

As trust in the guides and fellow pilgrims builds, the aliveness seeker becomes more open to seeing "whatever might be down there." He begins to accept his powerlessness to resolve or think through the disillusionment on his own. At this point, with an openness to the heart and with guides to accompany him, the pilgrim embarks on the journey to explore and understand his soul. He takes the first downward steps toward greatness.

Stories of Encounters at the Edge of Fear

Each encounter at the edge presents an opportunity to step consciously into a place of truth and, likely, pain, with no guarantee of a cure, healing, or even reduction of the torment. Usually the anguish will even increase, at least for a time. The alternative is a return to the denial, bargaining, or escape tactics that blur the truth and anesthetize the hurt. The only promise for going through the edge is a heightened awareness of the truth about ourselves, the real *source* of the pain. The more times we back away from this edge, reverting to defenses and diversions, the more numb we become to life and the more difficult it becomes to change.

My period of numbness manifested in clinical depression. For nearly two years I experienced my world through a fog. I felt chained to the bed each morning, dreading the downward spiral of problems awaiting me at the office. Arriving at work, I hunkered down, crafting correspondence and calling friends, minimizing contact with my management team, hoping they would somehow figure it out themselves. We would chat and joke, but we avoided the tough topics of downsizing and cost cutbacks until we had no choice but to take drastic action. But drastic action required rescuing, which was far better than wallowing. At least I was taking charge.

The combination of depression and the company unraveling brought me to the edge of powerlessness. Certainly I had some impact on the destiny of both my company and my life, but not much. Having led a relatively charmed life for 40 years, this edge terrified me, and I refused to confront the pain of possible failure. I couldn't meet it without experienced mentors, men who had faced their own depressions, failures, and worthlessness demons—and had survived the encounters.

I realized I needed help. I assembled a diverse "personal board of directors" who had each navigated their own derailments and train wrecks. They encouraged and guided me to, and then through, the edge of my fears. As I heard their stories of loss (the death of a child, living in a hateful marriage, being sucked under in the quicksand of a bankruptcy), I found solace and hope—especially seeing their aliveness on the other side of their failures.

My key breakthrough required facing head-on the prospect of losing the company and my entire investment of 12 years. I visualized the worst-case financial scenario of this loss, and extrapolated even further—imagining myself and my family as homeless, living in a cardboard box under a viaduct. By expanding my woes to the point of absurdity, my current situation seemed lighter—I could even laugh about it. I also accepted that, even with my clever brain and great connections, my life path was ultimately out of my control. Paradoxically, this thought of not being in control was very freeing. Perhaps most importantly, I reopened my heart to a Power greater than my heart that accepted me even in my brokenness, no matter what happened.

This gradual relaxation of control constituted my breakthrough and allowed me to downsize the company and—after tense negotiations where my ego tried to sabotage the deal—eventually to sell it, and to emerge from my depression. I escaped the destitution scene under the viaduct, but gained the courage to explore myself and my wounds further. At 42 I came to grips with the sorrow, hope, and transformation that come from loss, and I was prepared to explore the disowned parts of my soul.

Stan belonged to a small group, a Young Presidents' Organization (YPO) forum, where he felt safe enough to gradually reveal his deeper self. They listened to and affirmed him as he told his story, divulging more detail as he felt safer among these colleagues. Over time Stan came to realize that his edge involved facing the losses in his life: his father, his company, his marriages, and perhaps his ability to sire children. The breakthrough came as the members of his forum created the space for him to grieve the death of his father. Supported by others, he gained the courage to begin exploring the venom—and the untapped greatness—that had been stuffed inside him for most of his life.

Fletcher's turning point occurred at a retreat with his executive small group, when the others confronted him on his rudderless life. As he prepared to deliver his standard defense to these stodgy fellow presidents, he saw their sincere concern for his well-being and stopped cold. This was the first time he could recall *anyone* caring for him without wanting a piece of him. He returned from the retreat knowing he must shed his addictions, but still terrified of entering an honest, intimate-without-sex relationship. He came to understand the price of living in the truth. He had arrived at his edge: Was he willing to risk rejection by a woman of character and depth after she saw the real Fletcher?

Fletcher's breakthrough required the tentative first steps toward sobriety. After 20 years of hedonism and chameleon-like behavior, he prepared to walk into the naked truth about his vulnerabilities. With the support of his small group and a fledgling faith in God, he entered a stage of sexual abstinence and substance sobriety, open to explore his shadows and, perhaps, find his soul.

Peter had become close to a couple of members of his small group, who saw through the mask of humor and duty he wore at their monthly meetings and elicited from him the truth about the guilt, shame, and fear that kept him toiling in the family business. When these emotions surfaced, he was overcome by a sense of unworthiness—"Now even these guys know I'm a loser"—and offered to withdraw from the group: "I really don't have much to contribute. I'm sure you can find another member with more experience and energy. I'd better leave."

One man in the group sensed that Peter was close to a breakthrough and invited him to join him for a weekend getaway, where Peter could tell his full story from the inside. As his friend simply listened, Peter's story came pouring out—the wounds from his childhood, his love-hate relationship with his father, and his fear about leaving the business. By simply listening, Peter's friend gave him permission to explore his emotions and find his life.

With the completion of his vacation home, Larry's primary diversion switched to the clandestine affairs that numbed him from the sameness of his work. Fortunately, the YPO small group he had joined saw through his rationalizations and lovingly confronted him about his life. With the help of their tethering he closed off his current affair and began to explore different spiritual traditions, seeking the grounding and courage he would need to consider opportunities outside the corporate womb. The real breakthroughs came at a series of retreats where he raged over and mourned his fragmented spiritual upbringing and his relationship with his father. He was ready for the inner-work root canal.

With television, movies, and a general lethargy Thad numbed his anger and sadness over his and Rachael's infertility. He hated being a mercenary in the insurance firm and was frustrated at not being able to use his strategic, mentoring, and motivational skills. The small voice of inferiority from his childhood plagued him: "You're not good enough to play in the big leagues. You're a failure—you've disappointed your father." Deflated, he spun in the downward spiral of depression.

Yet Thad's wife and YPO forum did not give up on him. They loved and valued him, affirming his gifts and giving him a place to grieve and be angry. They gave him permission to be a man. Gradually, he began to set aside his past betrayals by authority figures and to trust these new guides, who encouraged him and held the miner's lamp as he began the fearful tunneling into his soul.

Marty regressed into the security of his associate pastor role, doing his job and staying small. Only embers of his vision of church leadership remained when his breakthrough came—via a family crisis. His son's drug habit had escalated to a dangerous level, and the family arranged an intervention. At the intervention, the focus suddenly shifted from his son to Marty. The wrath and sense of betrayal of both his wife and son cascaded onto Marty. Once they had spoken their truths, he marshaled the courage to share his own shame about his life, his fears of abandonment, and his yearning to run his own church.

Marty had always "had God," but now he finally began to believe that "God really cares about me, even with all my baggage." He and his wife participated in communication workshops, and he attended men's retreats where he could "work on his stuff."

Though Susan escaped through her work and the illusion of being superwoman, she was aware of her own deteriorating mental and emotional state. "I can't continue to live this way—or can I?" She oscillated between her need to recapture her life, possibly by getting out of a torturous marriage, and her duty to fulfill the responsibilities she felt toward her children. "If this marriage dies, we will destroy three little people. But either the marriage changes or *I will leave*."

All this whipsawed through her head when John asked her to attend a weekend Transition workshop with him to "sort through their life together." Wrathful and stubborn, at first she declined. But the loneliness and hopelessness of their situation finally compelled her to attend. She sensed this would be a direct confrontation with her fear of failure, of not being able to successfully "figure out" and "persevere through" a situation. She vowed that she would either break through the communication logjam with John or leave him.

The breakthrough occurred. They bared their souls to one another and discovered they didn't really hate each other, only what had happened to them. They honored each other's worth and became support for each other—to explore themselves, their marriage, their vocational destinies, their roles as parents. After expressing both their tears and their rage, they became open to whatever might come.

It was a huge step for Susan to acknowledge her powerlessness—and a joyous relief to discover that she now had a partner on her pilgrimage to re-define her life.

III

UNDERSTANDING the SOUL

13

UNDERSTANDING the SOUL—INTRODUCTION

Introduction to Greatness

Our success-oriented culture defines greatness using measures of wealth, achievement, and victory. We are so obsessed with comparison that self-contained greatness is never enough. People aim to be bigger than, better than, richer than, greater than others, whether a political leader guiding a nation, a corporate executive amassing profits, an athlete winning championships, a scientist finding cures, or an evangelist saving souls. The inevitable comparisons quantify and calibrate the individual's greatness: "Oh yes, he was richer than/smarter than/on a par with/close to Roosevelt, Welch, Jordan, Salk, Mother Teresa . . . "—pick your metric. And when the old standard-bearer is eclipsed, he or she becomes "old news," just another name in the annals of has-been leaders who were "great in their time."

I propose to you a new definition of greatness that defies comparison (though many of us will still try to concoct metrics) and may offend the many grade givers. There is a depth of greatness that has more to do with a person's essence or core than with outer accomplishments. It is tied more closely to what someone is and expresses than to what one achieves. Consider that this greatness is centered in the ability to receive and give love. The foundation of knowing that we are loved—by ourselves, by others, and by a higher Source—frees us to unabashedly offer our gifts to the world in loving stewardship and service.

I realize that it seems easy and naive to say, "Just learn how to love, and you'll be great." But, while this recipe for greatness appears simple, the path of self-discovery, awareness, and surrender that leads to it is arduous and terrifying. This is why so many disillusioned Western leaders, with noble intentions to plumb their psyches and find themselves, balk at their edge of fear, believing they are unlovable, incompetent, or just not good enough. Learning how to truly love requires an inward journey through the betrayals, shame, grief, anger, and anxieties accumulated over a lifetime and banished to the subconscious by our culture of cordiality. Love demands the truth, but spin doctors everywhere conspire to cloak the truth in a facade of comparison, affluence, supposed significance, and success. The image makers of our world then have the gall to call this *greatness*—and we buy it!

The following chapters map the journey across the edge of fear into what appears at first to be the frightening chasm of the subconscious. Figure 13.1 outlines the process of Understanding, Tunneling, and Transformation, and the frightful edge of confronting our shadows. I offer you this hope: If you persevere through these dark inner canyons, shining the light of awareness, forgiveness, and then love on the suppressed sludge heap of your disowned self, a transformation will occur. As you increase the light on and love for *all* of your soul, you'll find the abyss is really a treasure mine, and the rejected tailings are the nuggets of your greatness, simply waiting to be rediscovered, loved, and deployed joyfully in service to your world.

The Quest

In Chapter 12 we left our cadre of pilgrims at their own unique edges of disillusionment and angst. For myself, after 12 years of focused tower building, I had sold my company and entered a midlife sabbatical period. I sought a blueprint for the second half of my life and antidotes for the depression that had stunted my relationships and sapped my energy.

Betrayed by his 10-year business partner and held ransom by his second wife, Stan grasped for an identity beyond being an entrepreneur and a husband. He pondered, "Who am I in all this mess?"

Flush with wealth and supposed freedom after selling his business, Fletcher faced the emptiness and loneliness of encounters—he could hardly call them relationships—with a string of shallow sexual partners. Could he

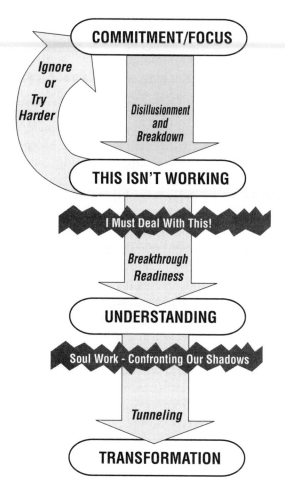

Figure 13.1 Understanding, Tunneling, and Transformation.

ever enter an honest, intimate-beyond-sex, substance-free relationship? Could anyone truly love him without his false bravado and the trappings of his lifestyle?

Peter had likewise reached a financial plateau that assured his material security. Yet he remained mired in a multigenerational legacy that mocked his true talents. He continued to serve as the titular CEO, but he was torn between fulfilling his responsibilities to the family business and pursuing his own dreams.

Larry had goals beyond the corporate monolith. But approaching 50 and not yet financially independent, how could he walk away from his comfortable financial package and perquisites? In addition, Larry knew he must face the splintering effect of his serial affairs on his marriage. He could no longer rationalize his oversize libido as the excuse for seemingly harmless infidelities. Larry knew if he didn't change, he would go numb, and likely lose his marriage.

In an autopilot job, Thad had ample time to ponder his scattered career and childless marriage. If he didn't make an independent name for himself and achieve substantial wealth, he would never meet his father's standards for success. And the specter of a life without his own children—and grandchildren for his parents—left him paralyzed in despair.

After nearly two decades of constant travel and fund-raising within the youth ministry, Marty had finally found some stability as associate pastor within the megachurch. Sarah was more supportive now and relieved to have Marty at home more, especially now, when their son required more attention and love as he worked through his drug addiction. They needed time to rebuild and strengthen their family. But Marty still passionately longed to launch his own church. Could he risk his steady paycheck, his marriage, and the well-being of his child to pursue a nebulous dream?

Susan, the survivor, neared the edge of her sanity. Her superwoman perseverance wore thin around her sniping in-laws and her husband's perpetual melancholy. Her children needed a loving mother, and she yearned for her own solitude and reflection time.

These eight protagonists, plus the hundreds of CEOs who have shared their stories at my retreats, invested their 20s and 30s building their monuments, and in midlife realized that their quests for a secure, happy life had become blocked. Perched on their towers of accomplishment, they questioned their identities ("Who am I?"), their purposes ("What is my life for?"), and their relationships ("Who could really love *me*?"). Research, tenacity, and perseverance failed to resolve these questions. Transformative change demanded that they face loss (of relationships, prestige, squandered years), confront the anger and sadness of prior betrayals, forgive their betrayers, and shed their pretense that everything is fine. These steps trigger the birthing pains of awareness, and none of them promises healing or even a better life.

I have encouraged hundreds of executives, professionals, and people in ministry to name their disillusionments. Many are willing to approach their darkness and can even name their blocks to a richer, truthful life: their anger, pretense, selfishness, worry, numbness, vengefulness, or low self-worth. Yet only a few muster the courage to push through their fears and explore the roots of these debilitating barriers to greatness.

Three common threads exist among these inner-work pilgrims. First, they recognize that lasting life change requires a shift from conventional upward-and-outward thought to more abstract, mystical, down-and-in experiences. The soul journey may begin with a cognitive understanding of the inner landscape, but the transformative work engages the emotions and the body. Few Western culture leaders—saturated with the comparative success ethic of the material world and imbued with the intellectualism and disdain for ambiguity of Western religious traditions—can bear the mystery and uncertainty of soul exploration. Most want answers and can't accept that transformative awareness and growth are always found in the questions.

Second, aliveness seekers recognize the need for a supportive, safe community of fellow pilgrims. They know that the inner journey requires guides and, as Henri Nouwen describes it, a "fellowship of the broken."[1] Yet our culture offers few havens of safety for lost, betrayed leaders. Everyone wants a piece of the man or woman in leadership. Oases of confidentiality and anonymity are rare. Sadly, even most religions, while they offer venues for prayer, worship, and experiencing Spirit, rarely provide the guidance and safety for exploring and experiencing the deep wounds of the soul. But many shattered pilgrims have found places to share their stories without judgment or shaming, in the small group meetings of the recovery movements, in therapy groups, and in the integration groups of the men's and women's movements.

Spirit and Soul

The third requirement for transformative exploration of the soul is some kind of spiritual foundation. Soul and Spirit are not the same. *Soul* relates to the psyche, experiences, particulars, and the self. *Spirit* tends toward the mind, universals, absolutes, and God. We observe the soul by understanding; we grasp it through experience. The "masculine" path to the soul is through the mind: ideas and understanding. The "feminine" path is through the senses: images, mythology, symbolism, ritual, and experience. For several hundred years Western religion has tried to mute the soul, focusing our minds on Spirit. Avoiding or negating soul won't get us to Spirit; instead, we get cheap, head-level religion.

Spirit keeps us open to the transcendent, which we ultimately call

God. The Spirit in us seeks the Spirit of God. Without at least some openness to a spiritual dimension and the possibility of a Higher Power or Source that blesses and orders all things, exploring the subconscious and soul regresses to "engaging psychology." Our explorations may yield some insights into the origins of our baggage, and maybe a little intellectual or emotional enlightenment, but only minimal, usually temporary, life change. Without surrendering to a Higher Power, the inner-work pilgrim often becomes an inner-work junkie, continually seeking a higher transcendent experience or a holier guru, in the elusive search for lasting peace.

For many the concept or person of God engenders great peace—a Father/Mother who is omnipresent, who holds and loves us unconditionally. For others God is synonymous with church and implies a weekly Sabbath obligation. This ceremonial God offers occasional contentment, but is a lower priority during our tower-building years. We call upon Him/Her for help in crises and blessing during celebrations. For some in the Western world the concept of God or the existence of any spiritual realm conjures images of hypocritical ministers and negative religious experiences from childhood. These past betrayals breed either apprehension or anger around anything that strays from the material or cognitive realms.

Before we launch into soul exploration I want to acknowledge your beliefs—and your fears. The models and approaches presented in the following chapters are for your consideration, not your conversion. They are food for thought, not a new doctrine of life or a twenty-first-century gospel. To consider these models and the follow-on action steps, I ask you to set aside the judgments and preconceptions of your faith or nonfaith, and at least be open to broadening your beliefs and awareness.

If you have previously considered and then rejected any spiritual realm, or if you have been betrayed by religiosity in the past, I invite you to reconsider or at least reexamine your position. By pondering the "spiritual talk" perhaps you'll gain some insights into why you are feeling anxious or disillusioned, as well as some tools for a deeper engagement with life.

Perhaps you have a spiritual belief system, Western or Eastern, traditional or nontraditional, that works for you. In your mind you have found the way, are at peace with your beliefs, and don't want to learn another way to look at your life. You might experience sorrow for others who don't have your faith. You may feel compelled to convert or at least educate them.

Regardless of your belief source or your ministry toward others, I applaud your spiritual journey. I ask you to relax your judgments toward other traditions, systems, beliefs, or absence of beliefs, and open yourself to an even larger, more encompassing concept of God than you have considered. Can you be open to new and different ways of knowing or experiencing the unknowable? Is it possible that you are making God too small?

The following chapters ask you to examine concepts and models that may at first appear to be either evangelism or heresy, depending on what you believe or don't believe. But the goal here is simply awareness, which comes from patiently steeping in the questions rather than seeking quick or rigid answers. These chapters offer an entry-level map for exploring and transforming the vast terrain of the subconscious. To talk about this realm requires the use of metaphors, nonlinear thinking, and openness to our senses and emotions. While the models and gateways may trigger your defense mechanisms, they may concurrently offer paths out of your delusions and disillusionment.

The tangible, material world thrives on order and control. The inner world resonates with myth, ambiguity, paradox, ritual, wonder, and not-knowing. Only a Higher Power, the ultimate Source of the inner world, can bring order to this realm of mystery. As you weigh the models and tools of the following chapters, set aside your creed, your biases, or your unbeliefs. Consider this an archaeological expedition that is never finished, yet always complete. Try to find solace and meaning in pieces, clues, and glimpses. The purpose of this work is not to "feel good" or "have a happy life," but to integrate truth and love into our lives and to consider that our deepest calling in life is the discovery and alignment of our one total Self with one all-loving Source.

The Light and the Dark

> I do not understand what I do. For what I want to do, I do not, but what I hate, I do.
>
> —*St. Paul in his letter to the Romans*[2]

How often do we have all the right intentions, but sabotage our efforts at the last minute? We sense the uniqueness and wonder of our giftedness, yet block, divert, or shame ourselves from deploying these gifts.

Part II showed how commitment to the construction of our personal tower masks the telltale signs of discontent until, typically in midlife, they will no longer be denied. When we confront the fearful edge of a life that is no longer working, we begin to ask, "Why do I undermine myself and mute my gifts? How can I stop doing this?"

In my own life I have the ability to galvanize and inspire others in the pursuit of a goal, yet my desire to be significant and my fear of failure often sabotage my efforts. I tend to second-guess my tactics, ignore my intuition, or use manipulation and bluster instead of truth. Nothing I do ever feels complete or right.

Stan is a gifted strategist and a tenacious warrior—a get-it-done guy—who can also organize and motivate a team toward greatness. However, in his relationships with women Stan falls prey to the voice of unworthiness and defeat, and either closes down into numb subservience or escapes through infidelity.

Thad is an insightful, reflective, broad thinker, and a skilled story-teller. But when Thad encounters hostile environments that require a leap of courage, he tends to acquiesce to others and stay small.

Larry is a natural teacher with compassion for the underdog. With his work ethic and passion for a goal, you'd think he would be unstoppable. Yet he has trapped himself in a secure, comfortable lifestyle, which he puts at risk with his promiscuity.

Fletcher is a born leader with an unquenchable work ethic. When focused on a task, he is indomitable. But his internal compass is unstable as he battles his addictions to work, substances, and sex, never getting enough. He oscillates between pleasured-filled fantasy and acute loneliness, wondering if anyone could really love him beyond the haze of the alcohol and the allure of his wealth.

Marty has a natural ability to captivate an audience and nurture struggling souls as he presents the gospel of Christ. However, the insecurities of his youth, when he was either the sidekick or the sideshow, convince him that he must perform and be special, and can't risk just being himself. He has no rest. He drives himself to tackle the hard problems, and pushes himself to the edge of his abilities. He must win, or he will be nobody.

Peter can deliver under pressure. When the stakes are high and disaster appears imminent, he rises to the occasion, diligently does his homework, rallies his teammates, weaves a spellbinding and impassioned story for the audience he is serving, and, normally, averts the crisis. But outside of an emergency, Peter slips into the quicksand of unworthiness and fear that hold him captive until the next crisis.

Susan's determination, attention to detail, and directness make her a natural for the precise, focused work of her practice. Her communication skills and compassion for her patients allow her to excel in her field. Yet even with her frankness Susan can be deceived and victimized by others.

As penance for her lack of judgment she simply works harder and ends up overcommitting herself to income targets, causes, or relationship triage. When her superwoman persona breaks down, she lashes out in anger, normally at her loved ones.

Our self-sabotaging parts will continue to dominate and detour our lives until we face them head-on. The following sections present models for looking at the parts of us we admire and desire to manifest in the world, and the parts we try to ignore, hide, or banish.

The Whole Human Being

The first model, conceptualized by Bob Sloan,[3] assumes that every human being is conceived by a Power beyond himself or herself to be perfect, whole, and completely known. Each of us is the embodiment of love, which flows into us, through us, out of us, and within us. Since everything is known, innocent, and perfect, there is no shame. The egglike depiction in Figure 13.2 represents this perfect, original self.

At some point in human history this whole self became split. In the Judeo-Christian tradition this was called the Fall, when man came to know the difference between good and evil. Figure 13.3 depicts this split. Above the line are the parts of us we wish to manifest in the world. Mythological and religious traditions use different names for these parts, including *life, light, the seen, the known, the visible, beauty, goodness.* We tend to believe that these parts lead to our power, success, and significance in life. We want them to be in control. They represent our known, accepted, and affirmed gifts.

Below the line are our banished or disowned parts. We view them as inner guerrillas intent on undermining our gifts. Mythological and religious names for these parts include *death, darkness, the unseen, the unknown, the invisible, ugliness, sinfulness.* We believe these parts subvert our power, goodness, and holiness, that they cause us to be out of control, to hurt others or ourselves. Therefore we seek to suppress them. Also below the line with these banished parts is our unknown or disowned giftedness, the kernels of our greatness. The psychological term for the part below the line is our subconscious. Soul mediates between the conscious above and the subconscious below. Soul is the *whole* egg.

The iceberg-like depiction of the split between the conscious and the subconscious is intentional. Our subconscious realm—the parts we keep in darkness—is many times larger than the pieces we show to the world.

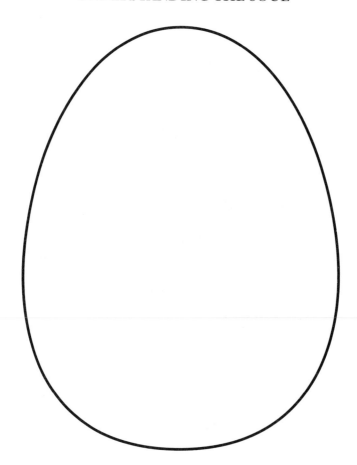

Figure 13.2　**The Whole Human Being.**

Evolution of the Subconscious

This model states that we emerge from the womb as wonder-filled, innocent, open, curious, truthful, totally dependent beings. Our greatness resides in ungerminated seeds, waiting to be watered and nurtured by our caregivers and our environment. At the time of our birth, most of our being is above the line.

Two factors, heredity and upbringing, affect which kernels take root and grow and which kernels languish below the line. Heredity causes both a physical and a psychic resemblance to our parents, grandparents, and ances-

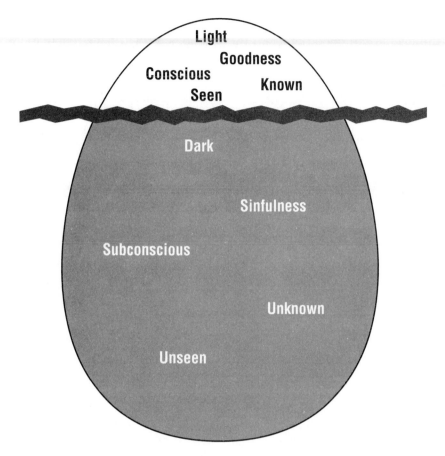

Figure 13.3 **The Split into Conscious and Subconscious.**

tors. For good or bad, we take on components of our progenitors' wiring: their brains, wit, gregariousness, shyness, artistry, and curiosity, as well as their learning disabilities, propensity for alcohol, anxieties, and anger. We are a mosaic of our lineage—the desirable and the undesirable.

Upbringing relates to our experiences and relationships, especially from childhood. As innocent, open children, we view *every* older person—parents, uncles, aunts, teachers, coaches, ministers, older siblings—as an authority figure. We believe them, depend on them, trust them, want to love them, and seek their love and affirmation. They are the mini-gods that shape our lives. Our malleable subconscious records their every word and move. The combination of all our encounters throughout childhood program the reactions we will have to situations and people in our adult lives.

Affirmation and truth-with-love from our caregivers helps keep more of our self above the line. Betrayals and confrontation-without-love push innocent parts below the line, or into *shadow*, defined as those parts of ourselves that we don't want others to see or that others deem unacceptable. When we push parts of ourselves into shadow, our conscious self disowns them, effectively saying, "That is not part of me." But they don't go away; they simply languish in the subconscious. Let's look at some of the ways that innocent parts of us are forced into shadow.

Trust

When we are children, every encounter is a test of trust. We experiment, look for affirmation and gentle guidance, and accept loving boundaries. We are dependent, vulnerable, and open to be shaped.

Well-meaning but insensitive caregivers are unaware that our psyche interprets their ill-timed reprimand or mild teasing as shaming. Group dynamics in school and playground settings often breed ridicule and hazing that push our openness and vulnerability into shadow. In adolescence and early adulthood we may be misled or abused by a coach, teacher, or minister; manipulated or abruptly dumped in a love affair; or cheated by a partner in a business deal. We conclude that trust leads to betrayal and pain.

So trust goes into shadow. We become outwardly nice, but distant and elusive. Eventually we live a controlled, guarded existence of antiseptic relationships, contingency plans, and legal backstops, withholding or avoiding anything that might lead to further shame.

Truth

As children we speak our truth oblivious of the impact. But a child's honesty and directness are often viewed by adults as embarrassing, discomforting, or impolite. Statements like "Look at the fat lady," "I'm bored," "I want to go home," or "I don't like you" often lead to a reprimand, a "Say you're sorry" admonition, or even physical punishment from our parents. Often worse than verbal or physical punishment are separation and the fear of abandonment. To a child, "I don't want to see you again until you can behave correctly" translates into "Be nice and hide your feelings, or we won't love you."

We're taught that our unfiltered truth is unwelcome and that anger and conflict are bad. If we speak what we *really* think and feel to our parents and friends—and later to our customers, spouse, or board of directors—we risk losing the relationship. So we become socialized, agreeable, and nice. Our honest reactions to pain, persecution, betrayal, and wounding are usually fear and anger. Since neither of these is acceptable in a polite society—or an abusive home—they go into shadow.

Loss and Sadness

Loss is an integral part of life. The great religious traditions acknowledge that loss begets grief, and expressed grief leads to acceptance and healing. But in our avoid-discomfort-be-happy culture we shun the vulnerability and pain of grief. We deny, rationalize, divert, or numb our grief, but rarely express it. In childhood, losses might include a close friend moving away, the death of a pet, failing to make a sports team, the death of a grandparent, or witnessing the divorce of our parents. These and a myriad of other minor and major losses trigger a gut-level sadness that could be released naturally through tears. The child in each of us longs to hear something like, "I see that you are hurt, that this is very painful. It's very hard. It's okay to feel sad. Your tears are welcome."

Since most people in our culture, especially men, feel awkward and embarrassed around grief, we divert it with gifts, excuses, or even admonitions designed to curtail the grief and blunt the tears. This is especially true for boys who are told variations of "That's nothing to cry about. It didn't work out. You'll have to move on. You'll just have to grow up. It's time to be a man. Suck it up. Get over it." They see the stoicism of their fathers in times of loss or bereavement and assume this is the only acceptable behavior. Since their grief is not welcome, they focus on building their tower and avoid situations or relationships that might lead to loss and emotion. Their sadness goes into shadow.

Our Bodies

As children we have a natural curiosity about our bodies and the bodies of others. Skin color, hair texture, penis or labia, smooth, hairy, sweaty—

they are all part of the human package to be explored, loved, and lived in. But somewhere along the line, progressive "civilized" cultures labeled the human body as shameful. The regimented church preaches that Spirit is good and the body is bad. Nakedness shifts from natural to embarrassing, and curiosity and wonder toward our bodies is branded as deviant. As a result we stuff the wonder and respect for our bodies and our sexuality into shadow.

The Need to Be Seen and Blessed

A society of tower builders breeds more tower builders. We want our children to have it better than we did. We orchestrate their lives so they have the best opportunities to discover their giftedness and succeed. We tend to measure and compare everything: school grades, playing time on sports teams, scouting ranks, chair numbers in the band, number of Bible verses memorized. Comparison breeds competition, and the drive to win often creates a subtle yet insidious erosion of self-worth.

As adults, our subconscious comes to believe that others will love us only if we perform to their high standards. We conclude that no achievement is ever good enough, and there's always the threat that someone else will do it better. As a result we become performers, pleasers, and victims whose identity and worth depend on the affirmation of others—parents, boss, spouse, coworkers. Without a natural grounding of self-worth, we feel under constant scrutiny to see if we measure up. Our playfulness and self-love go into shadow.

The Bus Analogy

The following analogy, conceived by Jim Dethmer[4] and depicted in Figure 13.4, describes the interaction between our conscious parts (above the line) and our disowned parts (below the line).

Imagine that our life is like driving a bus. In the first few rows of the bus are our chosen navigators. These are the parts that we want others in the world to see—the parts above the line in the egg/iceberg model. They might represent the parts of us that are articulate or compassionate, friendly or analytical, the good negotiator or motivator, the loyal, reverent parts that we want to share with the outside world.

In most situations we're able to choose whom we want to help steer

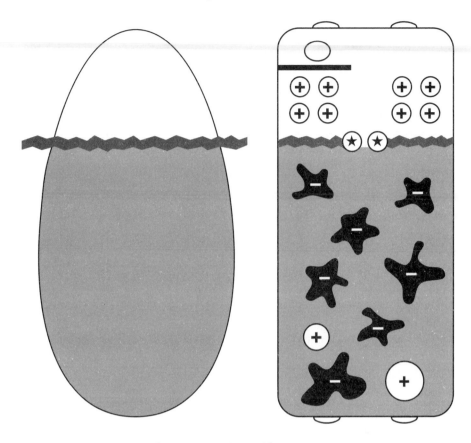

Figure 13.4 **Our Life as a Bus.**

the bus. When the road is paved and there are few distractions to the driver (our adult self), we call on these proven parts of our character to keep us on course.

A few rows back from the front of the bus is a thick curtain. Imagine that beyond this curtain, lurking in the back rows of the bus, are those parts that we hide from the world, our disgusting twin "brothers and sisters." These are the disowned parts that parental, societal, religious, or other authority figures have labeled as unacceptable or even dangerous. The back of the bus is windowless, and these repugnant parts are never allowed to look through or go through the curtain. Our security-conscious, success-oriented navigators in the front don't want them anywhere near the driver's seat.

Usually, these disowned parts are viewed as negative—for example, our pent-up rage, repressed sexuality, or chronic anxiety. However, they often include positive aspects of our wiring, like our curiosity, emotions, artistic talents, and sense of wonder for the world. In an overarching sense they represent "the rest of our truth," relegated to the back of the bus during childhood.

Consider that none of these characteristics, at least in their original form when they were sent to the back of the bus, is inherently bad or evil. But as they rankle for many years behind the curtain—in the dark canyons of our subconscious—they mutate into shadowy, sometimes dangerous saboteurs. They're similar to an innocent man imprisoned with hardened criminals. Eventually his original truth and innocence become warped and callous. He transforms into a seething stew of hatred, bitterness, malice, terror, helplessness, depression, narcissism, lust, addictions, duplicity, and worthlessness. And as he becomes more callous and abandoned, he resents the repression and seeks to express himself to the world—in any way he can. Any part of us that is rejected becomes a vengeful part.

When the road is smooth, representing times of low stress in our lives, subconscious sentinels guard the curtain. Their job is to shield both the world and us from the unpredictable, undesirable characters in the back of the bus.

However, when the road becomes bumpy or debris-laden, representing times of disillusionment, crisis, confrontation, annoyance, tension, wounding, temptation, or betrayal, the sentries at the curtain drop their guard to focus their attention on the road ahead—our outer crisis. In these moments of stress, usually at the most inopportune time, one of the disowned characters in the back bursts through the curtain, wrests the wheel away from the driver, and starts careening the bus down the road. If we're lucky, the disowned parts merely create diversions that delay or detour the bus along its journey (our life purpose). All too often, however, when these disowned parts seize control of our lives, they create explosions—affairs, vindictive or criminal acts, addictions, deep depression—that can damage or even destroy the entire bus (our life). Normally, after the crisis subsides, the curtain sentinels are able to regain control from the disowned part and reinstate a mature navigator. The saboteur is thrust again to the back of the bus, a temporary sanity is restored, and damage repair begins.

As a real-life example, imagine that you are an executive having a terrible day at the office. It's the end of the quarter, and you've spent most of the day placating an irate customer who has been berating you about a problem that is actually his. But you desperately need his business to meet your financial targets and to avoid an even worse harangue from the market analysts. So instead of speaking your truth and risking the loss of this important revenue stream, you smooth his ruffled feathers with a stream of vague promises. Your mounting indignation—"It's not your fault. Tell him!"—is gagged in the back of the bus.

Later that day an irritating, overpaid, yet key member of your management team struts into your office with a litany of accusations about your management style and your disrespect for his abundant talents. He concludes his diatribe by demanding a raise, or he'll join a competitor. You need him to complete a crucial project and, bluff or not, can't risk his knowledge of your company falling into the hands of a competitor. So you salve his ego and sweeten his bonus plan. Your integrity screams, "This is not right!" but your rising frustration is muzzled in the back of the bus. Your workday concludes with the discovery of a new dent in the passenger-side door of your car and no explanatory note on the windshield.

All the way home your anger is bubbling just beneath the surface. The curtain sentinels are working overtime to maintain some sense of civility as you greet your spouse coolly at the door. The whole family senses the "elephant in the room" as dinner begins. When your 10-year-old son spills his milk at the table, you erupt. All the frustrations and repressed anger from the day overpower the curtain sentinels, grab the steering wheel of your life, and lash out at this helpless child: "You idiot! Can't you do anything right? Look at this mess. You're a hopeless klutz. Go to your room until you can behave and treat the rest of us with respect!" Your freewheeling anger senses a helpless victim who won't push back, and you give him both barrels. The spilled milk triggers a lecture about his messy room, his disrespect for his mother, and the B's on his report card.

Later that evening, after the tirade has subsided and the mature adult is back in the driver's seat, you might go to his room, express your regret, explain about the hard day you had, tell him it's not really about him, maybe even ask his forgiveness. But the damage has been done, and you know it will take days, weeks, perhaps a lifetime to repair the relationship with your child.

This example is about unexpressed anger. Similar self-sabotage scenarios can be constructed for repressed sexuality, deep betrayal, unexpressed grief, and the desire to be loved. Much of Western culture as well as religious traditions tell us to ask forgiveness for our actions, redouble the guard on the curtain, and do whatever it takes to stay in control. But the harsh reality is that the shadowy characters in the back of the bus will *always* find a way to burst through the curtain, wounding those around us as well as ourselves.

Consider that the antidote is actually the opposite of what our culture and religions suggest. Instead of banishing these disowned parts, we need to visit the back of the bus, acknowledge them, greet them, and hear their stories. Invariably, when we can have a conversation with them, we find that they seek our well-being. Often they will lead us closer to God. The innermost desire of our repressed parts, our shadows, is that we be safe, truthful, and loved, which is exactly what they wanted for themselves before being rejected. So instead of berating and punishing our lust and anger, for example, we might *bless* these disowned parts, recycle them into healthy sexuality and clean boundaries, and seek their allegiance in finding and stepping into our greatness.

Richard Rohr suggests that the task of religion is to reunite our divided realities and baptize them,[5] which is really what Jesus did with the prostitutes, tax collectors, and misfits of his day. Over time, as we listen to and love these rejected parts, allowing them to be seen without judgment or condemnation, they begin to transform into the truthful, powerful navigators they were originally created to be.

Evil and the World

The bus analogy alludes to the innocent, disowned parts of us being locked up with "hardened criminals." Influenced by these criminal forces, the disowned parts shelve their concern for our well-being and seek an exit from the back of the bus any way they can. They want to get *out*, and if we or others get hurt in the process, that's the price that must be paid.

Consider that the negative influences of the material world and the evil forces in the spiritual world conspire to corrupt our innocent, disowned parts. Figure 13.5 shows how these influences and forces attack our shadow selves. One prominent influence in the material world is the media. The rituals of television, movies, and music purportedly seek to entertain the conscious mind and increase our awareness of reality. But most media target the subconscious because, as explained earlier, the subconscious actually runs our lives and, more importantly in a world built on commerce and profit, makes our buying decisions.

One way for the characters in the back of the bus to be validated is vicariously as we watch movies or listen to music. For example, if our authority figures (parents, clergy, teachers) denounce the expression of clean

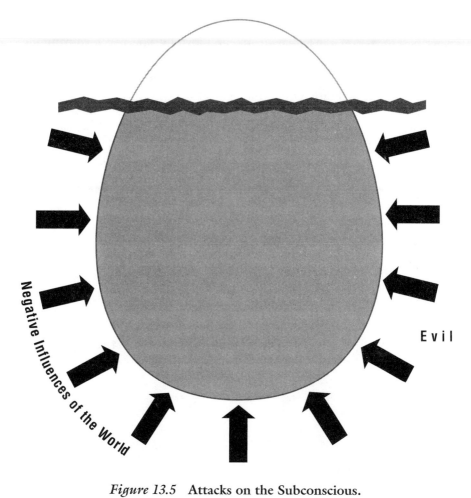

Figure 13.5 **Attacks on the Subconscious.**

boundaries and the wonder of our bodies, anger and healthy sexuality are shoved to the back of the bus. In movies, music, and magazines we experience, voyeuristically, the release of anger as violence and the transformation of healthy sexuality into erotic, deviant, or loveless sex.

If our self-worth languishes in the back of the bus, we will do almost anything to gain others' approval. Inflated, selfish people whom we seek to please will feed off our repressed need for approval. We become victims to the manipulators, tyrants, savages, and addicts of the world, doing their bidding to receive their approval and recognition, or their conditional "love."

Cliff Barry says, "Love is not something you do, it's who you are. You can't help it. If you can't love cleanly and joyfully, you will love painfully. But you *will* love."[6] Painful love—like accepting others' abuse, repeatedly allowing ourselves to be duped and manipulated, and committing wrongful acts in seeking the praise of unscrupulous leaders—is a symptom of a decadent and declining society, and perhaps one of the greatest threats we face in the world today. This fact is so clear to the subconscious, yet so foreign to the tower builders and intellectuals.

This is why soul work—exploring, touching, blessing, and transforming the subconscious—is so difficult in our culture. We banish or punish our shadows, while muting or occluding the truth—the reality—of our lives.

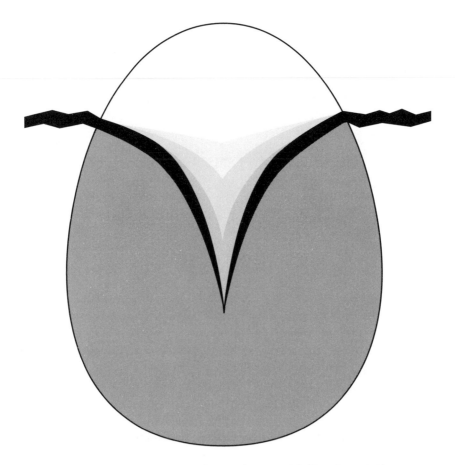

Figure 13.6 **Penetrating the Darkness with Truth and Grace.**

Recall my axiom from a little earlier: The shadow *always* wins. Our task is not to eradicate or exorcise the dark, disowned parts of our lives, but to bring them into the light and love them back to life. *Understanding* is about getting to know those parts of us below the line and in the back of the bus. We need to welcome them, hear their stories, and apologize to them for missing their hidden and noble concern for our well-being. When we grant them a full and unconditional pardon and ask their forgiveness in return, we reinstate their goodness and welcome them into the light. Figure 13.6 models the process of gradually opening the subconscious to the welcoming light of truth and grace.

The seeds of our greatness reside in the depths of our disowned parts. Only by searching these dark recesses of our soul will we be carried into our ultimate destiny and our deepest communion with Spirit. Before we can steward and deploy our gifts, truly serve others, and aspire to greatness in our lives, we must shine light into our darkness.

14

Our INNER ADVISORS

The egg and bus models in Chapter 13 show our whole self as being a combination of both the light and the dark, the known and the disowned, the accepted parts and the rejected or shadow parts. This chapter and the following four chapters present another model for mapping the conscious and subconscious, based on the concept of inner advisors. This model has origins in mythology, religion, psychology, and nature, and stems from the twentieth-century categorization of archetypes developed by Carl Jung.[1] It has been refined by Robert Moore and Douglas Gillette in their book, *King, Warrior, Magician, Lover.*[2] The reader is also referred to the groundbreaking experiential work of Cliff Barry and Mary Ellen Blandford, whose Shadow Work® Seminars help soul pilgrims understand, explore, and transform their shadows.[3]

Imagine the board of directors of a company, drawn together by an astute chairman to help ground and guide the business. Normally the members of the board will have diverse backgrounds and a range of financial, product or technology, manufacturing, marketing, human resources, and strategic skills. Individual board members advise the chairman when their specific expertise is sought, and the board works together on problems or opportunities that require unified input.

Now consider that inside us is a "personal board of advisors" who collaborate to determine our reactions to any situation. The trusted or mature advisors are like those parts of us in the front of the bus, the ones that serve us well and that we want others to see. The shadow advisors correlate to the parts of us behind the curtain, in the back of the bus, who divert or sabotage the best intentions of our mature advisors. Our inner advisory board guides all aspects of our lives: mental, emotional, physical, interpersonal, and spiritual. When the mature advisors are all "on line" and working in harmony, we feel centered, tethered, and aware. When one or more of the mature advisors is "off line" or underdeveloped, certain situations cause us to lose our groundedness. This misalignment is exacerbated when our shadow advisors, like the characters in the back of the bus, divert or sabotage the directions we get from the mature advisors.

All these advisors, all these parts, are inside us. The aware leader calls on the mature advisors but can get blindsided by the shadow advisors. Soul work calls us to acknowledge, meet, and bless the shadow advisors, transforming them into allies for our journey toward awareness and greatness. Chapter 20 will offer actions, experiences, and disciplines to help us do this work.

Figure 14.1 presents the connection of mature and sabotaging advisors with our adult self—the bus driver. The shadow advisors are connected to our ego by solid lines to indicate that they have more power than the mature advisors. During times of tension, anxiety, or duress, the shadow advisors, just like the disowned parts in the back of the bus, *always* win.

The Four Primary Advisors— Sovereign, Warrior, Magician, Lover

The characters in both the front and the back of the bus can be categorized into four primary advisory groups, as shown in Figure 14.2. Each advisor's primary role can be coupled with a "mythological example" from the original *Star Trek* television and movie series.

> ➤ The *Sovereign* (king or queen) makes decisions, initiates, guides, and sets the course. Captain Kirk carried the Sovereign energy in *Star Trek*.
> ➤ The *Warrior* accepts responsibility and gets the job done. The engineer, Scotty, was the primary Warrior in *Star Trek*.

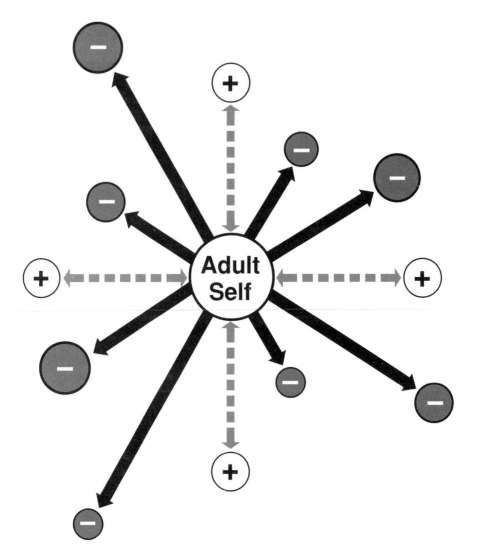

Figure 14.1 **Positive and Negative Advisors.**

➤ The *Magician* contains, assesses, stays detached, and offers advice. Mr. Spock was the Magician on *Star Trek*.
➤ The *Lover* connects, feels, and appreciates. Dr. McCoy was the Lover on *Star Trek*.

Each of these four advisors has a mature, centered component and two shadow components, a "deflated" shadow and an "inflated" shadow.

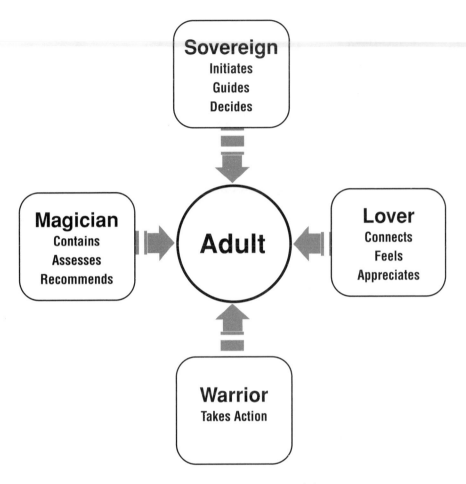

Figure 14.2   **The Four Mature Advisors.**

Figure 14.3 shows the interrelationship among the mature, deflated, and inflated parts. The mature manifestation or role represents the desired or "good" part of each advisor, embodying our healthy, open, and seen (versus hidden) aspects that keep us clear and truthful in our activities and relationships. Mature advisors acknowledge and love the self without denying or denigrating it (worthlessness) or, on the other hand, deifying it (narcissism). Their responsibility is to work both individually and as a team to keep us mentally, emotionally, physically, relationally, and spiritually healthy.

The mature adult balances two often-contradictory objectives: stewardship over our well-being and service to each of our realms. Realms may

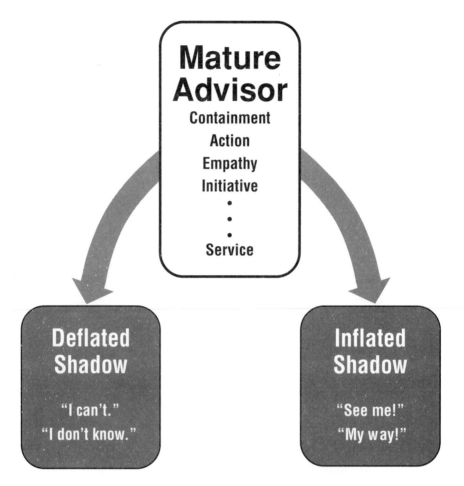

Figure 14.3   **The Mature Advisor and Shadows.**

include a business, a family, a marriage, an organization, the parenting of children, the local community, or the kingdom of God. The mature adult wisely recognizes, "The best way I can serve the realm is by first taking proper care of myself." At the same time, the mature adult realizes that whatever we do, it is ultimately in service to one of these realms. We don't really own anything. We are simply stewards of our gifts, asked to give them away in love and service to others.

Both the deflated and inflated shadow components of these advisors reside behind the curtain of the bus. Both types of shadow represent our rejected feelings and capacities, the parts that have been banished to the back of the bus and are no longer known directly. In a psychological sense, they are the parts of us that our conscious mind wants to neglect, ignore, deny, or bury. As the name *shadow* implies, they are elusive and difficult to comprehend.

Our shadows are not evil; they're just the unacceptable, dark side in everything we do. Ultimately, like the disowned characters in the back of the bus, they will not be denied. Until they are acknowledged, blessed, and transformed, these shadows lurking behind the curtain will continue to wait for that crisis moment when they can burst through, take control, and wreak havoc in our lives.

The deflated shadow of each advisor is best characterized as a victim. This shadow's mantra is "I can't. I don't know. I don't want to know." The deflated shadow is withdrawn, depressed, and never good enough. In difficult situations the deflated shadows cause us to become confused, helpless, and prone to abuse by others. As either victim or martyr, the deflated shadow undermines our health so that we neglect or abdicate stewardship of our realms.

In contrast, the inflated shadow has one overriding concern: *me!* Activities and behaviors focus on promoting, protecting, glorifying, satisfying—or abusing—*me*. This shadow seeks to be served *by* the realm, instead of acting in service *to* the realm. Unlike the deflated shadow, which closes down and finds any action difficult, the inflated shadow does everything to excess. Where the deflated scapegoat can't do anything right, the inflated zealot demands perfection from self and others. The deflated shadow is numb to all feelings; the inflated shadow is overwhelmed by emotions. The deflated shadow's cowardice is countered by the inflated shadow's savagery; deflated withdrawal is upstaged by inflated showmanship or buffoonery. Peter's inferiority around his father and his classmates and Marty's acquiescence to authority exemplify deflated shadows at work, while Fletcher's red convertible and nonstop partying, and Stan's orgiastic rampages typify inflated shadows.

Whether deflated or inflated, our shadows' origins are usually childhood betrayal or abandonment, stuffed or stilted truth, or times of deep shame. For a multitude of reasons, all stemming from fear, these childhood wounds could never be expressed to our parents or caregivers. The wounds spawned unworthiness and the ever-present dread that "I might be hurt again." So we adopted defense mechanisms—denial, diversions, escapes, numbing—to avoid the pain of shame, anger, anxiety, abuse, betrayal, and grief, and thereby keep ourselves safe.

Just like the parts in the back of the bus, our shadows' deepest desire is to protect us from harm, and, if at all possible, to experience love. While their actions or manifestations may be viewed as bad or even evil, the shadow advisors are not really dark, just apart. Our goal in shadow exploration is to acknowledge, transform, and reunite them with the mature advisor.

Since both the deflated and inflated shadows seek our safety, our actions may oscillate like a pendulum between deflated and inflated, depending on the situation. Recall the example in Chapter 13 of the executive's conciliatory behavior around the recalcitrant customer and arrogant employee, followed by his eruption into rage at his helpless son. The reverse of this is the sheepish husband who becomes a tyrant at work. The shy pleaser at the office may become an arrogant buffoon after a few drinks at a party. Stan's behavior epitomizes the swing between numbness in the face of confrontation (with the women in his life) and the accompanying sexual addiction to let off steam. Each of us has *both* the deflated and inflated shadows. While we may tend to manifest one over the other, they are both there.

Life on a Balance Beam

Imagine that your life is being managed by these four inner advisors. Envision that the mature components of these four advisors work together and form an elevated balance beam. Our adult self walks along this balance beam, as shown in Figure 14.4. When these mature advisors are well developed and work in harmony, the balance beam is wide and sturdy, allowing the person to keep his balance during times of life turbulence. When one or more of the mature advisors is either weak or overwhelmed by its shadows, the beam width is reduced and the footing becomes unstable.

On the left side below the balance beam are the deflated shadows, and the inflated shadows are in a similar position on the right. Each shadow has a line tied to our adult self and is constantly trying to pull the adult off the balance beam and downward to the level of the shadow. Underdeveloped mature advisors coupled with powerful, repressed shadows reduce the width of the beam and create a precarious balance. In the ideal sense our adult self balances on a wide platform and is sensitive to, but easily able to withstand, the occasional tugs from self- or realm-sabotaging shadows, especially during nonstressful life situations. However, an adult with weak mature advisors and wily shadows can be yanked from the balance beam during times of tension or crisis.

Figure 14.4 **The Adult Self Balancing Act.**

Consider the example of a mature husband, confident in his sexuality and living in a truthful relationship with his wife, to whom, in most situations, he can remain faithful while admiring a beautiful woman. However, after an unsettled argument with his wife, at the end of an unfruitful, multi-day business trip, nursing his ego (and a few drinks) at the hotel bar, he is highly vulnerable to the pull of his shadows and prone to either indiscretion or infidelity with any woman who takes an interest in him.

Stan stays clearheaded and makes rational recommendations during times of business crisis (mature Magician), defines and communicates a strategic direction for his organization (mature Sovereign), and is skilled and disciplined in accomplishing tasks (mature Warrior). Yet Stan either disconnects or escapes from his spousal relationships (shadow Lover). He can think, initiate, and execute, but he struggles with connection. This is a common pattern among successful businessmen, honored for their outward accomplishments and acumen, yet living reclusive or addictive lives. Three-quarters of Stan's advisors provide a sturdy platform for him to navigate life. But his Lover advisor, ignored and abused during his youth and never fully developed, shrinks his life balance beam to a tightrope when he faces sexual pressures or temptations. As a result he is easily pulled into one of his Lover shadows, becoming either emotionally or relationally numb (deflated shadow) or relationally overwhelmed (inflated shadow).

The Emotional Gateways to the Adult Advisors

Soul work invites those parts of us in shadow back into the light, where they can be blessed and transformed for our good. But this transformation requires more than simply understanding the shadow parts at an intellectual level. These parts have gone into shadow because we repressed emotion. We can't "think" them back into the light. *Releasing* certain emotions is the gateway through which the shadows come into the light.

Our "figure it out" culture generally disdains the emotions of fear, anger, grief, and joy. We have a hard time acknowledging them, much less experiencing and releasing them. Most of us were taught as children that strong emotions make others uncomfortable; they are inappropriate except, perhaps, in private. "You shouldn't be afraid of that. Don't be such a sissy!" "Be nice to her; say you're sorry. It's not nice to be angry." "C'mon, that's nothing to cry about. Be a big boy." Part of our personal truth is what we *feel*, and when our truth goes into shadow so do our feelings.

You may agree with me about fear, anger, and grief, but wonder why I say that joy is repressed. Aren't we encouraged to laugh and be happy? Isn't one of our primary life goals the pursuit of happiness? I propose to you that joy is the most difficult emotion of all for us to experience.

Happiness is a comparative and temporal term. We can say, "I'm *happier* than I was yesterday" or "This is the *happiest* I've been in several months." So happiness is a relative term bound in time; there is never enough, and it always ends. By contrast, joy is noncomparative and independent of time. Joy is full and complete in itself—an absolute.

Joy, as set forth in this model, encompasses the deep, foundational pleasure of existence. It can be described as a delight in and gratitude for being alive. Such joy is naturally accompanied by a sense of inherent self-worth, from which spring confidence and trust. While inexpressible in words, it is often manifested in tears: at the birth of your child, seeing a loved one after a lengthy absence, and truly loving sexual union. In some spiritual traditions the holy fool, the person in reckless, uninhibited abandon to God, is the only person who truly knows joy.

Grief and joy are flip sides of the same coin. The more deeply we can grieve, the greater our capacity to experience joy. In a stoic, pain-averse culture that disdains grief, we settle for cheap, temporal happiness and rarely experience the uninhibited, priceless ecstasy of surrender to the beauty and wonder of the moment.

Earnest pilgrims who seek to reclaim their disowned or lost selves, buried in shadow, must be open to welcoming their repressed emotions of fear, anger, grief, and joy. These four emotions are the gateways to the mature advisors.

Understanding the Individual Advisors

While the emotional experience is the necessary gateway to transformation, most pilgrims begin their exploration of the subconscious with an understanding, a map, of the inner advisors, including their characteristics, roles, and common manifestations in the material world. Chapters 15 through 18 describe the mature component, deflated shadow, and inflated shadow of each of the four inner advisors: Sovereign, Warrior, Magician, and Lover. Each chapter begins by describing the key characteristics and examples of the mature component of the advisor. The primary emotional gateway for each advisor is explained, along with the risks of exploring the advisor's shadows. Then the characteristics and examples of each shadow, deflated and inflated, are presented. The goal of these discussions is awareness of both the mature and the shadow components of each advisor. Figure 14.5 presents an overview of the four advisors.

As you review these descriptions, it's not a question of which components (mature or shadow) we have: *We have them all.* Sometimes one or more of the mature advisors' characteristics are so weak or suppressed that it seems as if one of the shadows is standing on the balance beam. You might be tempted to read these chapters with a mind-set of "How do I purge these shadows from my life, and focus on nurturing the attributes of the mature advisor?" Instead, I encourage you to shine the light of awareness on *each and every* attribute, both good and bad, knowing they are *all* part of you. Tremendous power resides in the energy of the shadows. When disowned or shunned, this energy works against us, subverting our lives and dragging us into a lukewarm, reactive existence. Acknowledged and brought fully into the light, the negative energy of the shadows can be blessed and transformed into the paradoxical alchemy of power and surrender that undergirds a truly aware life.

Any model of the subconscious provides only a glimpse of a phenomenon of both infinite vastness and utter simplicity. Chew on these descriptions, perhaps savor them, but don't venerate them. When individuals or movements preach their way as *the* way, they try to box in the infinite and thereby diminish that which they wish to define. They place human beings

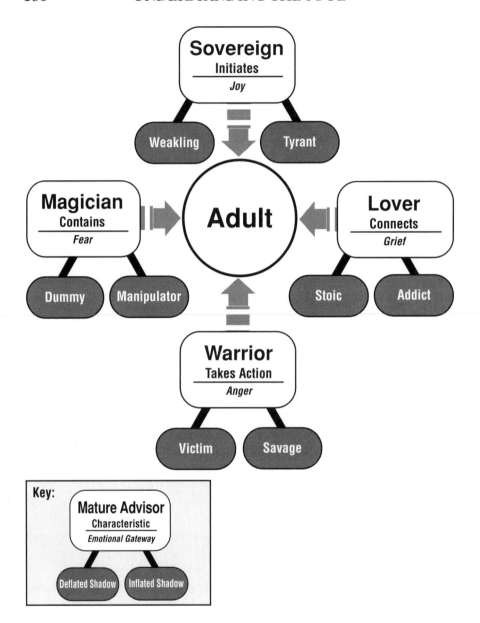

Figure 14.5 Summary of Inner Advisors and Shadows.

in tidy bins—"Oh, he's an I-N-T-P on the Myers-Briggs" or "She's a 5 on the Enneagram"—and miss out on the rich intricacies of what it means to be human.

Consider a few other reminders and caveats as you read these descriptions. The goal of soul work is not exorcising, fixing, or eradicating our shadows. They are not demonic. They are not our evil nature. Their *actions* may be evil or immoral when influenced by outside forces, but the shadows themselves, at their deepest level, are motivated by an inherent desire for our well-being.

These descriptions are not intended to define or refine psychological disorders, dysfunction, or trauma. They are offered to provide insight to "normal" functioning adults battling disillusionment and seeking deeper awareness and aliveness. Many therapists use these models in their work with deeply wounded individuals. The action steps presented in Part IV can be used by anyone.

The following chapters introduce the individual advisors serially—the Sovereign, the Warrior, the Magician, and the Lover. However, they all work interdependently and simultaneously with one another in our moment-by-moment lives. Try to grasp their interrelatedness as they are presented in succession.

I intentionally present the mature advisors in their best light and the shadow advisors in their worst darkness. Our shadows normally manifest in less dark ways. For example, the use of the term "Savage" for the inflated warrior may cause you to breathe a sigh of relief that you don't have *that* shadow to worry about. Consider, however, that there is a savage inside each of us. We may not be serial killers or Stalinesque tyrants, but our Savage comes out through "harmlessly" teasing our children or imposing our work ethic onto others while rationalizing that "Everyone should learn how to work hard." Most of the time our shadows sneak out, slipping through the curtain on the bus when the sentinels aren't looking. Only rarely, at least in a polite culture, will they explode out. But always remember that the dark, volatile shadow is still there. There is an ax murderer inside every pleaser, just as there is a terrified little boy, yearning to be loved, inside every tyrant.

The examples in Chapters 15 through 18 present Jesus as the archetypal man embodying the mature characteristics of each advisor. Examples from the protagonists and other midlife leaders are also provided, to depict the mature advisor and its shadows.

To help demonstrate their functions (and reactions to stress), each mature advisor and the deflated and inflated shadows will be placed in the following scenario: Uncontrollable market conditions have eroded a company's sales. It is likely that the prior favorable market conditions will return, but the timing is uncertain. By all common industry metrics, the company is overstaffed in several areas. Unless either sales increase or fixed costs decrease dramatically within the next six months, a cash flow crisis will occur and the company's long-term stability will be seriously threatened. The conditions call for a company downsizing. Each of the following chapters presents the actions the mature advisor and its two shadow advisors take in preparation for and implementation of a layoff.

15

The SOVEREIGN

Our inner Sovereign advisor charts the course for our life, makes decisions, and both receives blessing and gives blessings to others. He believes in himself and his abilities. He draws power from a Source beyond himself and knows he is loved regardless of outer accomplishments or faults.

The deflated shadow Sovereign is the Weakling. Feeling unloved and inferior to others, he has no personal power and is incapable of setting a direction for his life. He sees himself as unworthy or even worthless, and becomes captive to the approval of others. The inflated shadow Sovereign is the Tyrant, who sees himself as special, and sees power as being either self-generated or a birthright.

The emotional gateway to the mature Sovereign is the ability to experience joy. (See Figure 15.1.)

The Mature Sovereign

The mature Sovereign emanates power and grandeur, yet needs no crown. His sovereignty rests in his presence and clarity. He draws independence and strength from his dependence on a Source of Power larger than himself, which both transcends and complements his conscience and his common sense. He knows and accepts his present role, whether leader or follower,

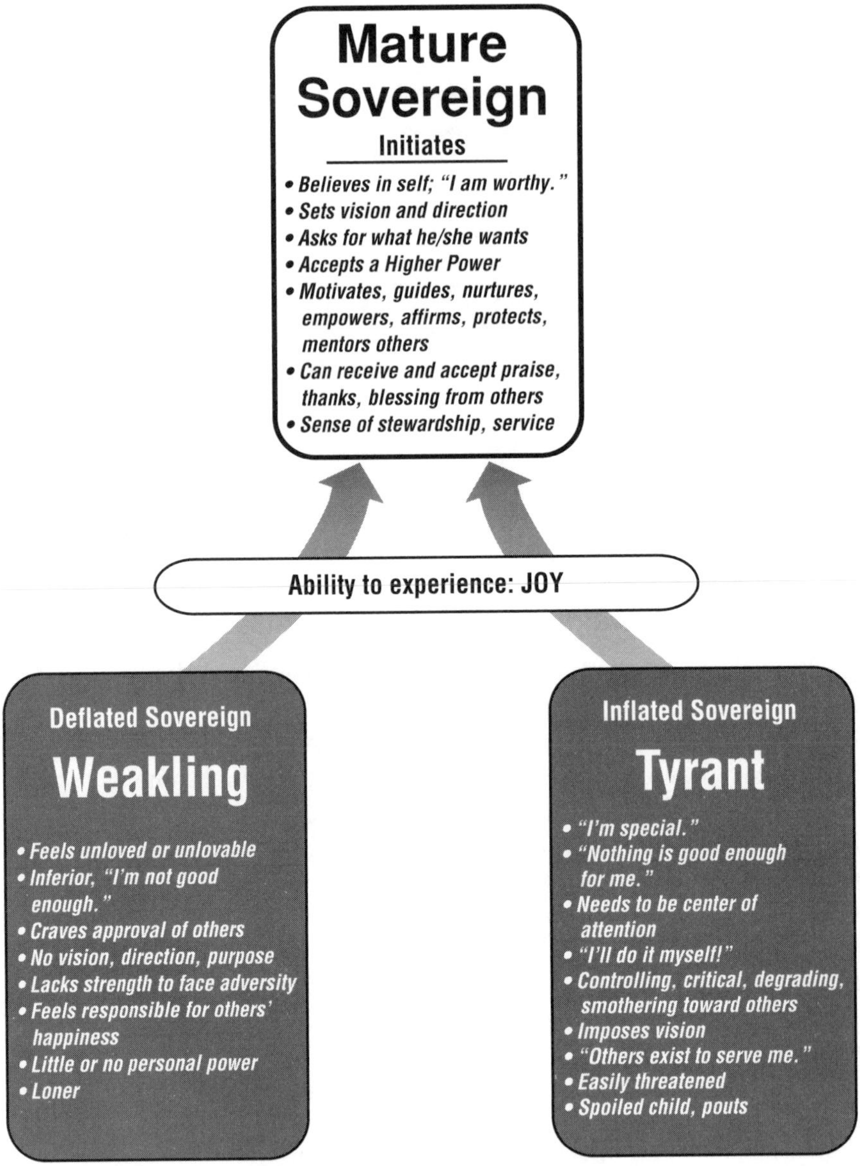

Mature Sovereign

Initiates

- *Believes in self; "I am worthy."*
- *Sets vision and direction*
- *Asks for what he/she wants*
- *Accepts a Higher Power*
- *Motivates, guides, nurtures, empowers, affirms, protects, mentors others*
- *Can receive and accept praise, thanks, blessing from others*
- *Sense of stewardship, service*

Ability to experience: JOY

Deflated Sovereign
Weakling

- *Feels unloved or unlovable*
- *Inferior, "I'm not good enough."*
- *Craves approval of others*
- *No vision, direction, purpose*
- *Lacks strength to face adversity*
- *Feels responsible for others' happiness*
- *Little or no personal power*
- *Loner*

Inflated Sovereign
Tyrant

- *"I'm special."*
- *"Nothing is good enough for me."*
- *Needs to be center of attention*
- *"I'll do it myself!"*
- *Controlling, critical, degrading, smothering toward others*
- *Imposes vision*
- *"Others exist to serve me."*
- *Easily threatened*
- *Spoiled child, pouts*

Figure 15.1   The Sovereign Advisor.

trusting that he is both loved for who he is and a channel for power despite his individual weakness. He is neither intoxicated by success nor depressed by failure. Grounded in a love from beyond himself, the Source of his self-worth, he receives success, praise, and thanks with humility and gratitude, and accepts failure with equanimity.

His ability to look another person in the eye and ask for what he wants, directly yet graciously, comes from an inner certainty of his worthiness to receive. When he asks, it is neither for self-aggrandizement nor to be rewarded for performance, but from a need to be internally alive or to be a channel of life to others.

Regardless of his span or level of leadership, the Sovereign is also a devoted servant, applying his intellect, possessions, and talents in service to the Source and to the realms, for ends that even he may not fully comprehend. Life is a rhapsody; he is the conductor and those in his respective realms are the orchestra. He assures that the realm is safe. He cares for his people.

Edson Bueno, for example, founded and leads the largest private health insurance company in his country, and he embraces his 1,500 employees as beloved family. Their education, physical security, and opportunities for growth are his overarching concerns. He is effusive in his affirmations and electric in his presentations on company vision—providing affordable health services to the people of his country. His rewards are unparalleled loyalty and, as a side effect rather than a primary motive, exceptional growth and profits.

Spiritual awareness allows the mature Sovereign to connect with and clearly perceive other people. The Sovereign (and also the Lover in Chapter 18) senses the woundedness, yearnings, and fears in others. He blesses their shadows and nurtures their suppressed greatness. By his example, he encourages others to find their own center, their own font of aliveness. He inspires and empowers others to achieve their highest potential, taking time to mentor younger Sovereigns and encouraging protégés to test their creativity, stretch themselves, and make mistakes. Often working behind the scenes, he is the "wind beneath the wings" of frightened eaglets—employees, colleagues, children, underdogs—lifting them patiently from their fear and uncertainty to their own unique self-realization. Stan's father constantly encouraged and challenged his son, in athletics, academics, and commitment to his work. Yet he neither pushed Stan nor sought to re-create him in his own image. Only after his father's death did Stan realize the man's impact on his self-confidence, loyalty to a cause, and ability to endure adversity.

The mature Sovereign embodies truth and is a beacon for veracity and order. He is just and unbiased in meting out consequences. While he may correct or punish to maintain order, he then forgives and forgets. He knows that repressed anger, malice, or grudges shackle and diminish both him and their targets. When others have harmed him and both parties desire to stay in the relationship, he receives their confession, acknowledges their sincere remorse, seeks reparation if needed, and then pardons unconditionally. When he has wronged others, he can confess, repent, ask forgiveness, accept the consequences, make amends, and move on. He also knows when certain relationships must end, and lets them go as cleanly as possible.

The mature Sovereign knows that the world is tenuous and fickle, that times and circumstances change, and that his role and position are transitory. He embraces what is healthy and good, and releases what must die. He views pain and loss both as opportunities to learn and grow and as portals into deeper awareness of his own dependence on and surrender to his higher Source. He therefore embraces change, remaining loyal only to the quiet voice of guidance and love within and beyond himself. At peace in his self-worth, he navigates his personal passages with composure and courage, and acts as a guide to others lost in the darkness of their own transitional wilderness.

While the Sovereign sets the direction, articulates the vision, and defines the boundaries of his realms, he also seeks out and values other advisors and mentors in his life. He relies on Magicians to offer counsel and watch his blind spots. He embraces the discipline of Warriors—those who implement the vision and enforce the boundaries of the realm—who encourage him to take action and tell the truth. He receives the spirit of wonder and appreciation from Lovers, who help him connect with others in his realms and mirror his own humanity to him. He receives the blessing and encouragement of other Sovereigns, who also remind him of his duty to serve his realms.

In the Academy Award–winning film *Gladiator*, the protagonist, Maximus, inspires his legions (as a general), his fellow slaves (as a fugitive and outcast), and, ultimately, the city of Rome. He leads without pedigree but by his raw presence, transparent truth, calmness under duress, and unswerving loyalty to the realm. His duty is first to the vision of his king and mentor, the elder Caesar, and then to the preservation of a Roman culture that serves the people. He would willingly give his own life in service to the realm, a cause greater than himself.

Jesus embodied Sovereign energy in his steward-leadership of his apostles, his emphasis on the truth, his clear delineation of right and wrong, and his unswerving obedience to and love for God.

In the downsizing scenario, the mature Sovereign faces the employees, the press, the customers, the vendors, the shareholders—all the company's constituencies—and tells the truth. He admits faults, accepts responsibility, and expresses remorse, but is not broken or crippled by guilt. He neither ignores nor wallows in the pain of the past. He releases past mistakes while painting the opportunities, the risks, and the potential of his new vision. He offers thanks and provides encouragement to displaced workers. He surveys the damage and the potential, and initiates the rebuilding of the kingdom. Under penetrating scrutiny from his critics, he accepts the pressure, bears up under the intensity, answers their questions, and maintains the new course for the organization, even when others fall away, threaten, or betray him. When it is time for him to surrender his mantle of leadership, he does so with dignity and without rancor or vendettas.

The Sovereign Shadows

Both the deflated and inflated shadows of the Sovereign covet the admiration and appreciation of others. The strongest pull against the mature Sovereign, drawing a person into his shadows, is his sense of unworthiness: "I can't. I'm not good enough. I'm undeserving." Typically, the person's parents or caregivers failed to provide him with the environment and tenderness that would foster self-worth and a sense of being loved without needing to perform. Whether the caregivers deliberately withheld the love or simply did not know how to give it, the child carried into adulthood the wound of feeling unloved. Betrayed, diminished, berated, abused, judged, or simply ignored as a child, the adult carries Sovereign shadows, which manifest as an insatiable hunger for recognition and approval.

The Deflated Shadow
Sovereign: The Weakling

The Weakling constantly seeks the approval of others. He has no personal power and only vague, malleable boundaries. Unwilling to ask for what he wants and fearful of disdain or disapproval, he'll do anything to maintain peace and get an occasional pat on the head. Thad modeled this behavior in both the public school system and his first job with the large law firm. He hated both environments but danced to the tune of the bullies and the bosses, fearful that they would reject him and he'd be either alone or out of work.

Rarely spoken, yet etched in the Weakling's countenance and evident in his actions, is his ingrained belief, "I'm not good enough." His first subconscious reaction to any assignment, challenge, or conflict is "I can't." Often manifesting a shy or passive demeanor, he may live vicariously through more powerful, visible, or famous personalities—often the inflated shadow Tyrants—siphoning some of their attention as an analgesic for the pain of feeling worthless.

The Weakling often appears to be a diligent worker, persevering servant, and peacemaker, and may be viewed and honored as one who deeply cares for others. In fact he so abhors conflict and disapproval that he will sacrifice himself to maintain harmony or resolve disputes. Rather than delegating tasks, he burdens himself with excessive responsibility, subconsciously believing that the more he takes on, the more people will like him. He becomes the long-suffering caretaker, rescuer, or martyr, typically working long hours at his job and serving on several nonprofit committees or boards while diminishing or ignoring his own needs—and often the needs of his family. Susan the superwoman cared for her husband, her practice, her children, and her medical association but, as her stress grew, allowed little time for herself. Weeds in the garden and dust on the piano were silent reminders of how her life revolved around the needs of others.

The Weakling in leadership often appears muddled or confused, trying to balance or ameliorate all of his constituencies (shareholders, employees, customers, vendors) while in reality serving none of them. He's like a plate spinner in a vaudeville act, trying frantically to keep numerous plates spinning on broomsticks above his head, skittering among them until at some point he collapses from fatigue. His plates—his life—shatter around him, substantiating his conviction of uselessness and unworthiness. His inner voice confirms, "I knew you couldn't do it. You can't do anything right."

Meandering through life without a rudder, the Weakling has no visions, convictions, or goals, other than to fill the needs of others and keep his many plates spinning. Having little or no belief in himself, he continually alters his course to suit the whims of others, compromising his plastic values in order to gain their approval. In business, for example, he'll overhaul company strategy based on the last lost sale, the vagaries of his partner, or a negative analyst report. Ironically, when recognition is given, a common pattern among Weakling executives is their inability to receive the praise they crave. They either deflect it, credit someone else, or meekly say, "It was nothing, really," denying themselves the very thing they long for.

The Weakling in leadership is often like the King of Hearts in *Alice in Wonderland*, holding a toy scepter while kowtowing to his tyrannical Queen. He may abdicate his power to others (a chief operating officer, a minority partner, or a general manager) and assume the role of benevolent chairman, distancing himself from the company's operational challenges and difficult strategic decisions—and his own possible failure. While the mature Sovereign can guide, motivate, and empower those around him, the Weakling either will seek to please or rescue those who look to him for support and encouragement or will withdraw to the safety of disengagement and uninvolvement. His blessing and motivation of subordinates is hollow and perfunctory, founded neither in inner strength and conviction nor in any external vision.

Spiritually, the Weakling either denies God or views God as a terrifying, punitive, unapproachable force, dictating orders, imposing commandments, and giving occasional pronouncements of adequacy. He often clothes his concept of God with the characteristics of his father, mother, or another caretaker, or his early recollections of judgmental religion. As an adult he may be fervent in his religious practice, but he finds it difficult to receive grace. Inwardly he bears the stigma, "Even God couldn't love *me*." Many deflated Sovereigns in ministry roles endlessly serve others yet neglect their own well-being.

In the layoff example, the Weakling cannot bear the weight of responsibility or close scrutiny, so he abdicates direction setting and decision making to others. Desperately wanting to be liked in the short term, he may seek some crumbs of approval from the displaced workers by offering excessive severance packages or outplacement programs that endanger the long-term health of the company. If the Weakling himself is laid off, he will not ask for a fair severance or defend his rights as a worker. He will accept whatever package is given rather than risk a bad reference from management as he seeks his next career.

The Inflated Shadow
Sovereign: The Tyrant

Like the Weakling, the inflated shadow Sovereign, or Tyrant, is plagued by a deep sense of unworthiness, but he shrouds his insecurity in an aura of power, bigness, and control. He is overt in his need for attention and approval—his activities and relationships seem to brandish a blinking neon sign that says, "See me. I'm special!" Devoid of humility, he covets the public's eye. Unlike the Weakling, who seeks only affirmation and acceptance, the Tyrant craves any form of recognition, whether for benevolence or malevolence.

Both the Tyrant and the Weakling may have had absent, abusive, or dysfunctional caretakers, who either never recognized him or only noticed (and then ridiculed or punished him for) his failings. But while the Weakling withdraws, becomes subservient, and passively desires the approval of others, the Tyrant determines to escape from his childhood abandonment, and does whatever it takes to appear prominent, powerful, and heroic as an adult. He often becomes a perfectionist, believing that love must be earned through accomplishment.

The Narcissist is another common manifestation of the inflated Sovereign. Fawned over or spoiled as a child, he received little discipline or guidance. No boundaries were imposed, and he never learned how to set his own, other than by pouting or tantrums. Selfishness and self-aggrandizement—"I'm special"—were acceptable behaviors. This "special boy" becomes the scheming adult who uses sulking, orchestrated fits of rage, sullen withdrawal, or bribery to obtain a position of distinction. He'll do whatever is necessary to get what he wants. The Narcissist emanates self-sufficiency, and either denies or diminishes the need for a spiritual life. He becomes his own demigod, prone to exploiting and abusing others to satisfy his own needs, while paradoxically seeking their adulation.

Perry flies friends to his ranch on his private jet for getaway weekends. He holds court in the evenings with his bawdy humor and droning stories of deals done, foes bested, or women satisfied. Most of his wealth comes from his wife's inheritance, and he is a willing investor in his friends' ventures. But woe to anyone whose venture fails to provide a double-digit return on equity. Perry can turn in an instant from benevolent host to enraged creditor and will smear the reputation or credit rating of anyone who fails to repay his debts or, worse, confronts Perry on his bluster.

The inflated shadow Sovereign, whether Tyrant or Narcissist, is the overachiever who has to "be the best" and is often obsessed with winning and dominating. Because his reign is safeguarded by his power and success, he needs others around him who are powerless and unsuccessful. Cocky in manner and rash in action, he finds scapegoats or excuses for his own failings and is easily threatened by people of truth and character. Often the Narcissist-Tyrant surrounds himself with Weaklings or sycophants who feed their own inadequacy off of his false power.

Although he exudes an aura of righteous invulnerability, this dark Sovereign is actually terrified of being unneeded, of being ordinary. He maintains the mask of power and perfection to avoid facing his own vulnerability and dependence. He must retain control over others, and does this by either micromanaging or doing the work for his subordinates, withholding empowerment or information so they become dependent on him. He may delegate responsibility to others, but then gives incomplete instructions or places subordinates in positions beyond their skills. In this way he predestines their failure, so he can be the magnanimous savior who intervenes just in time to rescue a doomed project. He may even arrange circumstances to ensure that he becomes the key man upon whom the success of a project hinges.

As a manager, the Tyrant believes that "Others exist to serve me." While he sees himself as a fatherly patriarch, he is really a dictator, manipulating the flow of information and smothering others' creativity so that he alone sees the big picture and controls strategy. He crosses the line from having authority to becoming authoritarian.

The mature Sovereign actively seeks the counsel of others, considers the long-term needs of the realm, sets and communicates the vision to his team, and empowers and blesses them to carry out the vision. The Tyrant, on the other hand, both immune to criticism and indifferent to coaching, spurns the truth and counsel of others, trusting no one but himself. He develops and imposes a vision that serves his own needs for power and recognition, and then leverages his position or title, commanding his subjects to execute his bidding.

Beneath his arrogant veil the Tyrant is stricken with deep loneliness and inferiority. He fears, hates, or envies the grounded, passionate life of others who have high self-esteem, a calm centeredness, and a spiritual connection. Even as he draws his power from the exploitation of others, inwardly he yearns for a blessing. Mature Sovereigns (in fact, all the mature inner advisors) sense the fallacious power of the Tyrant; they see that he is really the naked emperor, the foolish or dark king. The Tyrant knows this—that mature advisors don't just *see* him, they see *through* him—and he seeks either distance or their downfall.

Nate is a classic Tyrant. He grew his seven-state empire of retail building supplies franchises over a two-decade span through shrewd real estate negotiations and ironfisted management. Despised by his competitors and employees for his ruthlessness, he has come to relish the role of business despot. Alienated from his grown children and enduring a listless marriage, he bought an imported goods boutique for his wife to run—to keep her busy and out of his hair. Over time he has become a Scrooge-like loner, and he likes it that way. The only time he lost control was when a fledgling entrepreneur in his executive small group confronted him about the apparent emptiness in his life. "How dare this upstart call me unhappy! I'm in control. I've got it all!"

Mythology, literature, and movies often depict a noble underdog, an aspiring mature Sovereign (the "good guy") in conflict with an evil incumbent Sovereign (the "bad guy"). In the Old Testament this is exemplified by David and the aging Saul; in the New Testament it's Jesus versus Herod or Pilate. The evil foe may also be a negative force or social system. Contemporary examples of such conflicts include Nelson Mandela's lifelong crusade against apartheid in South Africa and William Wilberforce's successful battle to abolish slavery in Great Britain during the nineteenth century. In such cases it is easy to see the contrast between the broad, benevolent vision of the true Sovereign and the narrow, self-serving cruelty of the insecure Narcissist or Tyrant, or the blind selfishness of a nation.

In my work with company presidents and professionals I see some Tyrants who were raised in environments of poverty or abuse and then— through diligence, guile, obsession, or luck—rose to positions of substantial wealth and power. Most were thrust into the world at an early age and forced to survive on their own, having never experienced love or mentoring. They vow never to return to the pain of their youth, and gird themselves in the trappings of their wealth or position. They appear indifferent to or above the support or nurturing of others—to accept assistance would imply weakness or diminish their power. They begin to view themselves as self-sufficient and even impregnable, getting what they want by the sheer force of will. Often when they achieve their goals, the path behind them is strewn with the Victims and Weaklings they sucked dry to feed their lust for power.

Other business Tyrants either live off family trusts or lead second- or third-generation family businesses. Feeding at the trough of the family legacy, they have a false sense of their own importance and usually abuse their power. They manage by the aura of their surname or the thickness of their pocketbooks. Stripped of their pedigrees or bank accounts, many have neither the character nor the presence to lead. Texans have a wonderful euphemism for these people: "Big hat, no cattle."

The inflated Sovereign is the most common wound I encounter in my work with executives and professionals in transition. Unless they are at the helm with others serving them, they are lost and helpless. Most who sell their companies, retire from public life, or exit their practices, even those who have amassed fortunes, cannot bear time away from the limelight.

Their identities have become dependent on position, title, and trappings. To become ordinary or average—where the phone stops ringing and they are no longer asked to chair the fund-raiser or give the graduation keynote—is unthinkable. They must find a way to get back into the spotlight, usually by building another tower.

As the Tyrant ages, the constant need to compete and win in a hostile world plunges him deeper into his anxieties. He begins to eliminate people from his life whom he can't control or fix. He also eliminates those who reflect a divine image—the mature Sovereigns who might guide him out of his lonely abyss. Late in life, many Tyrants exist in gated estates or nursing homes, bitter, brittle, and alone.

In the company-downsizing example, the astute Tyrant has usually packed his bags and left town long before the layoff. If forced to act, he finds scapegoats to receive the blame, taking necessary steps to protect his image, especially in the short term. If the situation becomes truly dire, he acts solely out of self-preservation with little or no concern for the company. He may demand a large severance package, blame the situation on his subordinates, and then exit with bravado or false martyrdom, denying his own culpability.

Examples of the Mature and Shadow Sovereigns

All eight leaders introduced in Part I have the gifts to inspire and lead within their respective realms—entrepreneurial businesses and partnerships (Stan, Thad, Larry, Fletcher, and myself), family businesses (Peter), large corporations (Thad and Larry), professional groups (Susan), and ministries (Marty). They all acknowledge a Source of energy and grace beyond themselves, and feel some measure of dependence on this Source.

While Marty was prone to be a pleaser in high school and college, he set aside these tendencies and committed his life in service to God. He maintains a deep and selfless love for God's people and his assigned realm, the church. As a youth minister he drew on this love to guide and motivate young people toward a relationship with God, without imposing any personal agenda or expecting lavish affirmation.

Thad was a natural leader in his high school youth group. Both there and in his businesses he entrusted responsibility to others (classmates, employees) and motivated them to achieve their highest potential. His stature as a grounded man gave him the presence to encourage, guide, and bless all in his realms. They trusted him.

On the shadow side, Thad was always the sidekick as a child. On the few occasions he was allowed to shine, he was either betrayed by authority figures or bullied by classmates. Throughout his youth he felt continual pressure to excel (sports teams, youth group, academics, law school), and always fell short of his parents' expectations. These things implanted an "I can't" belief in him. As a result, he arranged his life so he occasionally got close but never reached his ultimate goals—the controlling presidency of a company and financial independence. Even in his late 30s, Thad the Weakling felt the shame of underperforming before the critical eyes of his father.

While Peter could rise to Sovereign leadership during times of crisis, he wallowed in insecurity during the ordinary times within the family business. He became his tyrannical father's pawn, doing his bidding out of fear of his ire rather than love for the enterprise. With no vision for his own life beyond laboring in the family trenches, he was always asking others' permission—"Is this okay?"—avoiding the responsibility of either failing himself or hurting someone else.

The shadow Sovereign often oscillates between Tyrant and Weakling, at one moment being the showman or buffoon exploiting and abusing others (the manic Tyrant), and later wallowing in worthlessness, feeling inferior to others, gridlocked, and helpless (the depressive Weakling). My own life in business reflected this pendulum swing between the two Sovereign shadows. Terribly averse to conflict, I would hide in my office, take lengthy road trips, and remain indecisive until problems escalated into crises. I would then launch into mega-control mode, micromanaging projects and firing executives, while seeking to be the savior/hero to the frontline employees.

Another client of mine was a classic example of Sovereign shadows in a high-profile leader. Maintaining a normally quiet demeanor, Arnold was always late to our sessions, offering deep apologies while being sure to mention the international crisis he had averted or life he had saved while we dealt with the mundane topics of our meeting. Oblivious to time constraints, he pontificated on his life accomplishments, dropping the names of the heads of state, entertainment kingpins, or spiritual gurus who regularly joined him on his yacht.

Arnold did have a good heart, backed by great wealth. He regularly offered to assist others in precarious financial positions. But their acceptance of his support created a dependency that somehow never went away. They became beholden to him, part of his chattel, never able to escape their own insignificance in the aura of his largesse.

Occasionally, mature Sovereigns confronted Arnold on his altruistic tyranny. He would crush the weaker ones with anger, blustering about their blindness to his generosity and caring. The few peers who challenged him were deflected by quick apologies for his insensitivity and promises to mend his ways and again carry the banner of leadership for which he was destined. Bluster, deflection, buffoonery, self-abasement—Arnold used these and other tactics to retain the illusion of control and power.

Closing Thoughts

Balanced Sovereign leaders in Western culture are rare. The pretense and success-focus of tower building lure the aspiring Sovereign away from stewardship and into the selfishness of personal security and recognition. Sadly, few corporate, public sector, and ministry leaders avoid the intoxication of business, political, or pastoral power. Conversely, the pressure to be liked and accepted can deflate them into assuming responsibility for the happiness of others. Many aspiring Sovereigns enter or rise to positions of visible leadership with the idealism to "make a difference." Most become worn down by the inexorable pressures and demands on them, as well as the temptations of rank. They forsake idealism—and possibly greatness—for fame, wealth, or security. They mortgage their souls.

Most modern-day leaders rule alone. Few have the wisdom and humility to convene a trusted group of covenantal brothers, sisters, and friends who will hold them accountable. Nor do they have the foresight during their tower-building years to find a mentor, elder, or guide, or to apprentice themselves to another Sovereign. So they stay highly visible, but unguided, untethered, and unloved.

They also live under the constant scrutiny of the media, which focuses on immediate accomplishments, harpoons long-term thinking and creative vision, and brands even the smallest shadows as fatal flaws. No wonder so many idealistic and capable young leaders lose vision, commitment, and passion for a life of public service or business stewardship, when they and their families are subjected to vindictive scrutiny and the media seek their downfall under the ruse of "telling the whole truth."

The great Sovereign leaders take a stand and are never lukewarm. Their honesty and conviction spotlight the weakness and duplicity of others' shadows. Grateful for, yet indifferent to, the praise of others, true Sovereigns are not ingratiating to the spin doctors, promoters, and power brokers who "make" successful people in our culture. Mature Sovereigns continually ask themselves, "What is my kingdom for?" In the end, their kingdom is always for service. It's never just so they can feel comfortable.

Great leaders have typically been vilified, caricatured, sabotaged, libeled, kidnapped, assassinated—crucified. Like the great prophets, true Sovereigns are normally appreciated only by subsequent generations. Yet our culture longs for the presence of grounded kings and queens. We need more heroes like Nelson Mandela, Mother Teresa, Martin Luther King Jr., Amelia Earhart, and Mahatma Gandhi, who capture a nation—or a neighborhood—with their vitality, vision, and humility. They *live* their ideals, without imposing their ideologies on others, and lead by their raw, pure presence. They've been tempered in personal infernos of betrayal, poverty, or ostracism, and have transformed their pain into character, graciousness, and service. They still have flaws, but their inner core exudes integrity and a fervent love for their realms.

If the gateway to Sovereign energy is joy, we must drop the obsession with self, as both the deflated, unworthy Weakling ("I'm not good enough") and the inflated, narcissistic Tyrant ("I'm special"). When we discard our obsession with ego and open ourselves to an infinite Source of love, joy comes flooding in, and with it genuine worth. The cost is high: the shedding of both our unworthiness and our narcissism, and then nakedly surrendering ourselves to this Love. The bounty is that we—and our realms—receive a new, loved, grounded, worthy self, whose calling is clear and whose presence is a beacon to others.

16

The WARRIOR

Men Wanted for Hazardous Journey

British Antarctic explorer Sir Ernest Shackleton
(1874–1922) placed this advertisement in London
newspapers in 1900 in preparation for the National
Antarctic Expedition (which subsequently failed to
reach the South Pole). Shackleton later said of the
call for volunteers that "It seemed as though all the
men in Great Britain were determined to accompany
me, the response was so overwhelming."

> MEN WANTED FOR HAZARDOUS JOURNEY. Small
> wages, bitter cold, long months of complete
> darkness, constant danger, safe return doubt-
> ful. Honor and recognition in case of success.
> —Ernest Shackleton

From *The Book of Virtues*,
Edited by William Bennett[1]

Our Warrior advisor takes action. Disciplined and committed to the
truth, the Warrior serves the Sovereign, dedicates himself to his assignments, and gets the job done. Well trained yet aware of his limitations,
the Warrior is dependable and loyal to the needs of the realm. The mature
Warrior has well-defined boundaries, which he communicates, maintains,
and enforces.

The Warrior exudes courage, persistence, and stamina for the cause. He shows up and does the right thing. His commitment transcends his personal ego, and he redoubles his efforts when he is exhausted. The emotional gateway to the mature Warrior is the ability to face and go through anger.

The deflated shadow Warrior, or Victim, represses or denies his anger and avoids confrontation or aggression. The inflated shadow Warrior, or Savage, is consumed by his anger, which leaks or spews onto others, especially Victims. The Victim has flimsy boundaries, easily trampled by others; the Savage ignores the boundaries of others as he pursues his own agenda. (See Figure 16.1.)

The Mature Warrior

While the Sovereign sets boundaries and direction, the Warrior defends boundaries and does the work. His role is to accomplish a task, as assigned, in the most direct way possible, using the full extent of his giftedness. He is thorough and focused in his preparation, be it hitting in the batting cage, preparing multiple drafts of a manuscript, studying in the library, or practicing the piano. Diligent in his execution, he plies his skills deftly and precisely, whether wielding a weapon or opening a new division of a company, and remains calm under pressure. He quietly translates theory into application, and with pinpoint focus devotes all his energy to the task at hand. He knows that long-term success or failure depends on his attention and awareness in the present moment.

Likewise, he recognizes that excellence comes only through perseverance and asceticism. He faces with equanimity his own pain and hardship, both psychological and physical. He maintains a quiet discipline and endures with neither flourish ("Look how hard I'm working") nor a need for sympathy or approval ("I'm willing to suffer so that others can succeed").

The mature Warrior is truthful to the point of bluntness. He communicates a clear, definite "Yes" or "No," and feels no compulsion to placate others. While never intentionally alienating another, he is more loyal to a cause than to a person. Personal relationships and the opinions of others take second place to his faithful execution of the task out of loyalty to the Sovereign and service to the realm.

The mature Warrior looks you in the eye, with a sense of clarity, simplicity, and honesty. To non-Warriors his transparency is often intimidating, especially when he speaks "what is," no matter how painful or harsh. He knows that the best resolution to difficult problems is to strip

Mature Warrior
Takes Action

- Gets the job done
- Skilled, disciplined, focused
- Grounded in the truth
- Direct, factual communicator
- Enforces own boundaries
- Honors others' boundaries
- Loyal, sense of duty
- Here-and-now oriented
- Can cut losses and move on

Ability to go through: ANGER

Deflated Warrior
Victim

- Avoids conflict, pain
- Weak boundaries; can't say "No"
- Helpless, pushover
- Undisciplined, unprepared
- No passion, vigor
- Anxious, nervous, depressed
- Overcommits
- Tells people what they want to hear
- Dilettante, dabbler, can't finish

Inflated Warrior
Savage

- Has to win
- Pushes or ignores boundaries
- Unpredictable, impatient, defiant, intimidating
- Perfectionist, workaholic
- Not open to criticism or advice
- Cannot tolerate weak people
- Short or volatile temper
- Rebels against authority

Figure 16.1 The Warrior Advisor.

away illusion and confront the hard facts. And while he has no need for enemies, he knows that evil and falsity must be confronted. He cherishes life, but is willing to look like a fool or even die for the Cause.

He'll go against the grain to take the right action and risk ostracism from his peers or even his realm—for example, the teenager who refuses to take drugs and alcohol; the public official who resigns his position rather than accept a kickback; the attorney who refuses a lucrative civil assignment that would compromise his values. In my own company several outstanding female employees turned down pay raises, flexible hours, and executive wooing to become full-time moms. Other accomplished women and men who loved their careers drew hard boundaries around their work hours to ensure having focused time with their families.

The Warrior is immune to emotional peaks and valleys, and neither revels in his successes nor wallows in his failures. While his deeds may be magnificent or dramatic, after the completion of a job he simply turns to the next assignment. He doesn't use drama or hoopla to draw attention to himself (e.g., no post-touchdown dances in the end zone). The Warrior also takes responsibility for his actions during times of failure, not self-shaming—"It was all my fault"—but honestly acknowledging, "I did my best. In retrospect I might have done certain things differently. It didn't work out. I will now focus on the next task."

Like the mature Sovereign, the mature Warrior knows when it is time to move on, and does so quietly and with dignity. He deals cleanly with the hard truth of loss. The Warrior in business resigns his position when he can no longer execute his duties at the required level. The Warrior athlete retires from his sport when his physical skills no longer allow him to compete. The mature Warrior leaves a relationship that has become either irreconcilable or codependent. Larry did this twice, leaving his original programming job when exploited by his bosses, and his real estate partnership when he lost his passion for it.

The mature Warrior has a sharp sword. Most of the time it is sheathed on his belt, but others can see it. On occasion his hand will touch the hilt of the sword; every so often he might pull it from its sheath. On rare occasions he will use the sword in swift, precise, definitive action. The sword represents the Warrior's clear vision and searing honesty, backed by his willingness to face loss or death in order to uphold the truth and defend the realm.

The Warrior receives his sword from an elder or mentor, a Sovereign figure in his life, who teaches the Warrior truth, integrity, right and wrong, good and evil, and the ways of the world, ideally during adolescence or young adulthood. Often this Sovereign figure is the father to a son or the mother to a daughter. Sometimes it is a coach, teacher, minister, or first boss who mentors the young Warrior in the discipline, conviction, and courage necessary to wield the sword, and the wisdom, character, and responsibility that underlie its use. The initiated Warrior then has the power and will use his sword in service to his realms when reality calls for action. He may not win or succeed, but he is willing to put his life on the line for the truth and the good of the kingdom. If he attacks, it is always for the goal of ensuring the safety of the realm, and never for imperialism or to impose his will.

Prototypical relationships between the Sovereign and the protégé-Warrior include the elder Caesar to Maximus (in *Gladiator*) and Obi Wan Kenobe to Luke Skywalker (in *Star Wars*). Stan's father and both of Susan's parents gave swords to their adolescent children, through their unswerving character, loving discipline, and the occasional one-on-one, heart-to-heart talks about life.

The Warrior is fully present, hungry for life, and willing to invest everything in the great adventure—his calling. He strives for something beyond his ego. Most indigenous cultures as well as practitioners of the martial arts understand this. Sadly, the materialism of our Western culture fosters the mercenary Warrior who fights only in exchange for money, power, and recognition.

Jesus embodied Warrior energy in clearing the temple and in his blunt encounters with the Pharisees. He taught his disciples, "Simply let your 'Yes' be 'Yes,' and your 'No,' 'No'" (Matthew 5:37).[2] His life was devoted to grounding and expanding the Kingdom of God on earth.

In the layoff example the mature Warrior tells the employees the exact details of the layoff, helps them clean out their desks, arranges outplacement, and handles all the ugly details. Afterward, he is also the manager or operating officer who says, "Okay, the layoff is over. We have a revised objective. It's time to focus our energies toward accomplishing the new goals. The bloodletting is over. Let's get on with rebuilding this organization."

The following excerpt from Oriah Mountain Dreamer's poem *The Invitation* captures the essence of the Warrior:

> It doesn't interest me to know where you live or how much money you have.
>
> I want to know if you can get up after the night of grief and despair, weary and bruised to the bone, and do what needs to be done for the children.

It doesn't interest me who you are or how you came to be here. I want to know if you will stand in the center of the fire with me—and not shrink back.[3]

The Warrior Shadows

As a child the shadow Warrior typically confronted authority and lost. Caregivers, teachers, or other authority figures devalued or rejected his words and his feelings, using verbal reprimands or physical abuse. He could never openly express his hurts. He often lived in fear of either punishment or abandonment—like Peter's childhood—or in a "nice" yet manipulative environment where excuses or rationalizations smoothed over all pains, and no one got visibly angry—like Stan's childhood. As an adult the shadow Warrior, both deflated and inflated, refuses to face hard truth.

The shadow Warrior either has no boundaries (deflated) or tramples the boundaries of others (inflated). Lacking mature Warrior and Sovereign role models in his life, the shadow Warrior never received a sword—that is, the integrity and discipline to defend the boundaries of his realms while respecting the non-encroaching boundaries of others. Western society's emphasis on comfort and security, coupled with the absence of clean, purposeful initiation rites, breeds adult children—needy, whiny Victims or pouting, selfish Savages—rather than grounded men and women.

Anger—The Gateway to the Mature Warrior

The mature Warrior has the ability and inner permission to express personal truth, no matter how embarrassing or painful—or loving. Wise caregivers can nurture and coach a malleable child in the clean expression of his truth without shaming the child or neutering his feelings. The child knows how he feels but is unskilled in conveying it. Guidance and modeling hone clean expression of emotion.

A wound occurs when caregivers and others ignore, reject, repress, or belittle a child's expressions. The repression of truth and feelings breeds anger, and when the anger in turn is repressed, it goes to the back of the bus, described in Chapter 13, where it festers and seeks opportunities for release. The longer it smolders in the back of the bus, the more venomous its expression when it finally comes out.

Where clean articulation is taboo, the anger leaks or bursts out on weaker loved ones (e.g., spouse or children) as teasing, sarcasm, or physical rage. When release is not possible or permissible (in a "nice" family or "polite" society), the anger toxins infect both the subconscious and the body, leading to depression or physical illness. As with all repressed shadows, the anger *will* manifest itself, either inwardly or outwardly, usually at the most inopportune time in the most debilitating way.

Violent sports and films have become popular partly because they provide a ritual outlet for our repressed rage. We identify with our maverick movie heroes as they humiliate inept or corrupt authority figures, enact vengeance for wrongdoing, and enforce justice. Sadly, many of us also revel in the savagery of adventure and horror films, which unleash, vicariously, the killer inside each of us. Competitive sport at all levels is the same: If *I* can't win, at least I want the other guy to feel some pain. Thank God for sports—better for the armchair quarterback to scream at the TV than to beat his wife. Sadly, too often both occur.

Mature Warrior energy requires the clean expression or release of anger. This does not mean that we must become angry people. *Anger* is an emotion to be acknowledged and expressed; then it is gone. *Angry* is a state of being where both truth and anger are repressed. The Warrior shadows are angry. The antidote is the safe expression of the pent-up anger. The resultant state is being grounded in the truth, where everything has been spoken and nothing is hidden. Specific steps for the transformation of anger into clean boundaries and truth telling are presented in Chapter 20 and Appendix C.

After the clean expression of anger, we learn to trust our fierce feelings, our sense of the wild man or woman within, and in that, the wildness and aliveness of God. We can then confidently dedicate our lives in servanthood where things aren't right, where people are oppressed, and where the truth has been concealed.

The Deflated Shadow Warrior: The Victim

While the adult Warrior exudes tenacity and perseverance, the deflated shadow Warrior, or Victim, is internally already defeated. At some point in his past, when he tried to take a stand and enforce boundaries for himself, he was intimidated or disgraced. When he showed disappointment or frustration, or simply spoke his mind, he was reprimanded, shamed, or beaten into a submissive state. He learned that standing up for himself led to pain or alienation. Unsupported, and unable to defend himself against physically overwhelming or authoritarian forces, the child learned to say or do anything to placate others and avoid confrontation.

As an adult, he subconsciously believes that he is powerless, and that any attempts to confront authority and stand on his own will lead to further embarrassment, futility, or pain. So, saying "What's the use?" the Victim denies his anger and often manifests the listlessness or resignation symptoms of depression. In times of tension or conflict he goes numb, and either acquiesces to others, runs away, or escapes (as we will also see later in the deflated Magician) into a world of fantasy.

Drained of spirit and stamina, the Victim lacks the desire and energy to discover and develop his talents. He becomes an undisciplined dilettante who dabbles in many projects or relationships, then abandons them at the first signs of stress or conflict. He often struggles to maintain his physical health, becoming overweight or out of shape and frequently indulging to excess in alcohol or food.

The Victim lives his life in reactive mode, waiting for direction from others rather than following his own desires or course. He is the pushover yes-man, content to do the will of artificially powerful or bullying people. Similar to his cousin, the Weakling Sovereign, he seeks the favor of others so they won't hurt him. He follows the current party line either because everyone else is doing it or to avoid making waves. His spiritual life is generally lukewarm or nonexistent. He may endure religious services as part of family tradition or because it's expected, but he lacks the energy and discipline for a committed spiritual life and the courage to stand up for his convictions.

The adult Warrior has a sword, is trained in its use, and will employ it when necessary. The Victim either never received a sword or had it shamefully stripped from him at an early age. Swordless and, for boys who grow up with abuse, emasculated, these men enter adulthood helpless, anxious, without boundaries, and constantly striving to avoid the wrath of others.

To compare the mature Warrior with the Victim, consider the following example. After working with wood, you discover a sliver in your finger. While not terribly painful, it's annoying, a constant reminder that something is not right with your finger. The adult Warrior acknowledges that the sliver is present, sterilizes a needle, and penetrates the skin to remove it. If the sliver is deep, the finger may bleed, followed by a period of pain, perhaps intense. Yet, because of the Warrior's swift action, the finger can be cleaned and bandaged, and will heal quickly.

The Victim, on the other hand, tries to ignore the pain. He does this by concentrating more intently on his work, or perhaps using analgesics (denial, diversions, escapes, numbness). He hopes the splinter will somehow come out on its own. On rare occasions this happens, but usually the splinter remains buried deep in the finger and begins to fester. Over time, the finger becomes discolored and infected. What could have been a brief instance of pain followed by a short healing period now requires a doctor's intervention (i.e., someone else is now responsible), followed by a longer period of suffering and healing. This is the Victim's preferred path: summon authority, surrender responsibility to a third party, and suffer.

In my work with family business executives I often see the patriarch or matriarch casting a dark shadow of intimidation over the heir-apparent son or daughter. Promises are made about surrendering the reins to the next generation, buy-sell agreements are structured, but ultimate authority remains with the parent. The Victim tolerates these inconsistencies and betrayals, seeking to maintain harmony in the family and, above all, avoid becoming the pariah that disgraces the family business by confronting or leaving Dad. This tolerance is perceived as loyalty to the family, as the heir abdicates his personal destiny for the sake of the family legacy.

Sometimes the hard-driving head of the family will anoint his son or daughter as the new president and ostensibly go into semiretirement. But instead of actually surrendering the reins to the heir, he holds the strings as a puppeteer, running the business from behind the scenes through his marionette son or daughter. The Victim struggles internally between loving service and indentured servitude, but avoids confronting the patriarch with his or her concerns.

Melanie's father had founded and grown his specialty import firm into a $100 million profit engine. She and her three brothers entered the business right out of college and had no work experience except under their father. Melanie was given a vice presidential title and supposedly ran marketing and sales. In reality, her dad called all the shots. She wanted to make some bold expansion moves, but he ridiculed her business plans and regularly reminded her of the good life she had. "Just be a good girl, do your job, and don't rock the boat. I'll take care of you." At 30 and ready to build her own tower, she felt more like a 12-year-old, sheltered and shackled by her father.

Another common occurrence is the conflict-averse entrepreneur who relishes running a rapidly growing enterprise, but balks at the competitive rigors and interpersonal tensions of the business world. Many of these unseasoned entrepreneurs crash their companies because they are unwilling to make the difficult decisions and take hard actions. In these examples the Victim leader either surrounds himself with parasites who sugarcoat bad news or surrenders the reins of his business to a Tyrant manager. Many

Savage or Tyrant turnaround experts feed off undisciplined and inexperienced Victim entrepreneurs.

Chris had built a comfortably profitable niche manufacturing business with a couple hundred employees. A shy inventor, he preferred the research lab to the manufacturing floor or boardroom, and was eventually blindsided by the automation and factory upgrades necessary to remain competitive. As his market share shrank and losses accumulated, Chris recognized his management deficiencies and brought in a mercenary workout specialist to relaunch his company. Chris gulped at the specialist's compensation and severance package, but surrendered the reins of his 20-year-old company to the supposed expert, who promptly fired many loyal managers, halved the R&D staff, and rebuilt the management team with his own bullpen of highly compensated managers—who knew little about Chris' business or customers. Within three years the company had missed major development windows, lost half its customers, and was flirting with bankruptcy. Meanwhile, Chris had personally guaranteed bank notes to keep the company afloat and was now a financial prisoner within his own company. He felt he had no choice but to keep paying the Tyrant "expert" in the fleeting hope that someday he might escape from the mire.

The mature Warrior confronts and goes through his anger. The pathway out of being a Victim is to understand, face, and *go through* the suppressed anger (often camouflaged as frustration, disappointment, or hurt), and emerge from helplessness into a sense of personal power. For most Victims, facing their anger is a terrifying prospect.

In the company-downsizing example, the Victim will often assume a scapegoat role. As an employee he may volunteer to be the first person laid off. As a manager he avoids the thorough research on possible tactics for the layoff—it's too hard and painful. Like the deflated Sovereign, he wants to placate the employee base so they'll still like him after the layoff. He may offer severance packages well beyond the means of the company to fund, or become a martyr, taking his own salary to zero. If the Victim is in a leadership position he may ignore the recommendations to downsize the company, preferring no action to any painful action.

The Inflated Shadow Warrior: The Savage

We have seen that the mature Warrior is disciplined and enforces well-defined boundaries, while the Victim is undisciplined and allows his boundaries to be trampled by others. The Savage goes beyond discipline to obsession in his actions, and either disregards or violates the boundaries of others. The mature Warrior expresses his truth, including his anger, like a surgeon using a scalpel, cleanly and precisely, so that the pain, while intense, will be brief, and healing can begin quickly. The Victim denies or suppresses his anger. The Savage spews out his anger as physical, verbal, or emotional abuse of others.

In work roles the Savage is an unpredictable insurgent, relentlessly pushing limits and attacking the status quo. He is compulsive and driven to action with an obsessive task orientation. Like the Victim, the Savage was often abused or shamed as a child. However, instead of becoming insular, depressed, helpless, or cowardly, he looks for something to kill and becomes the agitator or bully who wreaks his suppressed vengeance on the helpless Victims or Weaklings around him. His anger leaks or explodes onto others, usually defenseless loved ones, by taunting, sarcasm, teasing, and other forms of verbal and physical humiliation. Having previously experienced rejection or abuse for his own helplessness, he now loathes others who are hesitant or vulnerable.

Without Victims or Weaklings to ravage, the Savage may also turn his rage on himself, where it manifests as masochism, perfectionism, workaholism, bulimia, or other forms of self-imposed extremism. The Savage Warrior often works until he burns out, not for the approval of others (as with the shadow Sovereign), but as a warped way of punishing himself for his own powerlessness.

With no mature Sovereigns in his life, he learned at an early age how to dodge or undermine authority figures to get his way. He developed thick armor (similar to the deflated Lover, presented in Chapter 18) to ward off others who would seek tenderness and intimacy from him and in so doing might hurt or betray him. His subconscious mantra is, "I will not be hurt again."

While the Victim has no sword and the mature Warrior rarely uses his, the Savage always has his sword out. Instead of integrity, the Savage's sword represents self-interest and imperialistic control. Lacking the true Warrior's incorruptibility and care for the realm, he hacks and mutilates his Victims with the rusty, jagged edge of his rage and personal agendas. He is indifferent to the wounds he inflicts on others, and often draws a sadistic pleasure from their suffering, acquiescence, or mandatory homage to his will.

In the business realm, his approach to negotiation is, "I will win and you will lose—or both of us will die in the battle." In defeat or after failure, he is unable to let issues die. He gets even, carrying grudges and seeking re-venge on those who have bested him.

As a manager he demands that others labor at his own frenzied pace on ill-defined tasks, pursuing ambiguous goals. He manages or coaches by intimidation, subconsciously hoping others will fail so he may exact pun-ishment upon them, in distorted retribution for the way he was punished or abused. While management doctrine preaches "praise in public and criti-cize or coach in private," the Savage offers only backhanded or conditional praise, and enjoys criticizing or shaming subordinates in public.

The mature Warrior is a disciplined soldier, honing and deploying his skills in service to the mature Sovereign, and, if necessary, dying willingly for the good of the realm. The Savage is a mercenary, loyal only to himself. He sells his services to the highest bidder, indifferent to the good of his em-ployer's realm. He may be tenacious and disciplined, but only in serving his own ends. He takes care of himself and is unconcerned about the relational carnage left in his wake as he executes his assignments.

In the layoff example the Savage Warrior takes pleasure in the suffer-ing of others, relishing the "executioner" role. If 10 percent of the work-force needs to be cut, he might cut 20. If the equitable and affordable severance is one month's salary, he might offer no severance pay, and enjoy the prospect of possible litigation.

Examples of the Mature and Shadow Warriors

Most professional people (attorneys, physicians, accountants) manifest ma-ture Warrior traits. They have endured a weeding-out process along their educational path that only the diligent can survive. Their professions de-mand in-the-moment focus on the task, patient, or assignment at hand. They accept long hours and little recognition. Physicians, especially, must remain focused and unswayed by emotion when a life depends on the skilled application of their training.

Susan, as with many medical professionals, models Warrior energy in her commitment to her patients. Her arduous postgraduate educational path required perseverance and stamina over more than a decade. Susan thrives on tackling difficult goals or causes, whether opening her own prac-tice, battling managed care, or proving herself to her in-laws.

Fletcher learned hard work as a teen. He remained loyal to his first boss, the first real Sovereign in his life, when he could have easily left for more money. When he started his own service company he never considered the disloyalty of taking customers with him. While he aspires to "be the best" at every undertaking, and he expects recognition (his inflated Sovereign), he does the required homework and labors long hours without bragging about his work ethic. He is direct and sometimes abrupt with his language, and clean in expressing his anger.

Larry knows loyalty and closure. His discipline in the weight room and on the track earned him a walk-on position on the football team, where he stayed on the taxi squad, rarely seeing game time for two years. When the coaches began to abuse his commitment, he spoke his displeasure and quit. He worked long hours in his first programming job, studying and mastering new technology as new assignments stretched his training. Again, he fulfilled and usually exceeded his bosses' expectations, and left only when they took advantage of his loyalty. This pattern continued in his real estate management partnership and even in his current position within the large corporation. While he seeks deeper fulfillment in his life, he does not consider aborting his duty to his employers, unless they begin to abuse him. In his home life, too, though outwardly incongruous because of his sexual transgressions, he strives to remain loyal to his wife and family.

While Stan manifested multiple adult Warrior traits—his work ethic, devotion to his teammates and employees, duty to his employer—he became a helpless Victim around the women in his life. His mother had chastised and shamed him when he objected to violin lessons. Both of his wives ignored his wants and berated him verbally. His anger manifested through workaholism and hiring prostitutes.

Dutiful within and loyal to his ministries, Marty simmered with the rage repressed from his youth. As a teen and in college he was the designated fighter who literally lost consciousness as he physically pounded his victims. As a frontline worker in his ministry, with no one to abuse but himself, he worked until he burned out, and was bulimic for 10 years.

I see the Savage Warrior inside me. Throughout my childhood and into my work life I hated authority, anyone telling me what to do. My personal attitude in sports and later in business became "Win or don't play." Bred on competition, I hated (and still hate) to lose, and either sulked alone or lashed out at loved ones, rarely able to let go of a loss cleanly. Keenly aware of my own failings and weaknesses, my inflated Warrior still has little tolerance for the weaknesses of others.

One man from my retreat work stands out as a Warrior within a dysfunctional group. The other members, many more powerful or wealthy than Randy, prattled about how "connected and trustworthy" the group had become over a decade of meeting together. Randy sat quietly as he listened to their recounts of special celebrations or adventures and witnessed their avoidance of the tough, unspoken issues that stunted intimacy within the group. When his turn came to speak, he crisply laid out his perceptions of the hypocrisy and insensitivity within the group. In a calm manner he presented a litany of events that had hurt him and now caused him to consider leaving the group. Though initially painful, his "getting clean" brought the safety of truth to the group and gave the other members permission to get clean on their own unspoken issues, following the path he had blazed.

Closing Thoughts

We often oscillate between Victim and Savage, at one moment floundering in helplessness, inadequacy, and depression, and then flying into fits of anger or cruelty directed at others, usually loved ones. A common scenario is stuff-stuff-stuff-stuff-*explode!* In one area of our lives we play Victim; in another, Savage—normally not to the extremes painted intentionally in these descriptions, but in subtler, often undetectable ways. When we harbor anger toward another person, for issues that range from missing an appointment to wanting more sex to deep betrayal, we may nurse our buried splinter of frustration by going quiet, working alone, or simply avoiding the other person. Later, our subtle Savage manifests by criticizing in public, pouting in our office, feigning innocence, or giving "the glare."

I see many high-level leaders, seeking both to avoid confrontation and to gain approval, who promise impractical delivery dates, accept time-draining volunteer positions, and otherwise give away their time so that others will like them. After playing Victim at work or with other groups who request their time, the pendulum swings the other way as they vent their repressed anger on either themselves or loved ones—their surrogate Victims.

You have probably seen how this cycle cascades through relationships. If we yell at a child, he'll find a younger sibling or weaker child at school to tease or abuse. The cycle continues until someone has the courage to draw a boundary and say, "No, I won't do that. I won't accept that." Or, in the profound words of the cartoon world's archetypal Warrior, Popeye the sailor, "That's all I can stand, 'cause I can't stand no more."

To stay balanced and grounded as a mature Warrior requires a safe outlet for the clean expression of our truth and anger. The longer the anger is denied or repressed, the narrower the balance beam of clarity and the more prone we are to being pulled into either a Victim role or an explosive retaliation. The best way to broaden the beam is to have other mature Warriors and Sovereigns in our lives who can receive our truth and anger without judgment, knowing it is not directed at them. They offer a place for us to let off steam. They can also give us the courage and confidence to approach and get clean with those who have wounded us ("I didn't like it when you kept me waiting. I felt hurt.") or those to whom we have overcommitted ("I was wrong when I accepted the position. I can't fulfill your expectations and be true to myself. I must withdraw."). Lastly, they can support us as we endure the inevitable tension and perhaps lost relationships that are often the price paid for transparent honesty—being true to ourselves.

Domesticated Rebels

He was a difficult man. He thought differently and acted differently from the rest of us. He questioned everything. Was he a rebel or a prophet or a psychopath or a hero? "Who can tell the difference?" we said. "And who cares, anyway?"

So we *socialized* him. We taught him to be *sensitive* to public opinion and to the feelings of others. We got him to conform. He was a comfortable person to live with now. Well *adjusted*. We had made him manageable and docile.

We congratulated him on having achieved self-conquest. He began to congratulate himself too. He did not see that it was *we* who had conquered him.

A society that domesticates its rebels has gained its peace. But it has lost its future.

—*Anthony deMello*[4]

17

The MAGICIAN

The Magician advisor embodies wisdom, objectivity, penetrating insight, excellent communication skills, and the ability to deal with symbols, ritual, and mystery. The Magician's role is to hold the tension of disparate, sometimes contradictory information, feelings, and relationships, while remaining detached and clearheaded. The emotional gateway to the mature Magician is the ability to face, go through, and transform fear into an ally when grappling with difficult situations or relationships.

Unaddressed fear causes people to slip into one of the two Magician shadows. The deflated shadow Magician, consumed and confused by the fear, becomes gridlocked in his thinking and simply doesn't know what to do. This deflated shadow is characterized as the Dummy. The inflated shadow Magician is likewise held captive by fear, but shrouds it in a life of illusion, self-righteousness, and hidden agendas. The inflated shadow Magician is called the Manipulator. Both the Tyrant and the Manipulator seek to control situations. The Tyrant controls from a need to be visible and viewed as special, while the Manipulator is more sneaky and operates from a background position. (See Figure 17.1.)

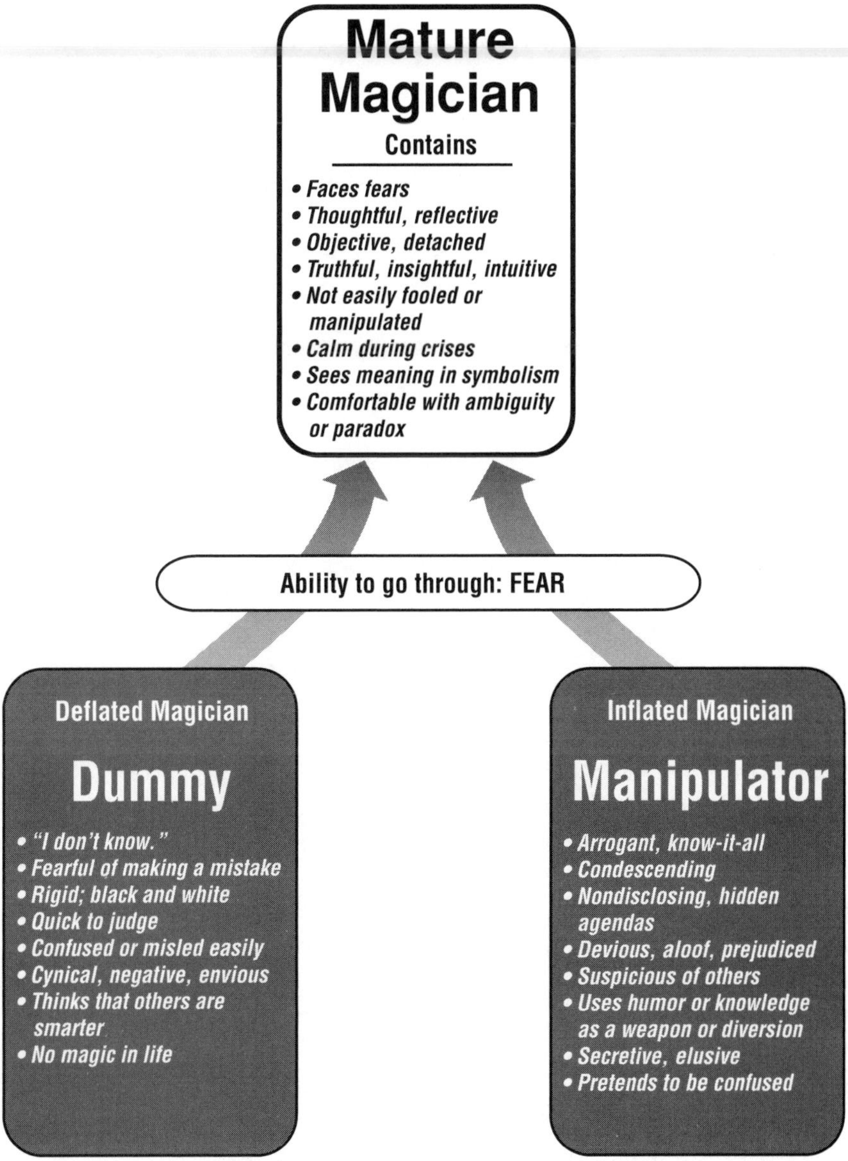

Mature Magician

Contains

- *Faces fears*
- *Thoughtful, reflective*
- *Objective, detached*
- *Truthful, insightful, intuitive*
- *Not easily fooled or manipulated*
- *Calm during crises*
- *Sees meaning in symbolism*
- *Comfortable with ambiguity or paradox*

Ability to go through: FEAR

Deflated Magician

Dummy

- *"I don't know."*
- *Fearful of making a mistake*
- *Rigid; black and white*
- *Quick to judge*
- *Confused or misled easily*
- *Cynical, negative, envious*
- *Thinks that others are smarter*
- *No magic in life*

Inflated Magician

Manipulator

- *Arrogant, know-it-all*
- *Condescending*
- *Nondisclosing, hidden agendas*
- *Devious, aloof, prejudiced*
- *Suspicious of others*
- *Uses humor or knowledge as a weapon or diversion*
- *Secretive, elusive*
- *Pretends to be confused*

Figure 17.1   The Magician Advisor.

The Mature Magician

> If you can keep your head when all about you
> Are losing theirs and blaming it on you. . . .
> —*Rudyard Kipling*[1]

The mature Magician is an advisor and teacher. He also serves the Sovereign as a researcher, strategist, or tactician. As an inner advisor his role is to sort through the data of a situation, alert to its nuances and idiosyncrasies; to conceive and assess reasonable options; and then to make sound recommendations. Decisions rest with the Sovereign; the Magician is a counselor.

He is a master of the technology available to him, from decision tree analysis to navigating the Internet to religious symbolism, and is able to deal well with abstract or multidimensional problems. He monitors and calibrates data without premature judgment and can penetrate to the heart of complex issues while being mindful of the subtleties. He embraces both yin and yang, and his instincts and insight, coupled with his dedication to study and research, give him a seasoned knowledge that transcends common sense.

He has a balanced blend of what can be termed "Big Mind" and "Small Mind." Big Mind sees the whole picture from a panoramic awareness. Small Mind sees the individual parts; it is pragmatic and goal-oriented and wants to explain, analyze, and organize. Small Mind needs Big Mind for context and perspective. Big Mind needs Small Mind to keep from getting lost in mystique and abstraction. In sports, Big Mind focuses on the strategy to win championships; Small Mind concentrates on the conditioning and play-by-play execution to win today's game. In business Big Mind sets and tunes the five-year plan; Small Mind focuses on making next quarter's earnings. In monitoring personal health, Big Mind is concerned with long-term wellness; Small Mind cooks tonight's dinner. Big Mind and Small Mind are often volatile partners, but the mature Magician holds them both without getting trapped in either.

This breadth of understanding allows him to remain objective and calm during times of uncertainty or crisis. His initial response to chaos or unexpected events is an unattached awareness that says, in effect, "Isn't this interesting. Let's see if we can find out what's *really* going on." Knowing that the obvious is rarely the full truth, he withholds judgment on people or situations, savoring his impressions without forming premature conclusions.

While the Warrior thinks in black and white, the Magician is comfortable not knowing the answer, and realizes that patience and detachment usually yield insight. His timing is measured and precise, recommending action—or no action—at just the right time.

Alex is a gifted professional manager who exemplifies the mature Magician at work. He separates himself from complex problems and company politics, staying calm, listening intently, and offering pithy advice to the corporate kingpins while staying detached from the fallout. During his long corporate tenure he has outlasted several management regimes and, like the grizzled master sergeant in the army, is the go-to guy for both the frontline workers and the corporate decision makers when either group wants insight about a situation or relationship.

The mature Magician is an accomplished communicator and teacher. He is skilled at weaving stories, telling parables, or using analogies to convey a message or lesson through colloquial language. His teaching tools employ all the senses, helping others learn experientially. His careful research and mental nimbleness enable him to speak extemporaneously or improvise appropriately for varying situations and audiences. He can tailor his teaching style to meet the learning needs of his students or to fit his environment (e.g., a classroom, a courtroom, an initiation ritual, the wilderness). Taking a metaphor from music, he is comfortable either playing off sheet music or playing improvisational jazz.

Because of his keen intuition he is rarely fooled. He acts as an inner lie detector, identifying blind spots and speaking the truth when no one else can perceive it. He directs light into shadows and illusions, his own and others', and often serves as a trusted friend, confidant, or guide to other men and women frozen in the complexity and turmoil of their problems. He can gently coax deflated shadows out of their fear and into the truth or deftly deflate arrogant ones without himself appearing egotistic or condescending. Therapists, lawyers, mediators, and facilitators are trained to see patterns in behavior. But, while seeing these patterns, the mature Magician refrains from judgment, staying detached and patient, knowing that the apparent answer is rarely the whole answer. This detachment allows him to contain tensions and emotions in a group, waiting for the right moment, when all parties are open to advice, to suggest routes out of seemingly insoluble dilemmas.

In relationships the Magician respects the viewpoint of another, putting himself in that person's shoes. He is a reflective listener ("Hmmm, let me see if I understand you. . . . ") who helps others feel at ease while encouraging them to experience and navigate their jumbled emotions. He applies his knowledge adroitly and tenderly, striving to nurture and guide others, always in service to a greater good. The mature Magician is also a savvy negotiator or mediator, able to assess moods and emotions, collate them with the data available, and recommend just the right tactic or message. He finds silver linings in dark clouds and creates win-win experiences or solutions in what had previously been bewildering, difficult, or even desperate situations. It was Peter's Magician skills that mapped the strategy, researched his customers, and developed tailored presentations to win back major accounts that had threatened to leave his business for a competitor.

The Magician's ability to remain unattached leads him into periods of self-reflection, self-awareness, and renewal of his own mind and spirit. He recognizes the limits of his understanding and is both patient and respectful in exploring mysteries, dichotomies, the collective unconscious, and his own shadows. He accepts the paradoxes of reality and stays in the questions rather than dispelling the tension by grasping at cheap, glib answers. Highly respectful of symbols and ritual, he incorporates them as tools for exploring emotions and encountering shadows. He can also create and maintain a sacred space—a safe container—for the self-discovery, renewal, and initiation of others.

Savvy ministers, therapists, elders, facilitators, and mentors embody the Magician's gifts of engendering trust and navigating fear. World-class facilitators, like Cliff Barry, Mary Ellen Blandford, Keith Fairmont, Kevin McHugh, Reneé Kauffman, Bill Evans, Jim Kochalka, Steve Mountjoy, and Dan Webster,[2] can meld total strangers into a unified group in which the participants feel safe with one another, with the group leaders, and with themselves. These facilitators use symbols, artifacts, music, drawings, sculpture, nature, and solitude as gateways and amplifiers for both experiential understanding and awareness of the subconscious.

In the spiritual realm the Magician (like the Lover in Chapter 18) learns from and aligns with nature. He appreciates, explores, and steeps in the awe and mystery of God, without trying to define the divine. While he may have a preferred spiritual path, he knows and honors other traditions (contemplative, charismatic, evangelical, Hasidic, ascetic) that help people perceive and connect with the Holy One. As a spiritual teacher he poses questions rather than proffering answers.

Jesus manifested the mature Magician as a teacher in the questions he posed to the authorities and the parables he told to his disciples. Like all the great prophets, he penetrated quickly to the core issues of both individuals and political systems, encouraging his followers to push through their fears and examine their hearts truthfully.

Most successful corporate and political leaders have strong Magician characteristics. Rise-through-the-ranks leaders must be able to manage their fears, hold and digest multidimensional information, and communicate clearly to diverse groups. Entrepreneurs and family business heirs who are catapulted into leadership by charisma, luck, or lineage often lack the mature Magician's breadth. For their careers to succeed they need a court of Magician friends who grasp the intricacies of the enterprise, acknowledge and contain the leader's fear, and guide him in making and then implementing wise decisions.

In the layoff example the mature Magician first digests all the variables (e.g., reaction of the press, the market, suppliers, lenders, the community, and other constituencies; impact on manufacturing, promotion, delivery to customers; financial ramifications). In areas beyond his scope of knowledge, he retains other consultants or advisors so that he has sufficient data before making his recommendation. He looks for innovative options (e.g., reduced hours and pay for all employees, debt restructuring). Neither making a hasty assessment based on a situation snapshot nor denying the problem (either to himself or to the ultimate decision makers), the mature Magician detaches from the turmoil and prepares a list of options, along with a recommendation on how to proceed. He acknowledges the severity of the situation (lost jobs, diminished view in the community, concerned vendors), while recommending the best long-term plan of action, even if it causes short-term pain.

If the decision is still to downsize, he crafts and tunes separate communications for each constituency, presenting the truth while offering encouragement and hope. The Sovereign or Warrior delivers these messages. The Magician then counsels laid-off personnel on their options, helping them find vocational alternatives equivalent to or better than their prior jobs. The Magician does not decide; he simply recommends. If his recommendation is not chosen, he is loyal to whatever decision is made and adapts his planning to fit it.

Fear and Our Risk Manager

In the physical world fear is the agitation felt at the presence of danger and is a valuable protection mechanism monitoring our safety. In the psychic and soul realm fear is the distress around the possibility of betrayal or loss. This distress often arises from the painful memory of a prior betrayal of trust or innocence, either to ourselves or to someone close to us, and the concern that "I'll be hurt again" or "I'll be hurt like they were."

The source of psychic-level fear is our terror of being rejected or abandoned, being insignificant or dependent, being alone or unloved. Common midlife fears include:

> ➤ My spouse, family, or friends will desert me (rejection, abandonment, aloneness, being unloved).
> ➤ I'll lose my wealth (dependence, insignificance).
> ➤ I'll lose my health (dependence).
> ➤ I'll make a major mistake and fail in my career (rejection, insignificance).
> ➤ I'll never reach my potential (insignificance).

Our deepest fears are always around aloneness and death. In my work with executives I'll invite them to go into their fears with the question: "Okay, suppose that happens—then what?" For example, "Suppose you fail in your career. Then what?" Their succession of responses to the "Then what?" question might be, "No one would ever hire me again. I'd run out of money. My family would leave me. I'd be destitute and have to rely on others to support me." Over time, as they begin to feel safe with me and other witnesses, most get to the heart of their fear: "I'd be unloved and alone. I would die."

As we'll see in Chapter 20 on Transformation, the antidotes for fear are truth and love. Fear, like shame, hates to be spoken, so voicing our fears to our spouse, therapist/confessor, or trusted friends dilutes their power. The role of these observers is to see and contain our fear symptoms, to help us explore the root causes and eventually release the fear.

The act of speaking our anxiety to others often engenders another, deeper fear—that they will reject or abandon us because we admitted our fears. The common response of "helpful" friends is often a variation of "You shouldn't be scared about that," which our subconscious translates into "Your fears aren't welcome here. I don't want to be around scared people. If you continue being afraid, I'll abandon you." At this point the diversions and defense mechanisms presented in Chapter 11 engage and we build another layer of armor (e.g., denial, cynicism) around our innermost self.

Cliff Barry and Mary Ellen Blandford of Shadow Work® Seminars identify a "Risk Manager" inside each of us, an aspect of the Magician that continually monitors situations and relationships, watching out for our physical and emotional safety.[3] The Risk Manager monitors *everything* in our lives as a possible threat to our security, continually building and updating subconscious danger profiles. When we consider any action that violates a threat profile, he sounds an internal alarm: "Don't go there. You'll get hurt."

In the bus analogy presented in Chapter 13 the Risk Manager is just behind the curtain. He maintains a data bank of all the pain, shame, and betrayals accumulated during our life. His overarching goal is our safety, and when he discerns potentially harmful situations or relationships, he triggers our defense mechanisms of denial, diversions, escapes, and numbness.

Welcomed to the front of the bus, he offers prudent caution as a valued component of the mature Magician, acknowledging and modulating past fears while not being consumed or regulated by them. He becomes our ally as we approach and pass through the edges of change in our life. Banished to the back of the bus (i.e., "Your fears aren't welcome here"), the Risk Manager amplifies the accumulated fears into a frenzied paranoia. All of life becomes a cacophony of warning signals; no action is safe, and no one can be trusted. We feel gripped by incessant anxiety as the shadow Risk Manager spurs us to create intricate safety nets, contingency plans, or escape hatches, yielding a labyrinth of supposed security. We surrender to our worries and forgo the wonder, challenge, mystery, and magic of life for fear of possible hurt.

The Risk Manager can divert or subvert change, and sabotage our will, all for the noble cause of keeping us safe. Besides protecting us from future pain, he doesn't even want us to examine past pain. While the mature Magician *requires* us to face and go through fears, to explore and probe the subconscious—below the line in the egg model of Chapter 13—the Risk Manager warns us that this will be very painful: "It's not worth it. You'll just relive the old pain and likely be hurt again. Don't go there." A banished Risk Manager will *always* mute the mature Magician and keep us "in our heads." He abhors change and drags us away from our edges.

The antidote, as with all characters in the back of the bus, is not to banish or bludgeon the Risk Manager, but to *thank him* for the ways he has protected and served us in our lives. For many abused and wounded adults, the Risk Manager *saved* their lives during childhood by creating diversions or escapes that protected the vulnerable child from the rage or manipulation of manic authority figures. Peter's Risk Manager told him to hide under the covers and become small and subservient around his drunken, abusive father, thus protecting him from physical harm.

So in order to step into and through our fear edges we need to honor the Risk Manager for his crucial, ongoing role of monitoring our safety, and enlist his support as an ally instead of condemning him as a bottleneck. We can then step into scary situations and sense his encouragement, knowing that if we are truly at risk, he is watching out for our safety.

The Magician Shadows

The common root of the Magician shadows—the Dummy and the Manipulator—is past betrayals that breed incessant anxiety and clog the flow of truth. Both shadows remember the pain or shame from the betrayals and vow, "Never again!" They strive to evade the truth through deflated confusion ("I don't know and I don't *want* to know") or inflated diversion ("Never let anyone else see the real me"). While the shadow Warrior carries anger about previous wounds, the shadow Magician is constantly fearful of failure, rejection, or being hurt again. Both shadows avoid vulnerability and intimacy, the Dummy by closing down and the Manipulator by his arrogance.

The Deflated Shadow Magician: The Dummy

The deflated shadow Magician, or Dummy, is best characterized by the phrase "I don't know." In times of uncertainty or crisis, this escalates to "I don't *want* to know" as he ignores warning signs in tenuous situations or relationships. He refuses to acknowledge the existence of a problem, hoping that if he stays busy and ignores it, it will either go away on its own or be addressed by someone else.

To dodge his anxiety he employs the denial, diversion, and numbing tactics described in Chapter 11 to persuade himself and others that there's nothing to fear. When forced to look at an ugly situation, he often focuses intentionally at the surface level, ignoring the subtleties and complexities and making flat, literal interpretations. He may push the problem back into denial ("There's really nothing wrong") and make ill-informed decisions.

The banished Risk Manager reinforces the Dummy and blocks him from going through his fear and facing the potential pain of change. As a result the Dummy isolates himself, disengages his imagination, and becomes both lifeless in his relationships and irresponsible in executing his duties. Frozen by fear and passionless in his own life, he is intimidated by the vitality in others. Yet he still seeks meaning in his life, and may devote himself to safe or anonymous fantasy outlets like video games, escape literature, or Internet voyeurism. He becomes an armchair adventurer with in-depth knowledge of maps and routes, but no experience in taking journeys.

The Dummy often has a keen intellect, but it gets channeled by his fears into narrow, linear thinking or quiet judgmentalism. He becomes rigid in his views and often envious or jealous of others. Prone to aloofness and cynicism, during times of organizational duress he'll lob grenades from the sidelines, but he rarely enters the fray. When negative outcomes occur, he takes a safe, detached position and offers sardonic comments like "I knew it would never work," or blaming, duplicitous comments like "I would never have done it that way" or "Can you believe how so-and-so screwed it up?!" This cynicism grows over decades until he doesn't even know it's there. After a while it suffocates his heart.

The Dummy in a leadership role avoids responsibility, has trouble grasping subtleties, and is easily fooled by others. In times of stress he buries his head in purposeless or diversionary activities, hoping that someone else will take care of things. If avoiding the problem doesn't work, he hunkers down, works harder, and tries to "figure it all out."

Dummy leaders have trouble dealing with uncertainty and complexity. In decision making, offering no recommendation is a better risk than possibly making the wrong one. When his own inaction finally forces him out of leadership, he tries to derail or block others who are making progress in his absence, and thereby shift blame from himself.

As you might guess, Dummies rarely rise through the ranks to become organizational leaders. Either market pressures or the demands of their constituency base block them from positions that involve ambiguity or risk. Some second-generation leaders who have inherited their positions in family businesses manifest deflated Magician tendencies, especially when the patriarch, who is often a Manipulator, is still actively involved.

In the company facing a downsizing, the Dummy may deny the existence of any major problems while focusing his energies on inconsequential tasks or diversions (e.g., developing a new procedure for the purchase of office supplies). He might assign others to a six-month data-gathering task force as a delaying, hope-it-will-get-better action. His approach to tactical problem-solving is "Ready, aim . . . aim . . . aim. . . . ."

Alternatively, he may make a quick decision to lay off 20 percent of the workforce without studying the ramifications. It then appears to the outside world that he's taking decisive action, whereas he's really avoiding the pain required to sleuth the best course of action from a range of painful options. Denial of the problem, taking no action, or taking spurious action are all better than facing the gravity of the situation, recommending a course of action, and enduring the potentially painful outcomes.

The Inflated Shadow Magician: The Manipulator

The inflated shadow Magician, or Manipulator, is haunted by the fear of being unmasked. Like the Dummy, the Manipulator fears others will reject him if he shows vulnerability or weakness. His trust has been betrayed, often viciously, in the past, and he vows to shield himself from further betrayals.

The Manipulator cloaks his fear with aloofness or arrogance, an outward attitude of "I know what's right." Often self-righteous or condescending, he deploys his knowledge as a weapon, implying, "I'm smarter than you are." He rarely seeks the advice of others, brushing off their counsel with a facade of self-assurance or bravado.

As with the other inflated shadows, the Manipulator looks out for himself ahead of the needs of his realms. He uses others to get his way, becoming devious, secretive, or elusive whenever his private kingdom is threatened. He is a shrewd negotiator who will stretch the truth or lie by omission to deflect scrutiny or to get what he wants. He'll do whatever it takes to win, and either he doesn't care what happens to the other parties or he wants them to lose.

Paul Newman and Robert Redford are archetypal Manipulators in the movie *The Sting*, in which they play con artists who set up an elaborate ruse to fleece their mark. As viewers we never know what is real. There are no meaningful, truthful relationships; everyone is out for personal gain, and all the participants vanish at the end of the movie as the Manipulators move on to find another venue for their self-serving genius. While the mature

Magician is comfortable exploring mysteries to understand himself better and to serve others, the Manipulator *creates* mystery and confusion to mislead or control others, capture what he wants for himself, and have his own agenda served. Like the mature Magician, he can hold impressions and interpretations of others, but he then seeks to use this information for his own good rather than for the betterment of others.

Wounded and vengeful from past betrayals, the Manipulator—often coupled with the inflated Warrior—seeks to get even, but in subtle, devious ways. He makes commitments he knows he cannot keep, then blames someone else for his own overcommitment. He instigates interpersonal tension among others and then relishes their infighting. He is a master at deflecting blame.

In public settings the Manipulator often becomes the clown or prankster who makes derisive jokes about others. He may make a statement with his dress, jewelry, or hair, drawing notice to the novelty of his image and deflecting attention from his insecurity and fear of betrayal. In small groups of peers, he uses humor or confusion as a diversion tactic when an intimate topic (e.g., a listless marriage, sexual inadequacies, or his own mortality) threatens to expose his long-denied emotions. He lives behind a smoke screen—a modern-day Wizard of Oz.

The inflated Magician can also become a kind of evil sorcerer who, instead of pointing to the Holy One, sets himself up *as* the holy one. He sometimes projects that he has a pipeline to God and stands on higher moral ground than others. In this role he is very dangerous.

In the layoff example the Manipulator never accepts responsibility. He works behind the scenes and, like the inflated Sovereign, finds a scapegoat to take the blame and handle the ugly details. He detaches himself from the situation, perhaps positioning himself as the benevolent spokesperson and company caretaker, while finding a Victim to do his penance.

Examples of the Mature and Shadow Magicians

Innate intelligence, a nose for the truth, and polished communication skills make Thad an accomplished Magician. As a professional manager in the insurance firm he calmly managed the company crises and understood the varying messages he would need to craft for the blue-collar employees and the family-business owners. He was a gifted sleuth who got to the core issues quickly. As the producer-choreographer-actor in both high school and law school productions, he used humor and pantomime to entertain and educate. In social settings Thad is a spellbinding storyteller.

Larry is sincere, articulate, and a natural teacher. Yet he also has a Manipulator streak. Touting his love for his wife and the strength of his marriage, he coached other men for years as they navigated marital duress, never disclosing his own string of affairs. He would also express deep interest in events or projects, create a stir of enthusiasm, and then vanish when funding was needed or a decision was required.

In my facilitation work I jokingly refer to myself as a recovering fearaholic. But it's no joke. As a child I was terrified riding the school bus and then sitting in the kindergarten classroom with 25 strangers. With impassive parents and older, absent siblings I had no one with whom to share this terror, so I either cried in the back of the room or went numb. Gradually I determined that if I was going to survive, I'd better "get a grip." As my confidence rose, through my school years I became friends with the popular kids and leveraged my athleticism and brains to stay in a control position—where I couldn't get hurt. I maintained a backup relationship or contingency plan if a friendship or project started to go sour.

Neil, one of the CEOs at a Transition retreat, epitomized the mature Magician. During our four-day seminar I admired his stately, quiet presence, as well as his ability to listen to others' stories, digest complex situations, and size up the diversity of the participants (leaders and spouses from several cultures with varying wealth profiles). As the participants each presented their most knotty issues, Neil assessed the data, acknowledged their emotions, and offered the key insight at the right moment that helped them break through their malaise.

At another retreat, Terry, a successful CEO with substantial wealth and a long-term member of his small group, had the clear respect of the other members of the group. As the participants dealt with their internal chaos, unexpressed anger, and distrust accumulated over more than a decade, Terry gently guided them out of their disparate generalities and into the specifics of their interpersonal conflicts. He then articulated a map for reconciliation and recovery that all parties accepted. Most impressive to me was his ability to build consensus and trust without wielding his longevity in the group or his wealth as clubs of power.

Evan, a brilliant investor who attended a Transition retreat, had accrued substantial wealth and sought a strategy for the second half of his life, but his entire view of the future was a derivative of his past. He epitomized the black-and-white thinker, virtually emotionless and unable to grasp subtleties in arguments. He would launch into rationalizing filibusters whenever the group suggested change. In discussions with his peers he was so set in his ways, argumentative, and oblivious to others' perceptions, they began to discount and then totally ignore his views. Evan's Risk Manager essentially declared that *anything* outside of the status quo was a threat. Without a major life crisis, this aversion to change, coupled with his financial independence, doomed him to a life of loneliness (no one wanted to be around him) and wheel spinning, searching for "something better," but never willing to cut the safety line that bound him to his lifestyle.

Of the four inner advisors, the Magician is least prone to swings between the deflated and inflated shadows. The Manipulator wants to know everything so that he's not surprised. The Dummy doesn't want to know anything bad or confrontational, rationalizing that "what I don't know can't hurt me." We adopt one of these defense mechanisms in childhood or adolescence, and tend to use it throughout life in fearful situations. A common exception is the Dummy around authority figures (e.g., boss, spouse, parents) who becomes the Manipulator around subordinates (e.g., employees, spouse, children). This parallels the swings of the Warrior between Victim at work and Savage at home. In both cases the shadow Magician doesn't want the other parties to know he's scared. The common thread in the two shadows is the Risk Manager's admonition to take some action so we don't get hurt again—either get small or get big, but avoid pain and betrayal.

Closing Thoughts

Our repressed Risk Manager fuels our fears, narrows our balance beam, and admonishes, "Confronting the situation will only hurt you, so save yourself—leave it alone." The mature Magician broadens the balance beam by both honoring the Risk Manager and confronting our fears. The wider the beam, the more open, aware, and connected we are to the truth. Grounded and stable on the balance beam, we can look chaos, potential betrayal, even death in the face and say, "I see you. This is interesting. Yes, it's scary, but I choose to stay here and see what gift you have for me." The mature Magician has the wisdom to leave when true danger threatens his physical or emotional safety. But his first inclination is to face the fear, hold the energy of the moment, and look for insight, connection, or wisdom.

Sadly, our Western society encourages the concealment of truth and the development of shadow Magicians. Our conflict-averse culture of moderation and "looking good" has caused most public sector leaders, regardless of their noble intentions upon entering office, to become Manipulators. Compromising their initial values to get reelected, they tell their varying constituencies whatever the voters want to hear so they can remain in office. In chameleon-like fashion, they sacrifice truth for the sake of image, popularity, and security.

The legal profession is similar. In litigation work, winning supersedes justice. Defendants or plaintiffs operating from a place of factual weakness strive, with bluster and obfuscation, to trumpet their own case and denigrate the opposing side. Most courtrooms are a manipulation circus where jurists must sift truth from innuendo. Much legislative action is defensive, designed to plug loopholes pounced upon by wounded Manipulators who seek to enhance their security and position while the taxpayer picks up the tab.

Many people entering the ministry professions bear betrayals from their youth. They may have outwardly forgiven the perpetrators but still carry the fear of sharing their insecurities and anger, which they mask by being in perpetual service to others. Sincere in their faith at the above-the-line, intellectual level, they preach love but remain gripped by fear of further betrayal. By counseling and praying for others in distress they vicariously touch their own unexpressed wounds.

For many betrayed or abused people, religious faith becomes a life preserver, insulating them from both the evils of the world and the evil they feel is buried inside them. A conversion experience marks their instant birth into a new life as their past is supposedly washed clean and healed.

While the conversion experience, or encounter with the grace of God, brings awareness and a degree of renewal, God doesn't heal what we refuse to admit. The patterns and programs stored over a lifetime in our soul and body cannot be truly healed or transformed until we acknowledge them face-to-face. A spiritual epiphany is just the beginning of sanctification, the intentional work of self-discovery, so that we may *know* all of ourselves, *bless* and *baptize* all of ourselves, and then *surrender* all of ourselves to God. We can't surrender what we don't acknowledge or what we keep in hiding. A conversion experience may be sincere and penetrate deeply into the soul—but it is only an entry.

Much of the Western religious world praises the catalytic conversion event, then focuses subsequent efforts "above the line," in learning about and studying the divine, God, and paths to God. We become expert soul and spiritual mapmakers, but few actually make the journey. The intellectual emphasis of Western culture prompts the spiritually hungry to become committed and zealous to the point of fanaticism for the tenets of their faith, while missing the personal encounters with God that happen in the back of the bus.

As we'll see again in Chapter 20 on Transformation, denied fear controls our lives from behind the curtain on the bus. When fear is not confronted, the shadow Risk Manager conjures up heinous scenarios that cripple our ability to think, lead, act, and love. When we speak our fears and begin to experience how temporary, ephemeral, ridiculous—or real— they are, we can begin to let love and grace whisk them away. I suggest changing the adage "Love is letting go of fear" to "Facing fear is the opening for love."

18

The LOVER

Our inner Lover advisor has the ability to connect and engage: with his own emotions, creativity, and sexuality; with other people at an intimate level; with the wonder and beauty of the world; and with the spiritual dimension beyond and inside himself.

The deflated shadow Lover is the Stoic, numb to his own feelings, ambivalent to or detached from any spiritual dimension, and unable or unwilling to connect with others. In contrast, the inflated shadow Lover is the Addict, overwhelmed by his feelings, obsessed with the pursuit of pleasure or passion, fanatically for—or against—the spiritual dimension, and either neurotic or codependent in his relationships.

The emotional gateway to the mature Lover is the ability to go through grief. (See Figure 18.1.)

The Mature Lover

The Sovereign proclaims his vision and provides leadership for the realm. The Warrior protects the realm. The Magician balances the ambiguities and paradoxes within the realm. The mature Lover holds the realm together with sweetness. The world is boring and legalistic without the wonder and

Mature Lover

Connects

- *Embraces feelings*
- *Appreciates beauty, wonder*
- *Spontaneous, playful*
- *Healthy sexual awareness*
- *Takes time for self-renewal*
- *Can be alone, reflective, introspective, contemplative*
- *Aligned, healthy spiritual life*
- *Sees into the hearts of others*
- *Able to celebrate*

Ability to go through: GRIEF

Deflated Lover

Stoic

- *Bored, listless, no zest for life*
- *Feels guilty, easily shamed*
- *Shuns intimacy*
- *Sexually inactive or impotent*
- *Can't/won't have fun*
- *Can't/won't connect spiritually*
- *Can't/won't connect with others*
- *Worldly, materialistic*
- *Hides in a fantasy world*

Inflated Lover

Addict

- *Lives only in the moment*
- *Consumed or overwhelmed by emotions or desires*
- *Prone to addictions (e.g., money, food, pleasure, work)*
- *In unhealthy relationships*
- *Sexually restless*
- *Prone to fanaticism or idolatry*
- *Afraid of being alone or abandoned*

Figure 18.1   The Lover Advisor.

spontaneity of the Lover. He provides music, art, communion, celebration, procreation, passion—life!

The mature Lover experiences his own feelings and honors the emotions of others. He knows that pain, loss, and death are an integral part of life, gauntlets and gateways offering deeper connection with ourselves, others, and God. Embracing life's interweaving of joy and grief, he rejoices with others during times of celebration and mourns with them in crisis, tragedy, or bereavement. He experiences others' pain and sadness, and touches their wounds with a tender hand without forcing advice, solutions, or cures. His mere presence can bring life to a dying heart.

The mature Lover is sensitive to and grateful for blessings that cannot be measured: beauty, creativity, sexuality, nature, and God. The natural world is his cathedral for expressing wonder and gratitude. The same awe-inspiring universe is open to him through the telescope or through the microscope, as he experiences perpetual wonder in the simple or complex, in a blade of grass or evolving galaxies. He views all of life as a gallery to be entered, experienced, and appreciated without having to be analyzed, apportioned, or owned. He doesn't *need* anything because he already *has* everything.

The Lover has a healthy appetite for the stew of life, welcoming the opportunities of every moment. He exudes a playfulness and creativity that exist simply for themselves, unpolluted by measurement or comparison. Neither dwelling on the past nor fretting about the future, he revels in the present moment, and the whole world comes to life. He sees life as a dance, figuratively and literally, and, in a positive sense, doesn't care what others think as he expresses his passion about being alive.

The Lover respects the temple of his body, regardless of its shape, color, age, or imperfections. He eats, drinks, and exercises wisely, knowing that physical vitality enhances mental acuity, emotional awareness, and spiritual openness. He is shameless and reverent in his sexuality and honors his fleshly desires without being controlled by them. The Lover respects the holy act of lovemaking, knowing that tenderness, kindness, and surrender transcend frequency, potency, and performance. He celebrates physical intimacy as a blessed component of the relationship between a man and a woman, while recognizing that it is only a component.

The mature Lover connects naturally and easily with other people and is always open to new relationships. He is trusting, nurturing, warm, and welcoming. He touches others and is open to being touched himself, physically, emotionally, and spiritually. The intuitive Lover trusts his gut feeling about people and situations. He relies on heart-level knowing rather than head-level judgment.

The Lover embraces the notion of community, whether a single intimate friend or a small group of covenanted brothers and sisters who remove their armor and risk betrayal as they share their fears, pains, anger, sadness, dreams, and joys with one another. He enlists advisors, mentors, confessors, and spiritual directors to whom he opens his soul and from whom he receives enrichment. The mature Lover draws strength from play, prayer, study, work, forgiveness, revelry, and worship with others. He exalts the oneness of humanity, while valuing the beauty and uniqueness of each individual.

At the same time the mature Lover finds deep fulfillment in introspection and self-renewal. He can party and he can pray. He treasures time by himself both for private reflection and for quiet communion with the divine. He engages in the disciplines of solitude, prayer, meditation, journaling, and fasting, regularly separating himself from the diversions and distractions of the world so that he can explore his soul, grasp his destiny, and connect with Reality.

As a contemplative the Lover takes a long, loving look at what is real, constantly seeking deeper and more vivid encounters with his soul. He longs to unite his conscious and subconscious parts, to let his whole self be known and loved.

Like the mature Magician, the Lover accepts and rejoices in the mystery and unfathomable nature of the divine. He has a healthy spiritual alignment, both within himself and beyond himself. His ultimate connection is with an all-loving, personal God. This spiritual union fans his fire of aliveness in his relationships and his work. He senses the divine in every aspect of life, and sees himself as a spiritual being having human experiences, rather than a human being having spiritual experiences.

The mature Lover welcomes *all* emotions as sentinels of the presence of God, and also knows that Spirit resides at the cellular level. He listens to his body for spiritual guidance; the conscience in his heart or gut distinguishes between right and wrong, often well before his mind does. He also uses his body as a conduit for spiritual connection and prayer—for example, through dance, yoga, and contemplative martial arts such as tai chi.

Jean is a staff member at many of my retreats with couples. She and her husband live a very modest lifestyle raising their only child, a daughter. When she was diagnosed with breast cancer, Jean endured a mastectomy. Since her brush with death, she has exuded a radiance and peace as she serves anxious couples who still cling to their possessions and position. She talks openly, with tenderness and without shame, about her breast prosthesis and her renewed sexuality. Her trials have blessed her with the gifts of empathy and connection, and she can sit quietly with fragile retreat participants during their raw, anguishing encounters with long-stuffed grief. Her gentle witness blesses them as they cry quietly or with the wrenching sobs that signal the release of deep, repressed pain. Having faced death and gone through her own grief, Jean can now freely support others with the compassion of the Lover.

Jesus embodied Lover energy in his compassionate encounters with the broken and the poor, and his open-hearted welcome of the playfulness of children. He invested his early-morning hours alone in prayer. He wept at the death of his friend Lazarus, mourned the decadence in Jerusalem, and anguished in the Garden of Gethsemane the night before his death. By opening himself to grief, he also experienced unbounded joy, both with his disciples and with God.

In the layoff example, the mature Lover acknowledges and expresses his own sadness over the situation. He supports a displaced worker during the awkward, often tearful moments while the person cleans out his desk. He acknowledges the fear and anger of coworkers or subordinates, neither coddling them nor being consumed himself by their pain. He receives their stories with empathy and compassion, and validates their emotions without imposing judgment, offering unsolicited advice, or becoming enmeshed in their feelings.

Grief—The Gateway to the Lover

Loss and regret breed pain and suffering. Grief is the emotion behind the suffering. *Any* loss or regret engenders pain and some degree of sadness. While "loss" is often used as a polite word for "death," there are many kinds of death besides the physical. When our teenager goes off to college the old relationship (parent to teen) dies. When we change jobs, voluntarily or involuntarily, our old vocational role dies. When our midlife body can no longer play team sports, when our libido fades, when the divorce papers are finalized, something inside us dies.

Regret—the futile wish that things had happened differently—is a close cousin to loss and also a form of death. "If Dad hadn't died . . . ," "If I had gotten the promotion . . . ," "If I hadn't been abused or betrayed as a child . . . ," "If I had studied harder in school . . . ," "If I had spent more time with my young sons . . ." are examples of regret. Regrets are often more debilitating than losses when they also contain guilt about our failure either to manifest what might have been or to do our part to prevent a negative event.

Grief and guilt are very different. Grief is the natural feeling of sadness over loss (including the loss of what might have been). Guilt is a gnawing feeling of self-reproach, failure, and shame. The expression of grief cleanses and purifies, while guilt festers and condemns. Grief can be a pathway to Spirit. Guilt is a downward spiral into darkness and self-condemnation.

To honor and cleanly express our sorrow about loss, regret, and death restores and even enhances the flow of life through us. Unexpressed grief and self-flagellating guilt constrict this life flow. To compensate, we turn to the diversions and escapes outlined in Chapter 11 and manifested in the two Lover shadows, the Stoic and the Addict.

Our culture of comparison and success refuses to acknowledge the tragic nature of life. We shun death, disdain the perceived weakness of grief, and instead wallow in the mire of our guilt. Rather than repent and grieve, we just try to get rid of the pain. We numb ourselves with pleasure and activity, running as fast as we can to escape the centripetal, damning pull of the guilt vortex. Our contempt for tears masks our real fear around expressing grief—that the whirlpool of sorrow is bottomless and the pain so enveloping that if we go into our grief, we will drown. We overlook the fact that, inside, we're already dead.

Yet we must enter the pit of our grief. We must experience our sadness, first in the head, next in the body, and finally in the soul, accepting grief as a mandatory station on the journey toward joy and aliveness, on the path from death to life. On the other hand, we are *never* called to languish in guilt, which is naturally eradicated from our being as we receive grace from a Higher Power and affirmation from our fellow human beings. Uplifted by this grace and blessing, we begin to accept our own imperfections and powerlessness. The ultimate antidote for guilt is the wondrous realization that, even with all our flaws, we are *still* lovable and loved. Then our wrenching tears of sadness are transformed into the holy tears of joy.

The Lover Shadows

The Lover shadows harbor the wounds of unresolved guilt or shame from the person's youth, as well as his ungrieved losses (e.g., personal failures, abuse, desertion, broken relationships). Both the deflated and inflated shadows carry deep fears of abandonment, by others and often by God. These shadows disconnect the person from his innocence—what is often called his inner child. As a result, he never learns how to love others joyfully or receive love from another.

The shadow Lover avoids sadness either by denial and repression (the deflated Stoic) or by the constant pursuit of external gratification (the inflated Addict). Untrained in how to face the searing grief of his past abandonment, wounds, or shameful acts, he blunts his pain by becoming either numb to life or consumed by shallow pleasures.

The Deflated Shadow Lover: The Stoic

The deflated shadow Lover, or Stoic, suppresses or denies his emotions, especially grief. The mature Lover knows that connection means opening up a little more of his wounds, helplessness, neediness, and powerlessness. This can be terrifying to the Stoic, who has experienced childhood betrayals and has zealously guarded his heart for a lifetime.

Many parents who are focused on their own tower building are unable either to express feelings or to model healthy relationships with each other, their children, or others. In Warrior-dominated homes, the child is often pushed toward greater academic rigor or athletic achievements while his parents diminish or mock his interests in music, poetry, the arts, or social sciences. During emotionally wrenching times (e.g., the death of a grandparent, parental divorce, or friends moving to a new city), the child's feelings may be either ignored or belittled. He may be told, "It's not that bad. Stop being a baby. Grow up," "Keep your feelings to yourself—don't bother other people with them," or "Keep this up and I'll *really* give you something to cry about."

As a result the Stoic becomes either unable or unwilling to connect at the heart level with the world, with others, or with a Higher Power. Seeking to avert emotional and interpersonal pain, the Stoic shuns intimacy and numbly insulates himself from any internal life, disdaining his own feelings and ridiculing the playfulness and serendipity of others. He chooses to live solely in rational, measurable realms, a cerebral world of facts and deeds. Anything that is unmeasurable or unfathomable—in nature, in his inner spirit, or in others—is considered a waste of time, if not an outright threat. He often becomes bored, listless, or depressed.

The deflated Lover's cynicism shrouds the void in his soul. Having underdeveloped or deadened senses may reduce his pain, but it also blocks his ability to savor the beauty of art, the taste of food, the smells of nature, the sounds of music, the rich tapestry of life. For example, he may sit on the bank of a beautiful mountain stream, computing cubic feet of water flow per minute, oblivious to the play of shadows on the water, the warmth of the sun, the sounds of the wildlife, the smell of the earth—the entire visceral experience.

The Stoic is also obsessed with cost and time, which further dampens his pleasure ("I've only got a little time to enjoy this—I'd better make it count"). He calculates the time when a good thing will end and his predictable life will resume its inevitable course. For example, I love to ski, but I rarely relax in the splendor of the mountains or simply enjoy the grace of the sport. I exhibit Stoic tendencies in my preoccupation with "getting a deal" on lift tickets and being on the mountain when the lifts open to get "maximum value." My altimeter watch closely monitors how many runs and vertical feet I ski each day. I fume at lift lines and slower skiing companions that cause me to wait more than a couple of minutes. And of course only perfect powder conditions are satisfactory. My kids gave me a T-shirt that reads, "No Friends on Powder Days." A more accurate line would be "Stoic Skier—Stay Away."

The Stoic's relationships tend to be mechanical and utilitarian, lacking serendipity, variety, and tenderness. Interpersonal contacts are made solely to achieve a goal, whether completing a project or conceiving a child. Absent a goal, he withdraws to the control tower of his intellect and becomes more a spectator of life than a participant. Within a group he avoids sharing personal stories and eschews any activities or discussions that might lead to intimacy. He prefers social, athletic, or adventurous engagements or events, where there is little danger of self-disclosure. When thrust into potentially intimate environments, his first reaction is to close down completely. Or, like the Manipulator Magician, he uses ambivalence, humor, or sarcasm as a deflection mechanism, intended to detour intimate discussions and keep the group at a shallow level.

While the mature Lover warms others with an aura of passion and a zest for life, the Stoic Lover chills people with the fog of indifference and fear that enshrouds his life. In my retreat work the Stoic Lover is often polite, but guarded, when we begin to explore potentially emotional topics. When others in the group encourage him to push through his withdrawal or diversionary tactics, or when he begins to sense the welling of long-repressed emotions, his Risk Manager kicks in and he may become angry or bombastic: "This touchy-feely stuff is stupid! Let's focus on some of the harder, practical problems and make some real progress here!" He may literally escape: "This is going nowhere! It's stupid and ridiculous, a waste of my time—all our time. I'm leaving!"

Lance's father died when Lance was 10 and, with three sisters and a needy mother, he immediately became the man of the house. He supplemented the family's meager income by working 40-hour weeks while maintaining the high grades that earned him a full-ride academic scholarship at the state university. A thoughtless remark by the local pastor at his father's funeral ("I guess God needed your father in heaven more than he was needed here") alienated Lance from any religious or spiritual pursuits. His life revolved around material security. He loathed the mental and emotional weakness of the other men in his small group, who gushed intimate life stories that were no one else's business and sought the empathy of the group regarding their depression and sadness in their marriages. He silently fumed at their frailty, inwardly screaming, "Deal with it. Get a life!"

The Stoic has a highly developed Risk Manager that protects him from the possible pain and betrayal of intimacy or ecstasy. The Stoic also harbors deep shame about his body and his sexuality (e.g., size, performance), caused by either misanthropic authority figures or the derision and duplicity of immature lovers. If he does engage in sex it is often solely to meet his pent-up needs and to receive momentary physical pleasure.

Spiritually, the Stoic may study philosophy or theology, attend church or synagogue, read prayers, and in general follow the rules of the organized religion of his youth. Similar to the Dummy, he typically disdains religious ritual and symbolism—anything that cannot be grasped, sifted, filtered, or filed intellectually—and scorns emotional displays of spiritual fellowship or intimacy. He may know *about* God, but he has a hard time *experiencing* God.

The deflated Lover may also express indifference, cynicism, or anger toward any kind of spiritual life. This often happens as a reaction to the fanaticism, dishonesty, selfishness, and other shadow behavior of misdirected religious leaders he has known. He then concludes that religious people are weak, manipulative, and phony. He may envision God as a punitive, puritanical shepherd who occasionally tosses crumbs of approval to His sinful, despicable flock. The betrayed Lover reacts with "Who needs that kind of God? That God is certainly not going to take care of me, so I'd better take care of myself." When he rejects this judgmental God, he also closes any doors to the spiritual dimension. Externally, the Stoic retreats to the controlled, measurable success of intellectual pursuits or worldly accomplishments. Internally, a spiritual void begins to form.

To counter his spiritual emptiness the Stoic must have a plan and be in control. Much of his life revolves around the accumulation of money for self-protection and relational independence, so he won't have to depend on anyone else—so no one can hurt him. He's miserly (the Addict is greedy) and follows the creed of "I've got mine. They can get theirs." He protects himself against financial and relational betrayal by hedge funds and prenuptial agreements. His life is bereft of trust—and hope.

The deflated Lover in leadership is often a brilliant recluse who does his work and delegates all employee connection to more relationally skilled managers. Directives, coaching, performance reviews, and even rewards for achievement are measured and communicated precisely, yet are bereft of any feeling or passion.

While his professional parents advanced their careers, Vic spent most of his adolescence in front of his computer screen, at first mastering games, then writing his own entertainment software. By his mid-20s he had become a world-class software author earning nearly $700,000 per year in fees and royalties. He tried to hire employees but was clueless on the human relations side of management, so they left him and he worked alone. He now leads a hermitic life, surrounded by cutting-edge technology and devoid of intimate human connection. He lives on less than a tenth of his income, hoards his wealth in municipal bonds and other low-risk investments, and never gives to charities.

In the layoff example, the Stoic Lover avoids contact with anyone caught in the emotional throes of the downsizing. He hides in his office, refuses phone calls, and works on the practical details of severance packages and outplacement. Disconnected from his own emotions, he also distances himself from the feelings of others. If forced into encounters with distressed employees, he either ignores their emotions or offers scripted words of empathy, attempting to distract laid-off workers from the painful realities of lost jobs that must be acknowledged, grieved, accepted, and finally released.

The Inflated Shadow Lover: The Addict

While the Stoic ignores or represses his feelings, the inflated shadow Lover, the Addict, intensifies his. He is consumed by his desires for pleasures, possessions, causes, or beliefs. Seeking immediate and constant gratification, the Addict can never get enough—food, drugs, sex, money, pleasure. He doesn't know lasting joy, so he inoculates himself with temporal happiness.

The Addict loves to push and exceed his "edge," driving himself, and often others, toward the ultimate and continuous high. He becomes compulsive and obsessive in his pursuit of pleasure or his escape from reality, and either can't or won't say no to himself or his desires. Untethered by the wisdom of the mature Magician or the boundaries of the mature Warrior, he feels invulnerable and scoffs at the idea that negative influences might hurt him. Especially for people in power, the opportunities for tainted sex and money are rampant. With no soul-level guidance system to counter these lures, the Addict is easily wooed into damaging pleasures and relationships that catapult him farther into the ozone of denial and fantasy.

At some point in his life the Addict drank from the font of pure joy. He experienced the rapture of real love—filial, sexual, or spiritual—perhaps in a friendship, a romance, or a close encounter with the presence of God. But somehow, through betrayal or abandonment, the experience or the relationship was lost. The Addict's life then became an obsessive search for this lost grail of love, which he once experienced but can no longer find, or perhaps even define. Without a guide to assist him in his search, he settles for shallow substitutes and cheap disguises for the elusive love he so desperately seeks. His first taste of love created a voracious appetite for more. But since he can't feast at the real banquet, he gorges on fast food.

Barry, a mid-40s CEO with nine digits of net worth, personifies this frenzied search for meaning. Like Fletcher, he races fast cars, pilots sleek planes, sleeps with beautiful women, and cuts big deals. He's already halved his net worth twice in acrimonious divorces, yet he's now considering a third marriage. In a rare moment of self-reflection he shared how much he still loves his first wife, but how a single indiscretion on a business trip early in his career caused such shame when discovered by his wife that he chose to escape rather than face the truth and do the work required for forgiveness and reconciliation. He now lives his life on the run, evading his grief at the loss of the love and serenity he abandoned in his 20s.

The mature Lover has an alive, flowing connection with his spiritual dimension, a healthy, grounded relationship with a Higher Power, which he quietly manifests in his daily life, often without words. Conversely, the Addict is consumed by his beliefs and imposes them on others. When a nonspiritual Addict has a spiritual experience, he often transfers his obsession with self-gratification into radical fervor for his new beliefs. This switch is often coupled with an immediate and intense intolerance for the contrasting behaviors and beliefs of others—especially those people who remind him of his old self. Hank, a born-again, recovering alcoholic, epitomizes this transference of addiction. Spouting Bible verses, handing out leaflets, damning those in the lifestyle he just left, and badgering his friends to come to his new church, he overwhelms and alienates others who haven't made his leap of faith.

Nonspiritual inflated Lovers try to fill their spiritual voids with things, people, or experiences. Where religious wounds run deep (e.g., verbal or physical abuse from religious authority figures), the Addict's innate yearning for a Higher Power becomes twisted into the idolatry of possessions, power, or position. When his facade of control bursts, he is often flung from his illusory tower of success into a well of despair—and the higher the tower, the deeper the well. Prominent suicides—"The guy had everything. Why would he go and kill himself?"—often match this profile.

Sometimes an inflated Lover becomes a soul work junkie. He buys every new self-help book or tape set and travels the country attending encounter retreats and awareness workshops. Where the Stoic avoids his feelings, this enlightenment seeker dives in to experience all the ranges of emotion. Every book, retreat, or workshop yields a new cathartic insight or high, but the effects are short-lived. Soon he's again mired in confused feelings and needs the electroshock of another soul fix.

The Addict's moods can also change based on the emotional swings of others. Where the healthy Lover can *be* with another person in times of grief or joy, the codependent Lover either engulfs others in his emotional vortex or becomes enmeshed in another's instabilities and addictions. Restless, compulsive, and possessive in his relationships, he can be at one moment sensual, tearful, fawning, or totally subservient, and in the next moment abrasive, angry, possessive, or unfaithful. He can swirl endlessly in the maelstrom of his emotional fragility.

The inflated Lover's addictions invariably contaminate the people around him. Relentless and clinging, he draws from the vitality of those with whom he is in relationship. He persistently calls, nags, whines, and babbles his story to others, seeking any connection to their energy, oblivious to their boundaries. Inflated Lovers may appear attentive, affectionate, and deeply interested in the stories or counsel of others. But in their hunger to connect, they impose themselves so forcefully or obtrusively that they lure other Addicts, Victims, or Weaklings into codependent relationships and block healthy interactions.

The inflated Lover is unpredictable. With no rudder for his life or boundaries on his lust, he lives a life of anomalies and contradictions. He will often reach a position of leadership or responsibility in an organization based on his intellect and creativity, accompanied by the cunning and manipulation skills of his inflated Magician. He may oscillate between addiction and stoicism, in one moment being the fanatical commander (manic Addict), and in the next moment slipping into despondency and seclusion (depressive Stoic). The Addict shadow in a leader often aligns with the Tyrant and Savage shadows and manifests in angry tirades, smothering praise, and long mourning periods over missed opportunities or failed projects. Victim and Weakling employees vicariously feed off his energy and become devoted disciples, beguiled by his charisma and tolerant of his whims. More grounded employees, if they stay, are wary of his volatile moods, constantly wondering, "Where is this guy coming from?"

For his organization to succeed, the inflated Lover must be surrounded by pragmatic colleagues, managers, or partners who can harness and channel his creativity and zeal. Since the Addict is so scattered relationally, others within the organization must provide healthy connections, boundaries, and order within the realm. Without such containment, the organization will either implode or explode, similar to the way the Addict ruptures his other relationships.

In the layoff example, the inflated Lover manager may take on the emotions of the laid-off workers, vicariously expressing his own feelings through their duress. Rather than acknowledging their grief, fear, and anger and helping them get on with their lives, his obsessive nature may escalate their grief into despondency, their fear into paranoia, and their anger into vengeance.

Lover Examples

Grounded in her mature Lover, Susan holds a deep appreciation for the arts. She relishes great literature and both experiences and plays the music she loves. Her garden is her sanctuary, offering a return to the earth in a blend of solitude and service at the most basic level. In her medical practice, she takes the time to offer tenderness, empathy, and comfort to frightened patients and their families.

Growing up in a rough neighborhood with embittered parents, Fletcher had no models for healthy intimacy as a child. Work and pleasure became his two outlets, and eventually his addictions. He regularly pushed the edge of sanity and safety through extreme adventures—flying, motorcycling, mountain climbing. His mantra of "Anything worth doing is worth overdoing" was his self-endorsement for his addictive behaviors. His fantasy world of recreational toys, drinks, drugs, and nightly conquests created a bubble of intimacy that burst every morning as he woke up, hung over, in bed with what's-her-name, wondering, "What am I doing *here?!*"

Fletcher also embodied the spiritual fanaticism of the Addict. Zealous religious types ignited his anger—they seemed so self-righteous and phony, and their plastic enthusiasm disgusted him. But when Fletcher got his own glimmers of a connection with God, *he* became the zealot, attending multiple Bible studies, buying inspirational tapes and books, hiring a private meditation instructor, and leading his own small group. He had found the *answer*, and by God, he was going to make sure everyone else got it, too!

Stan oscillated between addiction and numbness in his relationships. He sought indulgent, volatile women who took him to sexual ecstasy. He "fell in lust" quickly with his first wife, sensed it was wrong but stayed in the codependent relationship, both out of duty and because any relationship was better than being alone. When he could no longer get the sexual high in his marriages, he sought pleasure and release, often deviantly or violently, through call girls. When the momentary satisfaction wore off and the shame for his infidelity set in, he became the numb whipping boy for his marital partners.

As a mature Lover Marty always had a connection (though not always healthy) with people and a love for nature and art. During his youth his connection with people was often abused, as high school friends led him into delinquency and fraternity brothers used his fighting skills for their own sick entertainment. Mentored by the youth group leader as an adolescent, he developed a personal relationship with God, grounded in wonder and worship, not in obligation or fear of punishment. But Marty gravitated toward addictive extremes as the zealot for bringing young people to Christ within the youth ministry, bracketed by his 10-year secret bout with bulimia.

His parents' indifferent marriage and his father's absence gave him no models for close relationships with women. After his whirlwind courtship and marriage to Sarah, he again immersed himself in work, ignoring his wife's need for intimacy. Only when his teenage son's addictive behavior forced an intervention did Marty begin to see how his own obsession with ministry and detachment from his family had been the root cause of his son's explosions.

Pat, a recovering alcoholic who had sold her business and now concentrated on spending time with her family, was the "soul" of her small group. Though uninvolved with the group's leadership—the high-powered wheeler-dealers controlled the direction—she carried the feelings for the other members. Unassertive (weak Warrior), inarticulate (weak Magician), and always seeking to please (weak Sovereign), she was the touchstone whenever someone needed an emotional fix. Distressed members would take her aside to vent their pent-up anxiety, anger, or dejection during breaks or after the meeting. When her own tears overflowed, either in regret about her abusive first husband or around the many squandered years of her life, there was a sense in the room that she was weeping for all the members' broken relationships and wasted years. Otherwise, she was ignored.

Closing Thoughts on the Lover

Most leaders are prone to swinging between addiction and stoicism as they explore connection with themselves, others, and God. For untethered Addicts the pendulum swings between fix and withdrawal—the void of withdrawal, whether from substances, work, or other addictions, breeds such loneliness or shame that they again seek a fix. Spiritual swings, like Fletcher's, are similar, ranging from total denial of the spiritual dimension to fanatical evangelism.

Sadly, some celibate men in the pastorate have no open expression for their sexual needs and no one with whom to share their desires, longings, and emotions. Without an acceptable outlet, many revert to pornography, and some become sexual abusers or pedophiles. The problem is not limited to celibates. Many married people in ministry as "noble men of God" are compelled to maintain a "glittering image"[1] of propriety in their marriages. When the pressure becomes too great, they escape through alcohol or affairs, and then wallow alone in their shame.

By contrast, many celibate pastors, people in religious orders, and some unmarried men and women have "fallen in love" with their personal God. Their contemplative nature both blesses and redirects their sensual energy into an intimacy with the divine that surpasses any fleshly experience. God becomes their one and only Lover. Some fortunate couples have found this transcendent intimacy together, where sex is the complementary physical component of a far deeper connection. These men and women are the truly great Lovers and are all too sparse in a carnal world.

It's especially arduous for the Lover to find balance in a materialistic culture that diminishes emotions and endorses accumulation. The profit-hungry corporate world applauds and rewards the cunning, calculating leader who immerses himself in his work and consistently exceeds his quarterly financial targets, to the neglect of the rest of his life. Many communities and the media venerate successful entrepreneurs who build skyscraper towers in record time. I counsel these leaders a few years after the media hype is over, when their tower has collapsed and they are in the throes of disillusionment, desperately seeking an honest connection.

The alliance of the mature Warrior and the mature Lover is a potent combination, rare in Western culture. Mother Teresa and Gandhi were examples of the Warrior-Lover: disciplined, resolute leaders who proclaimed and lived out their values while manifesting a love for and connection with the downtrodden. They both had a raw presence and passion for their realms that dwarfed the tyrannical or manipulative world leaders of their eras. The tough and tender Warrior-Lover leaders connect with their disparate constituencies, bracketing and holding together families, neighborhoods, communities, or nations with truth and love.

In my experience with Western culture CEOs in confidential retreat settings, the Lover is the least developed of the four mature advisors. Lover energy is unnecessary for, and often inhibits, financial success and recognition in a materialistic world. Most Western leaders have spent from 16 to 22 years in an education system that teaches them how to solve problems and make money. They've invested little or no time learning how to connect with and love one another. These leaders force their cognitive talents into intangible, mysterious, and emotional situations that require a sense, feel, and connection beyond raw thinking skills. Their natural inclination when they encounter interpersonal tension is to assess the situation, assemble options, and initiate a solution. Most of these leaders are so intellectually gifted and so relationally naive with their spouses, children, parents, and friends that they can't conceive how the softer approach of the Lover can serve them or their realms.

This naïveté is actually a well-developed yet subconscious defense mechanism used by their shadow Risk Manager to avoid facing the emotional pain of past betrayals. Subconsciously they rationalize, "If I don't let myself feel it, it can't hurt me." The armor around their feelings has become so thick that their hearts seem rusted shut.

In their 50s and beyond, many of these leaders become brittle and caustic curmudgeons, devoting their lives to physical comfort, wealth accumulation, and portfolio diversification. They worship at the shrine of independence, security, pleasure, and control. They coexist with their spouses, buy extravagant homes, travel to the right vacation spots, and socialize with their peers, becoming content in lukewarm conviviality, in the listless world of temporal pleasures and guarded relationships. Most are terrified of dying, and much of their conversation revolves around the topics of health protection, life elongation, and beauty retention. They may ponder the existence of life after death but ignore the opportunities for life *before* death.

Few antidotes exist for these aging, underdeveloped Lovers. The occasional breakthroughs come through a major personal crisis of powerlessness, a loving intervention by caring friends or family members, or an unexpected encounter with God. For change to occur they must get to a point where they can't think, talk, or buy their way out of their disillusionment.

Reuniting the Advisors

All of us reject one or more of these archetypes, typically the ones we feel most threatened by. Most, though certainly not all, Western men reject or diminish the Lover, relying instead on the cognitive skills of their Magician, the discipline and action orientation of the Warrior, and the decision making of the Sovereign. Most, certainly not all, Western women have poorly developed Warrior energy. They are untrained or unwilling to set and enforce boundaries or to risk the loss of a relationship by speaking their truth. They try to compensate through the intuition of their Magician advisor and empathy of their Lover.

In *Listening to Midlife* by Mark Gerzon[2] and the *Passages* books by Gail Sheehy,[3] the authors speak of significant midlife shifts, in which earnest tower builders seek to rediscover their lost Lover energy, and dutiful, empty-nest spouses become flush with Warrior zeal, eager to leave the home and make their mark in the world. Subconsciously, midlife men generally begin to move from their inflated shadows (winning, control, manipulation, selfishness) toward their mature center (patience, appreciation, connection, mentoring of others), while women transition from their deflated shadows (subservience, responsibility, pleasing) toward their mature center (clarity, direction, taking care of myself). A mature spouse will sense these shifts in his partner and affirm and bless the transition, recognizing that their relationship may change radically. A controlling midlife person, living out of his shadows, may admonish, punish, or leave his partner, fearful or angry about the inevitable change in their relationship. Consequently, many midlife marital explosions are caused by leaking shadows that blunt the truth about change and endeavor to redirect the path of the partner.

In this Sovereign-Warrior-Magician-Lover model, the goal is to achieve harmony among all four mature advisors and transform our sabotaging shadows into mature allies. Chapter 19 introduces a parallel model on energy that complements the shadow paradigm. Chapters 20 and 21 offer suggestions and tools for reinvigorating our less-developed advisors and reclaiming the gold buried in our shadows.

19

ᚖᚖᚖᚖᚖᚖᚖ

ENERGY

ᚖᚖᚖᚖᚖᚖ**The Energy Conduit**ᚖᚖᚖᚖᚖ

At my retreats many midlife executives lament to me, "Everyone views me as successful, but my passion for life is at low ebb. I feel slow and sluggish. I'm going through the motions in my work and my relationships. I don't seem to have any energy. How do I feel good again?"

This chapter introduces a model for energy—both positive and negative—as it flows into us, through us, and out to the world around us. It also explains how our refusal to acknowledge the shadows described in Chapters 15 through 18 leads to the formation of blocks or coagulants to this flow of energy. These blocks drain our passion, both for our work and in our relationships. The model was conceived by Bob Sloan and has evolved from our executive coaching and retreat work with executives and professionals.[1]

As a paradigm for this energy flow, picture your life as a conduit and the energy flowing through you as fluid flowing through the conduit. The pipe has both an opening and an outlet, either of which can be closed off. The diagrams in this chapter illustrate this pipe analogy.

As we begin to explore this model for energy in our lives, consider that an infant emerging from the womb has a purity and innocence as yet unpolluted by the world. Unpretentious and helpless, the infant is

215

naturally a wide-open conduit. He receives love and nourishment from his parents and, despite having no apparent ability to repay this gift of care, mirrors this love out to others simply by existing. As adults we long for the child's innocence, simplicity, and total security in the love and support of an external source. Perhaps this is why most of us smile and become childlike (e.g., goofy faces and coochie-coos) in the presence of a newborn.

Imagine that an unquenchable flow of pure, positive energy is available to us at every moment. As shown in Figure 19.1, the energy comes from a source outside ourselves. We might also think of this energy as love or grace—the unmerited favor of God—that flows into us, through us, and out to others. So energy, love, and grace are all like pure water flowing into the pipe. In childhood we may have welcomed and accepted the flow of energy from a source beyond us (parental or spiritual) as a wondrous gift that sustained us in our stark dependence and gave us a sense of aliveness, awareness, and purpose.

Also consider that we are merely conduits for this energy; it goes through us, but it is *not* us. In the pipe analogy, envision this energy as fluid flowing unimpeded into the pipe at the inlet, through the clean pipe, and out to others at the outlet. As the energy emerges from us it may carry the imprint of our personalities, but it is not ours to keep. We did not create it, and we don't know or determine where it goes once it leaves us. We are simply the conduit, the means by which energy, love, and grace are manifested in the world and shared with others.

As a "flow of life," this unimpeded energy offers vibrancy, clarity, and presence to every situation and relationship in our lives. It reveals who we are—our identity—and what we are supposed to do—our calling.

Closing Off the Inlet of Energy

Many midlife leaders have closed off their energy inlets. This closure usually began in either childhood or adolescence when the youth began to feel distant from or unworthy of the love of his parents or of God. Still seeking love and approval, he developed a pleaser or caretaker behavior and generated his own energy, which flowed immediately out to others without first nourishing his own being. Over time, the unlubricated pipe became dry and shriveled, representing a numb, rudderless life, devoted to others but devoid of its once-inherent aliveness.

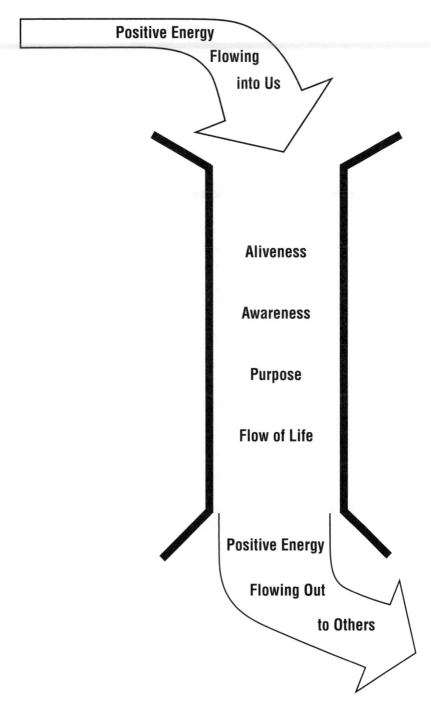

Figure 19.1   Energy Flow Into, Through, and Out of Us.

Closing Off Both the Inlet and Outlet of Energy

Equally common among midlife leaders is the closure of both the inlet and the outlet, representing a mind-set that "I take care of myself. I don't need anybody else." The inlet closure stems from a conviction of unworthiness combined with a false sense of independence—a belief that the energy for life can be self-generated. This self-reliance normally begins during the tower-building commitment stage of life discussed in Chapter 9.

The outlet closure reflects either selfishness or a mind-set of scarcity: "There is only so much money, time, and love to go around. I'm going to make sure I always have enough for myself." With no external source of energy to replenish what might flow out to others, it's easy to see why many affluent, supposedly secure leaders focus on creating their own opportunities while zealously guarding their possessions and maintaining control. This protectionism often emerges after a betrayal, where possessions were seized or a relationship was broken by force or deceit. Having once been either betrayed or made to feel powerless, they vow never to surrender control again.

With no inward flow or outward release of energy, the "waters of life" in the conduit become inert, like a pond with dams at both the inlet and outlet. A life without some manifestation of service and giving (outflow) eventually deteriorates into selfishness and loneliness, a putrid stagnation that poisons the soul. Facing the inevitable breakdowns of midlife, the doubly dammed leader yearns for a rejuvenated, flowing life. Most, however, have neither the courage nor the support community to dynamite their dams—to receive no-strings-attached love and support from a Source outside themselves, and then to freely give of themselves to others, requiring nothing in return. Without a major physical or interpersonal crisis, many "successful" and "secure" leaders swim out their autumn years in the emotional, relational, or spiritual stagnation of their polluted pond.

Flow Constrictors

Refer back to Figure 19.1, where both the inlet and outlet of the conduit are open. Assume some inflow of unmerited energy fuels our lives each day and that we are open to having at least some of this energy flow out to others. Yet even with open inlets and outlets we may sense some drain of energy; our lives lack flow, nourishment, and passion. The flow is being constricted, as with arteriosclerosis in our arteries or sediment buildup on the inside of a pipe.

The sediment buildup parallels the waning of vitality, awareness, and purpose in our lives. Midlife leaders lament, "If I'm so successful, why do I feel so blocked and empty?" Boredom and self-indulgence replace the vigor and innocence of youth. They ponder, "Where did my energy go, and how do I get it back?"

Several flow constrictors and pollutants lead to this sense of blockage and emptiness. Figure 19.2 models the sediment buildup on the inside of the conduit. Love and grace are still available to us, but their flow through us and out to others is constricted by this buildup of deposits. The following sections look at the combination of residues that reduce the flow of energy through us.

UNTRUTHS

The flow of life through us depends on our acknowledging and communicating the whole, undiluted truth. *Any* untruth, whether overt or by omission, restricts this flow. We normally create deceptions for one or more of these purposes:

➤ To protect what we have or to get what we don't have, usually possessions or position.
➤ To obtain or keep the approval of others.
➤ To gain or maintain control.
➤ To avoid embarrassment.

Examples of untruths among midlife leaders include:

➤ Telling a prospective client, "Sure, we can make that delivery by the end of the month," knowing that manufacturing is hopelessly behind or that critical raw materials are missing.
➤ Telling one's spouse, "I'll be home for dinner, honey," knowing that an important client meeting will drag into the evening.
➤ Telling a key employee, "You're next in line for a vice presidency," knowing the board will never approve it.

We initially rationalize, "No one will get hurt," or "I'll fix it before anybody finds out." However, any untruth creates a secret, and protecting a

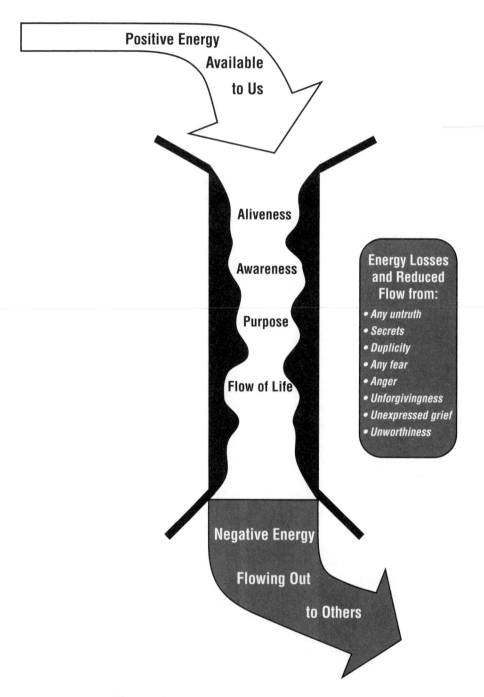

Figure 19.2 Blocks to the Flow of Energy.

secret requires energy. Invariably, the original white lie escalates into a web of deception that takes considerable energy to maintain.

Perhaps the most volatile secrets among midlife leaders revolve around money and sex—manifestations of their greed and lust. The obsession to accumulate money is typically viewed as a zero-sum game: There's only so much to go around, and you have to get your own first. People will lie or withhold information as necessary to get more money and protect what they have. Infidelities and hidden sexual acts breed fear, shame, or guilt that must be hidden from both unsuspecting loved ones and scrutinizing constituencies (e.g., shareholders, church members, political base).

Maintaining a secret is like holding an inflatable ball submerged below the surface of a pool. The ball of untruth may originally be the size of an orange, but over years of deception, secrets can easily grow to the size of beach balls (as in multiple marital infidelities) and often require all of a person's energy to keep them submerged and undetected.

Duplicity and gossip are first cousins to untruths. In sharing with a friend our negative judgments about another person—feelings that we don't have the courage to share to the person's face—we force our secret on the friend. In realms with many secrets, a blanket of distrust envelops the members, creating a state in which no one is trusted and everyone is watching out for themselves. Being on guard against betrayal becomes another draining consequence of lying and secrecy.

I regularly encounter duplicity and hidden agendas in my facilitation work with small groups of executives. The members are polite and nice with one another—what M. Scott Peck calls "pseudo community"[2]—but the emotional climate is pungent with caustic humor, innuendo, and unspoken friction. Pea-size conflicts from five years previous have swollen to elephant-size boulders that hinder the safety, honesty, and productivity of the group.

Larry and Stan concocted elaborate ruses so their wives wouldn't know about their affairs or hookers. They also lived with the constant anxiety of being found out—through an ill-timed call to their home, an unexplainable credit card receipt, or the wrong name spoken during sex with their wives. Marty concealed his bulimia from his wife and coworkers for 10 years, regularly excusing himself after a meal and escaping to a nearby bathroom to vomit, always fearful of being caught and humiliated.

FEAR

Fear is often characterized as the opposite of love and, like untruth, is an insidious drain on our energy. Fear consumes energy in two ways. First, when we are anxiously running worst-case what-if scenarios in our minds, it's hard to have productive thoughts about anything else. Second, it takes energy to hide our fears from others, to appear calm and unworried when we are scared.

The most common fears among midlife leaders are:

➤ Fear of loss: "Everything I have accumulated, including my relationships, will be taken away or squandered."
➤ Fear of failure: "My efforts will be for naught, others will suffer, and I'll be responsible. I'll be ashamed."
➤ Fear of being unmasked or rejected: "I'm not as successful, intelligent, or clever as I pretend to be. Someday, I'll be found out and ridiculed. If you knew my background or who I *really* am, you would desert me."

All of these fears cascaded on me as my company floundered in the early 1990s. I envisioned my tower, 12 years in construction, collapsing into a pile of rubble. I foresaw ex-employees avoiding me in the grocery store or mocking my ineptness behind my back, and anticipated the ignominy of being seen as the bungling leader of a struggling company. Perhaps most of all I feared being unneeded, unwanted, and unknown—yesterday's news.

I expended considerable energy hiding my worries from employees and customers, putting on a "game face" every day at the office. My anxiety manifested physically through depression, weight loss, and reduced sex drive. The fear had unraveled my persona of invincibility and reduced my former flood of energy to a trickle.

ANGER AND WITHHELD FORGIVENESS

Another major flow constrictor develops when we repress or cling to anger. As discussed in Chapter 16, the root cause of anger is betrayal or some injury caused by another person. Untreated, this wound festers. Our inability to speak the truth or "get clean" with others about our hurt leads to pouting, duplicity, unforgivingness, even hatred. I often hear leaders who have been deceived exclaim, "I've put the incident behind me, but I'll never forgive them."

The most common sources of the betrayal wound relate to money, sex, and shame. Whether cheated or embarrassed by a partner, competitor, or loved one, or hurt by any infidelity or humiliation, the wounded person can often become consumed by the negative energy of vengeance. Their "I'll get even—I'll make him pay" vendetta siphons energy from work and relationships and discharges negative energy onto others.

Sometimes the hatred leads to a resolution that "I'll never let anyone do that to me again." The combination of refusal to forgive and fear of betrayal gives rise to gated communities and legal scrutiny of every deal and relationship. A past betrayal causes many people to live isolated, insulated lives, protecting what they still have and buffering themselves from further hurt.

Susan harbored deep anger toward her in-laws for the ways they diminished her mothering skills and degraded her husband, John. At times her anger blocked her love for John and even leaked out at her children. She regularly fantasized the demise of her in-laws and vowed never to forgive them for their duplicity and insensitivity.

UNEXPRESSED GRIEF FOR ANY LOSS

Forgiveness of a wound or betrayal is a form of release. Similarly, to deal cleanly with any loss requires that we first acknowledge it, *grieve* it, and then let it go. Most of us associate grief with the death of a loved one or the loss of a significant relationship (e.g., a divorce or the dissolution of a lifetime friendship). However, we need to grieve *every* loss if we want energy to flow through us unrestricted. Examples of other losses include bankruptcy of a business, a child leaving home, aging, reduced sexual drive, and never having had a childhood.

Grief is normally associated with pain, so we try to divert our sorrow by:

- ➤ Denial: "It's really not that big a deal. I'm over it. I'm fine."
- ➤ Bargaining: "If I just work harder, try harder, pray harder, or seek out an expert, I know I can fix this."
- ➤ Anger: "Why is this happening to me? This is not right. It isn't fair. Someone has to pay!"

The diversions of denial, bargaining, and anger often cycle and detour us around our pit of sadness. In reality, expressing grief is the only way off this treadmill of distractions. Forgiveness is to anger as grief is to loss. They are the only long-term antidotes.

In my work with executives I encounter many "deaf, dumb, and dead" men and women, deflated Lovers who have sealed themselves off from their emotions, especially grief. They become fix-it experts, immersing themselves in a whirl of activity and fabricating excuses or rationalizations for every lost deal or relationship. To grieve requires a vulnerability and trust that are inhibited by past betrayals and a shadow Risk Manager. Yet if they would make the journey through it, on the other side of the grief they would arrive at acceptance, a surrendered, "let it be" mind-set that releases the past, cleanses the wound, and initiates healing.

My mother's memory problems surfaced when she was in her early 70s. My father, siblings, and I became frustrated at repeatedly having to answer the same questions, but we stubbornly denied the existence of any problem beyond the forgetfulness that accompanies old age. As her state worsened and she forgot the names of her grandchildren, we sought advanced medications and better neurologists to "fix her." When my father could no longer care for her and the reality of Alzheimer's disease hit us, we collectively raged at the unfairness: "Why *my* mother/wife? What did she/we do to deserve this?" Every time I reflected on her slow decline I seethed with anger.

For 15 years Stan, too, ignored the pain around his father's premature death. Whenever it surfaced, he rationalized it away as "something that happens" and told himself to "get over it" as he immersed himself in his new company. Sometimes his suppressed grief erupted as rage toward his dad—his best friend—for dying so young and leaving him alone. Ruminating on his father's death was a subtle daily reminder that his life was incomplete, that he was lost.

UNWORTHINESS

Perhaps the most debilitating energy constrictor of all is a conviction of unworthiness, the damning inner voice that drones, "Whatever I do is not good enough. I just don't belong. No one could love me." As discussed in Chapter 15 on the Sovereign advisor, many leaders view the Source of energy flowing into them as conditional. They envision a stern CEO God who scrutinizes their every action. They structure their lives to avoid His punishment rather than to receive His grace. Since they can't or won't accept love and grace from a higher Source, and they don't have any inherent self-worth, they invest their energy in seeking the recognition and approval of others. They place a filter over their energy inlet to block or restrict the flow of love and grace into them—they either don't deserve it or simply don't believe it's there.

Often the source of our unworthiness is not the perceived condemnation by God, but an ill-conceived message during childhood from parents or pastors, teachers or friends, coaches or siblings, that crushed our spirit. Our shattered little boy or girl was shoved into the back of the bus, cordoned off from the flow of life- and spirit-giving energy, convinced that his or her life doesn't matter or that he or she doesn't even exist.

Loss of Energy—An Example

In this contrived example, imagine that you have 100 units of free energy available to you at the beginning of every day. It is meant for your good and there's nothing you can do to earn it. All you need to do is receive it.

But you've had a bad quarter in your business. Sales and profits are down, you're experiencing inventory shrinkage, you've lost two key customers, and your stakeholders (investors, partners, board members, family) are concerned about your company's financial performance. If you tell them the truth about these issues they will begin to question your leadership and perhaps force your resignation. So you massage the financial statements and tell the stakeholders that the company is on track and that you will make your numbers. Assume it takes 10 units of energy to shroud the truth from your investors. You're now down to 90 units.

You and your spouse are at war. Every encounter is a potential confrontation. You have sex only when the physical desire cannot be muted by cold showers or masturbation. On a business trip you meet an engaging woman who takes a keen interest in you as a person. You form a pact with her that she is never to call you at your home. Whenever this individual calls your office, you immediately get up and close the door. You no longer let your secretary screen your e-mail messages, concerned that a provocative or flirtatious message might come and be intercepted. You orchestrate trips to her city and stay over the weekend, ostensibly to get a better airfare or see more customers. The relationship is not physical, yet. Your wife is not suspicious—yet. But your secret is becoming more and more difficult to contain and siphons an additional 20 units of energy each day. You're now down to 70 units.

You see a personal trainer three days a week and consume $250 a month in nutritional supplements. The hair implants have finally taken root and look almost natural. You play in the noontime basketball game with the college kids, can barely walk in the evening, and have a 1,200-mg daily ibuprofen habit. Yes, you yearn to be healthy, but you still think you should be able to do it like a 30-year-old even though you're 55. Your world worships youth, and you still crave the adulation. This obsession with physical appearance and stamina, though laudable for health retention, distracts you from the inevitable sadness of aging and drains away five units of energy every day. You now have 65 units left.

You moved regularly as a child and then began working in your father's store at age 12. While all your friends played together, you worked nights and weekends, being responsible and helping to support your family. Your father died suddenly while you were in your 20s; you assumed his responsibilities and became, by default, the family patriarch. You had neither the time nor the support from loved ones to grieve the loss of your childhood or to fill the emotional vacuum that arose from your father's death. So every day you return to the materialistic, accomplishment-oriented world to continue building Dad's tower, taking care of others, and ignoring the well of emptiness in your gut. Every day the ungrieved loss siphons another 15 units of energy away from your potential. You're now down to 50 units.

During your childhood an insensitive adult (coach, youth group leader, minister, teacher, parent, etc.) humiliated you in front of your peers. Maybe this adult mocked your clothes, blamed you for letting down the team, blasted your sinful behavior, or ridiculed you for your low grade on the chemistry final. You felt betrayed and belittled. Ever since that time—and the similar times when you were shamed or made to feel not quite good enough—you've endured a daily spasm of unworthiness. Today, the failure and worthlessness demons are out in full force, pummeling your self-worth. It takes another 20 units of your energy to keep them at bay, so you can function at work and appear normal around your family. You have 30 units left.

It's been seven years since your divorce and the huge settlement. She moved across the country, and the judge gave her custody of your kids, whom you now see on occasional weekends and six weeks every summer. You've rebuilt your net worth and have an empathic, engaging new wife and a reasonable relationship with your two teen sons, and part of you wants to close the wound and move on in your life. Yet every time you fly over your ex-wife's city, you want the plane to make a bombing run on her house—actually *your* house. You burn her saccharine Christmas cards, refuse her phone calls, and slur her integrity at college reunions. You'll never forgive the shrew, and many hours a week you daydream about ways to get even. Even after seven years it takes 20 units of your energy every day to hate this woman. You now have 10 units.*

You've spent the past 25 or more years building your tower and accruing security for your family. And by all outside standards you've made it. Yet while you've far exceeded the financial targets you set in your 20s, every day you remember the penury, teasing, and abuse of your youth and subconsciously vow never to return to that place of being confused, subservient, vulnerable, or powerless. Your fear of rejection, failure, ordinariness, and poverty now governs every action in your life. Seeking to insulate yourself from future betrayals and to protect what is yours, you have a personal attorney on retainer, a prenuptial agreement, and tax-sheltered overseas bank accounts. Yet even with legal protections and wealth preservers, you still awaken regularly at 4:00 A.M. gripped by anxiety and loneliness, longing for a friend you can trust, someone who doesn't want a piece of you. The accumulation of these fears—and your preoccupation with ensuring your safety—drains 15 more units of energy from your life every day. You now face an energy deficit.

This energy shortage often manifests in the body. Numerous books chronicle the impact of anxiety, stress, anger, and depression on the body: heart disease, cancer, neck and back pain, gastrointestinal disorders, reduced appetite and sexual drive, among others. Many affluent Western leaders spend vast sums of time and money investing in antidotes for these bodily symptoms, without considering, much less exploring, their subconscious root causes. They go to the Mayo Clinic for damage control in their 50s when they really needed a soul clinic for well care in their 30s and 40s.

---

*This is the reciprocal side of the divorce: It's been seven years since you discovered his string of affairs, endured the legal humiliation, and received a pittance of a settlement. Thank God you were awarded custody of the kids. You moved yourself and the kids across the country, away from his lascivious lifestyle and incessant verbal abuse. You invest two months in damage control with your teen sons every time they return from their six-week summer binge with their father. You gave him the best 20 years of your life and he discarded you like an old lamp. You've returned to work, you actually like your job, and you're seeing a delightful man who has befriended your boys. Part of you wants to close the wound and move on in your life. Yet every time you fly over your ex-husband's city, you want the plane to make a bombing run on his house—actually *your* house. You refuse his phone calls and slur his integrity at family reunions. You'll never forgive the bastard, and many hours a week you daydream about ways to get even. Even after seven years it takes 20 units of your energy every day to hate this man.

Negative Energy Sources

People with deficit energy somehow make it through life. Many seem to thrive. We all know a duplicitous, secretive, rageful, or unforgiving person who never gets sick and exudes boundless energy. We wonder, "How does he do it? Where does he get his energy?"

When we deny or reject the pure Source of positive energy, grace, and love, we must get energy from somewhere, and we often turn to self-generated, temporary, and usually negative sources. Figure 19.3 depicts the flow of these negative energies into us. These sources of polluted energy are related to the energy blocks: untruth, unforgivingness, unexpressed anger, unexpressed grief, and unworthiness.

Vengeance, an offspring of anger and withheld forgiveness, is a potent fuel. Attitudes like "I'll show them," "I'll get even," or "No one will ever do that to me again" are powerful drivers to the wounded leader building or rebuilding his life tower. This occurs regularly among Savage-Tyrant leaders, diminished or betrayed as children, who vow to get even—first with their parents or caregivers, and often with the world. Since they were never allowed or able to receive cleanly, they become takers and abusers, deriving both pleasure and energy from their unquenchable thirst for revenge or to prove someone else wrong. When Stan's boss at the international software company told him he'd be a failure in his new start-up, Stan worked 80-hour weeks for eight years to prove him wrong.

Pride and *pretense* help neutralize the pain of unworthiness, providing the temporary strength necessary to maintain secrets and the illusion that everything is fine. Pretense, shame, and anxiety often combine as potent drivers for the person who has suffered failures or betrayals. The desire not to be found out—for a criminal offense, unplanned pregnancy, business failure, childhood poverty or abuse, or a sexually transmitted disease—motivates him to push through adversity and inner angst, and maintain the mask of normalcy to the outside world. Max, a successful investment banker, lived in an affluent community with his wife and two athletic, popular teens, and served as a church elder. His wife sat on nonprofit boards, and the couple regularly cohosted fund-raising banquets for local charities. By all outward appearances, Max was a pillar of the community. He was also gay. The trappings of his comfortable world spurred him to maintain a pretense of familial bliss and to conceal his sexual identity.

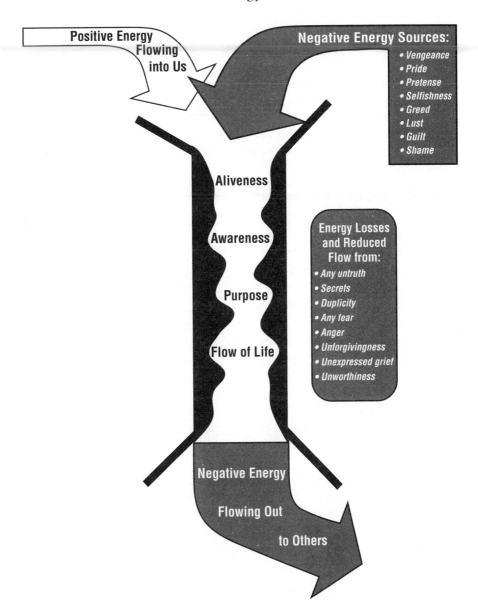

Figure 19.3 Negative Sources of Energy.

Selfishness and its most common manifestations, greed, power, and lust, are toxic energy sources. At the soul level the selfish person suffers from some combination of unworthiness, anger, and the fear of being abandoned. His anesthetic is the drive toward pleasure and independence. As a result he uses others and has no desire or need to serve anyone. Fletcher's immersion in work started as a commitment to achievement and recognition, but soon evolved into an addiction to power and the incessant need for more: money, women, and independence. He maintained 100 percent ownership in his company and absolute control over all aspects of his business. He closed off both the inlet and outlet of his energy conduit—all he cared about was himself and his tower.

Guilt and *shame*, close cousins to unworthiness, are based on a deep yearning for other people to like us. A person with low self-esteem often appears to have boundless energy as he pursues the approval of others. In the business setting this is the person who seemingly lives at the office and has a huge capacity for work. He is praised for his loyalty, work ethic, and accomplishments. Inwardly, however, he suffers from such a low sense of self that the only approval meaningful to him is what comes from others, and he'll do whatever it takes to keep getting it. Shamed or guilt-ridden people are reluctant or unable to set boundaries, because saying no may cause others not to like them—and the disapproval of anyone can be devastating to a fragile self-image. Marty was unstoppable in his devotion to youth ministry. The kids loved him, and his donors and superiors marveled at his charisma and work ethic. Despite all this affirmation, he saw himself as a stupid clown, and worked incessantly to be reassured by others of his worth.

Selfishness, greed, lust, revenge, pretense, pride, guilt, and shame are potent but destructive sources of energy. They may fuel us for a time, generate affirmation from others, and often feel good in the short term, but they are toxic to the soul. Over time they contribute to the sludge buildup on the inside of the energy pipe. Beyond just inhibiting the flow of positive energy through us, these negative energies spew out onto others, polluting the lives of the people in our realms (loved ones, employees, coworkers, clients, congregations, constituencies).

Leaders who reach their mid-50s and have not yet confronted their energy constrictors and toxic energy sources are often beyond human help. They have drunk from the polluted sources for so long that the toxins have taken over their system. They think their way is the right way and the rest of the world is insane. They may be aware of detoxification programs, and may even have a sincere desire to change, yet they consciously choose to stay in their numbed or fantasy state, fearful that the pain of confronting reality will be too great.

Part III has presented several models (the egg, the bus, the inner advisors, the balance beam, the flow of energy) for understanding the causes of midlife disillusionment. If Part III outlines the map for the journey toward greatness, Part IV offers specific action steps for launching and continuing the journey. Chapters 20 and 21 present practical tools for confronting our shadows, as well as several antidotes for neutralizing and transforming the blocks to positive energy flow and eliminating the negative sources of energy. In this sense these chapters help us "get clean." Chapter 22 then paints the upward and outward path toward greatness.

IV

ALIVENESS

20

TRANSFORMATION

Armed with our maps and models, we are now ready for the actual journey into the soul. But first, a couple of caveats. These concluding two chapters are about waking up, not about getting fixed. The temptation after the Understanding stage of Part III—after we've had a glimpse of what's lurking in our darkness—is to tiptoe back to the front of the bus, put together a to-do list of cognitive remedies, strap on our figure-out-the-soul tool kit, and think we're enlightened. If that works, we'll be able to continue along the familiar road and hope that the beasts in back will remain dormant. But to reclaim our greatness requires that we steer away from the heavily traveled route of quick fixes and courageously open ourselves to whatever frightening encounters and transformations may occur in the back of the bus—and, in doing this, approach the ultimate goal: the full and free expression of all that we are in service to the world, from a solid foundation of self-love and communion with our Source.

To begin, we will revisit the barriers that inhibit us from soul tunneling and the value of moving through them. We will look at specific antidotes for the energy constrictors and negative energy sources presented in Chapter 19, as well as examine catalysts and amplifiers for maintaining a constant, open flow of positive energy and love through us and out to others. These antidotes and amplifiers are also the catalysts for transforming our illuminated shadows from saboteurs into allies, restoring their original,

235

positive intent for us so that we may return to our outer realms (family, business, community) with clean hearts and renewed spirits.

Chapter 21 looks at surrender, gratitude, and remedies for the midlife disillusionment of leaders across the five areas presented in Chapter 10: identity, purpose, money, balance, and connections. These final three chapters will guide us to the discovery of the gift that lies within the "hole in our souls."

The Hole in the Soul

That part of ourselves that we most hate, that we are most afraid of and most reject, is the poor, oppressed woman or man within. That hated person within holds our greatest gift. Our poverty has the key; it offers the breakthrough moment for us to wake up. It's the hole in the soul, that place where we are radically broken, where we are powerless and therefore open.

—*Richard Rohr*[1]

The New Edge of Fear

We are now at the second edge of soul work: entering the dark side, confronting these shadow parts on their own turf, and hearing their painful stories. Many people arrive at this place of understanding, either through books like this or in therapy sessions, and balk at further exploration. Simply understanding is safe and doesn't require change. But the prospect of actually *entering* the emotional gateways and *encountering* our negative energy and shadows involves risk and emotional vulnerability. Transformation triggers greater angst in that when we understand "why we are the way we are" we can no longer deny the solutions.

Our shadow parts contain painful memories. We fear resurrecting the anguish of the original wounds—and the longer the part has been in darkness, the more misery there will be to face. Why risk disturbing these lumbering, threatening giants? Let's just leave them alone. For most of us in the Western culture our emotions are untrod ground, full of sinkholes that might suck us into oblivion. We don't know what we'll find by going into our fear, anger, grief, shame, and unworthiness. If we shed the control armor that we have forged and worn over a lifetime, emotional openness might overwhelm, fracture, or destroy us.

We may lay bare our souls and embark on major life course corrections, and then . . . nothing will change, or our lives will get *worse*. At least the dull pain of our current life is manageable. Why endure what will surely be a torturous excavation that may end up being fruitless?

Another impediment to starting the journey is that many religious traditions in our culture see the recesses of our subconscious as demonic, to be viewed from a distance and perhaps exorcised or eradicated, but never to be explored, experienced, welcomed, and blessed. We ought to be able either to conceive a resolution to our malaise or to pray our way into healing, without delving into the pain of the past or our "evil" shadows.

Perhaps our deepest fear prior to exploration is that something *will* change and life *will* be different. The likely outcome of inner work is a deeper awareness and honesty about ourselves. As we take responsibility for our lives, forgiving and releasing the past, we can no longer plead ignorance or confusion. We can't hide out as victims of the world. Patterns, behaviors, relationships, and protection mechanisms developed over a lifetime must be jettisoned as we follow our new blueprint for greatness. Others may reject us for our sudden change—our apparent insanity.

Until we acknowledge and welcome the shadows into the light, they govern us. We may fear losing control if we confront them, but the reverse is actually true: The shadows own us until we meet and know them. As a parallel to the bus analogy, consider that our shadow is like a wild, unbroken stallion restrained in a corral. We're terrified of its power and seek to contain it within fences. But the stallion is a crafty animal and always finds a way to escape the corral, damage the grounds, and spook the other, working horses (i.e., our mature advisors), no matter how high we make the fences.

The solution is not bigger fences, but rather mounting and riding the stallion. The terror may be overwhelming at first, especially if we have never ridden an unbroken horse (i.e., experienced deep emotion). We may be thrown the first few times we try to ride him. If we do stay on, he may take us for a wild ride, going where he wants to go, and all we can do is hang on and follow. But over time, as we acknowledge the strength of the beast, feel our legs on his flanks, clutch his mane in our fingers, synchronize our breathing with his, and welcome his power, we can begin to *guide* the horse in the directions *we* want to go. If we feed him and love him, he'll come to trust us and serve us, and no longer seek to escape the corral or spook the other horses. The demanding task is to honor the shadow without identifying with it. To get a taste of this, substitute your anger for all references to the stallion in this paragraph.

The tamed yet spirit-filled stallion becomes our ally and perhaps the manifestation of our greatness. Our shadows may be impacted by negative influences in both the material world and the spiritual realm, but they are not evil, just disowned. The challenge of inner transformation work is to greet them, let them lead us where they will as they express themselves, and then bless them for their good intentions and their love for us. We must encourage them into the light where they can work positively on our behalf—as they were originally intended to do. For example, disowned anger brought into the light and honored can be transformed into clean boundaries. Table 20.1 shows examples of our shadows that, when acknowledged, honored, and received into the light, can be transformed into gifts that we share with our realms.

The remainder of this chapter describes specific action steps for dealing with negative energy, our shadows, and midlife disillusionment. Consider that the steps you *least* wish to take are likely the ones most important for your own transformation. For example, if the prospect of making amends with the people whom you have hurt in your life is frightening to you, or if the idea of forgiving someone who grievously harmed

Table 20.1 Transformation of Shadows and Sins into Gifts

Shadows and Sins	Gifts
Judgment	A loving mirror to others
Controlling others	Mentoring others
Profanity	Clear, articulate communication
Duplicity, cynicism, or degradation of others	Wisdom
Impatience	Compassion
Unworthiness	Blessing and passion
Sabotaging relationship	Nourishing others
Greed	Generosity
Lust or deviant sex	Sacred intimacy
Shaming	Forgiveness
Secrecy	Transparency
Pride	Encouragement
Rage	Boundaries
Fear of death	Gratitude for life
Fear of life	Exuberance for life

you is offensive, these are likely the critical steps you *must* take on your journey toward aliveness.

Negative Energy Cleansers, Antidotes, and Amplifiers

Chapter 19 described the flow of positive energy into us from a Source beyond us, showing how this energy is the font of our aliveness and how it flows out to others in the forms of service, vision, blessing, and love. The flow is constricted by our repressed shadows, including untruth, fear, unexpressed anger and grief, unforgivingness, and unworthiness. And when positive energy is restricted, we turn to negative sources such as vengeance, pride, pretense, and selfishness.

Fortunately, cleansing agents exist that, when deliberately and consciously applied, scour away the sediment buildup on the inside of our energy conduit, restore the pure flow of love into our being, and open clogged outlets so that our life energy may flow out to others. These agents also serve to transform our sabotaging shadows into supportive allies. Figure 20.1 presents the antidotes that reduce the sediment buildup and lead to energy gains in our lives.

These antidotes do not work instantaneously. Just as it takes time, exercise, and dietary discipline to restore unhindered blood flow through corroded arteries, so shadow transformation requires patience and discipline. Further, there is no single antidote that removes all the sediment and eliminates all of the negative energy. Over time we must utilize the full suite of cleansers if we wish to restore full energy flow and feel equipped to face all of our shadows.

At first, the coagulants and negative sources of energy will react or rebel against these cleansers. The shadow sediment prefers to stay in the darkness, avoiding the pain implicit in purification. The pressures of the world and of our own vanity and misplaced passions conspire to lure us back to the toxic sources. Like the human body battling addictions, the person seeking to purge the sediment and toxins from his soul will experience withdrawal pains.

TRUTH, CONFESSION, AND MAKING AMENDS

Truth may be primarily perceived by the mind, but our full truth is stored in our subconscious, in our emotions, in our bodies, and, at the deepest, purest level, in our souls. But we live in a culture of lies. Subtle omissions,

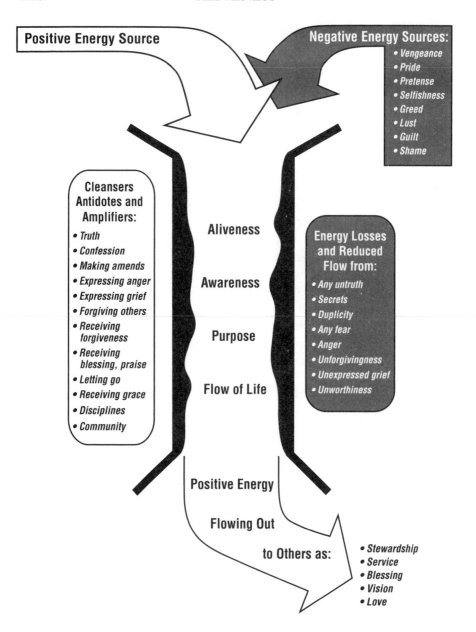

Figure 20.1 Energy: Removing the Blocks.

rationalizations, hidden agendas, don't-hurt-his-feelings, there's-no-problem-here, nobody-will-ever-know, just-between-you-and-me, we'll-fix-it-next-quarter, it-will-all-turn-out-okay-in-the-end are all part of the duplicity and web of secrets that gag the truth and supposedly keep us safe. We hate these lies in advertising, election campaigns, and annual reports, yet we pretend they don't exist in our own lives. We've become a society of polite, nicey-nice subjects flattering naked emperors.

Clean truth forces us to confront both facts and fear: that you won't like me, that this committee isn't working, that our ministry is failing, that our children need our presence, that our children *don't* need our presence, that I won't get reelected, that the business is in trouble, that this marriage is dying, that I can't pay you what I owe—the list is endless. The *only* way to begin the soul work journey is by taking this first and mandatory step in speaking the truth about what *is*: I'm scared to death; I want to rip his head off; I feel totally worthless; the loss of my father feels like a bowling ball in my gut; *I am in pain*. Hidden emotions derive their power over us by remaining unspoken, by being stuffed, by our pretending they aren't there. When we deny them, *they rule us*. Welcoming these emotions into the light of truth defuses their power.

Speaking the truth is a bedrock characteristic of all four inner advisors. The Magician communicates his fears. The Warrior identifies his wounds and declares his boundaries. The Lover expresses his emotions. The Sovereign asks for what he wants. The phrase "getting clean" encourages leaders to reveal the dishonesty, deceit, secrets—any withheld truth.

In the recovery movement, truth is embodied in all steps, but most evidently in Step Four of the Twelve-Step program: a searching and fearless moral inventory of ourselves. This inventory covers three areas of our lives: (1) where we have wronged or wounded others, or made bad choices that have hurt others or ourselves; (2) the fear surrounding the issues and dilemmas in our lives; and (3) where we have been betrayed or injured, and our resultant anger, grief, unforgivingness, and unworthiness.

The first truth expression is *confession*, the disclosure of our full truth about where we have wounded others or made hurtful choices. It forms the core of the recovery movement's fifth step: admitting to God, to ourselves, and to another human being the exact nature of our choices. Confession of wrongdoing begins to dislodge the sediment in our energy conduit. To fully remove the coagulants caused by our transgressions we need to *be willing to make amends* to others whom we have wounded, and then, wherever possible—except when to do so would injure them or others—to actually make reparation. Making amends is a crucial step on the critical path to aliveness, and is Step Nine in the recovery movement's Twelve Steps. In many religious traditions it is expressed as "penance" or "atonement."

Confession and reparation can be daunting and terrifying prospects to us as we review the list of people whom we have abused, wounded, violated, deceived, or shamed in our lives—the people with whom we need to "get clean." Too much thought about this process of getting clean breeds negotiation, rationalization, and lukewarm confession and reparation. Common rationalizations include, "Well, I didn't hurt her *that* badly," or "He's probably forgotten about it, anyway."

The best approach to confession and reparation is to just do it. It may require a long, slow, embarrassing process to clean up the toxic waste spillage caused by our transgressions, but truth allows no shortcuts.

Fletcher was smitten by his new girlfriend, who he thought could be "the one." His first truth experience was to meet with her clearheaded, not under the influence of alcohol or drugs. Without the glib patter and rich-guy toys, he would just show up as himself—and he was terrified.

He also knew that if the relationship was to have a chance, he had to come clean with her about his life, something he had *never* done with a woman since his early high school betrayal. He saw the huge gap between what he felt for her and what he had told her. "Man, I was scared out of my mind: 'This is not *like* me. I work these girls. I get what I want. I'm gonna blow this.'" Fletcher broke through the fear and told her "the full-tilt truth, from A to Z, the selfish relationships, the whole ugly side." Emptied of all his dignity, he became like a small child, "like a feather." And then she began to speak her own fears: that he would leave her; that she was just an "experiment." The dam burst as they both shared their shadows and became free to explore new heights—and depths—in their relationship.

If confession can't be made with loving integrity to the person we have wronged, we can still speak our transgressions to a person or within a group, and ask their accountability as we seek reparation.

Richard's sole marital infidelity happened on the tail end of a grueling business trip when, after a few drinks at a ribald party, he gave in to the seductive overtures of an attractive woman. A simple one-night stand, in a faraway city—she didn't even know his name. No one would ever know.

But the shame haunted him. He had been faithful for the 15 years of their marriage, and he loved his wife deeply. Confessing his indiscretion to her might free his conscience, but it would likely devastate her. Wracked with guilt, he found the courage to share the story, in absolute confidence, with a lifetime friend, who listened without judgment and then mirrored back his fear and shame. Richard determined that, for his situation, telling his wife would be more harmful than good for their marriage. As reparation, he chose to abstain from alcohol and never be in a potentially compromising situation again. He asked his friend to hold him accountable. The friend offered to be available 24/7 for a phone call if Richard ever again felt tempted. Richard also committed to love his wife as the most precious being on the planet. He continued to feel deep regret for his actions, but he was able to move ahead in renewed commitment to his marriage.

In these examples of "getting clean," both Fletcher and Richard found a way to speak their shame and guilt, bringing it out in the open and admitting full responsibility for their actions.

The second truth expression is to *admit our fear* around a situation, issue, or dilemma in our lives. Fear is the main block to the mature Magician energy described in Chapter 17, and includes fears about facing or making a decision. While we know a dilemma exists, we often subconsciously *don't want to know* the alternatives. We prefer to live in the confusion of the dilemma rather than confronting the truth required at a decision point.

When we confront the fearful truth about our knotty issues head-on, we can no longer use confusion as an excuse for delaying action. When the truth is known, we must decide either to stay in our current situation or to change. Both are conscious choices, and we *always* have a choice.

Facing fears about our dilemmas yields clarity. The first action step is to express them—get them out of our heads and onto paper. In my retreat work a participant writes out a pressing dilemma in his life as two or more opposing "voices" that argue back and forth in his head. Each voice strongly defends its position on the issue. Writing out the voices forces the participant to *look at them.*

Most leaders are trained in developing pro/con charts or decision trees to evaluate decisions. While these cognitive approaches are valuable tools in many business situations, they ignore the emotional or intangible sides of most personal issues—including the shadows, which defy quantification. And ignored or repressed shadows always find a way to foil our well-conceived plans. Several example dilemmas, with no clear solutions, are presented in Table 20.2.

The next action step is to speak both sides of the dilemma to another person, in specific detail, including the fears. Often just speaking the fears around an issue results in a solution emerging, like an invisible trap door, deep in the darkness, miraculously opening into the light. When speaking

Table 20.2   Example Dilemmas

Side 1 of the Issue	Side 2 of the Issue
Make your mark. You're gifted. Build a company—a legacy. Now is the time. You've prepared your whole career for just this time.	**Spend time with your family.** They're only young once. You're a great mom/dad. This is your real calling. They don't care about your "legacy"; they want *you*.
You have a destiny. Step into it. I believe in you.	**You can't do it. You're just not good enough.** You'll never be good enough. You'll fail.
Get your life back! Face the fear. C'mon! You need to find and fix those ugly patterns that sabotage your life. *Just do it!*	**It's too scary.** Suppose there is nothing there? You'll just get hurt again.
Forgive them. Let go of the past; reconcile; they did their best; they didn't know any better; love them; if you don't forgive them, you'll live in anxiety and anger the rest of your life.	**They hurt you. Get even.** You'll just get hurt again; cut them off. Screw 'em! They OWE you!
I want my own life. It's my turn! I'm tired of serving others. I'm tired of being responsible for everyone else, always putting them ahead of me.	**You're being selfish. Others are counting on you.** You *are* responsible. Besides, this is all you know. Just be quiet and do your job. You'll fail if you change. You'll lose it all.
Don't stop! Focus! Make your money. Now! Get the financial security. You'll never unravel your past. You're too screwed up. Just work and live for today. You'll be just fine.	**You're out of control.** You know your life can offer so much more. Keep working on your baggage. It's okay to fail . . . to be "ordinary." Let yourself be human (a man/a woman). Step into your fears.
Step into your creativity. You're a gifted artist/teacher/author. This is your real passion. You know it. The people around you—your loved ones—will feed from your energy. Get your space! Step into your genius. Do it!	**You'll lose everything you have.** You'll be alone; others will shun you—even loved ones. You're not a kid any more. You're an adult with responsibilities. Just stay where you are. This is what you know. It's safe.
You don't need spirituality or God. Don't fall for this religious stuff. Spirituality is for weak people who can't take care of themselves. Know what you want, and go after it. Don't trust the spiritual types; you'll just get hurt.	**Your life has a void.** In your heart, you know this. Investigate something/someone—a Higher Power—beyond yourself. Fill the loneliness. Nothing else is working—try spirituality. Perhaps you'll fill the void. Be open.
You need money. Get the security. Take care of yourself (and your family). You	**The money is a drug, and you know it.** You're addicted. The money's not

Table 20.2 *(Continued)*

Side 1 of the Issue	Side 2 of the Issue
don't want to end up like Dad. You're not even close to financial security yet. Work now and get your money. Money gives you options. Everything else will follow.	important. Do what you love; find yourself; get connected. In your heart, you know this is right.
Just figure it out. You're a bright woman/guy. Just think it through. This "soft stuff" is for weak people who haven't got the guts or brains to work through tough issues. Besides, you don't know how to do touchy-feely stuff, anyway. Stick with what you know.	**"Thinking" isn't the answer. Go into your heart.** You're working too hard. Slow down. Even your head tells you this is the right thing to do. You don't have to "figure it out." If you can just trust and let go; the answers will come naturally. Don't force it. Be patient. Trust.
I want to be loved by God. I want to know God. I want a connection with God. I want peace and serenity in my life. I long to experience joy.	**How could God love YOU?** You are unlovable. You are worthless. Look at what a screw-up you are. A loser. The world is tough. Get used to it.
You hate what you're doing. Get out. You know it's not the right path; you just try to rationalize. Make your life count; make an impact.	**Stay where you are. It's safe.** Look, you're just a little rattled. Others really like you. You're good at what you do. It will be *very* painful to change. If you leave, you'll let down a lot of people.
You need to be married. You're getting old, and you're alone. You've got plenty of money. You've gotten everything else you've ever wanted. This is just another problem to solve. Figure it out. Put together your criteria; find somebody; fall in love. You want a family and a relationship. *Just do it!*	**You've got a great life. Don't complicate it.** Maybe there's a reason you're still single. You run through relationships, chew 'em up, spit 'em out. No woman/man can handle you. Besides, you can't really love anyone. It will just end in misery.
It's okay to express your pain. You've been holding so much pain for so long. No person is meant to hold that kind of pain. If you let it out, you'll feel so free and clean.	**It's way too risky. Don't let anything out.** You don't know how deep this goes. Don't show any vulnerability. You'll just get hurt, again.
Marry her/him. He/she is the one. Time is running out.	**Don't rush this. You'll be sorry.** Remember what happened last time. Wait!
Dump the loser you are with. He/she is sucking the life out of you. Your whole life revolves around his/her whims. You have no life of your own. You are dying! Get out while you can!	**He/she is all you have. You'll be alone if you leave.** If you stick it out, maybe he/she will change. Just give it some more time. To leave now will be a disaster. Live with it.

all sides of the dilemma fails to yield clarity, other participants might help the person refine the voices down to their most basic, pointed message, as shown in bold in the table.

Louis, the third-generation CEO of a family business, kept vacillating on whether to sell the company, which would allow him and his wife to explore other interests. After he wrote and spoke the crux of his dilemma (a variation of the "Get out" versus "Stay where you are" dilemma shown in Table 20.2), he chose not to explore the "Get out" option, at least for a time. He was simply not ready to examine the side effects of selling the family company. He chose to postpone the prospect of leaving and instead focus on shedding several outside interests and finding more time for himself while continuing to run the business. His conscious *choice* was to defer any examination of the issue, saying, "The family situation is a mess. I see that now. I'm angry about it, and I know at some point I must deal with this, but not now. I can come back here when I'm ready." In this way he acknowledged the truth about his underlying resentment and also his fear about dealing with the dilemma.

By modeling our dilemmas as two or more voices reverberating in our heads, and then "bringing these voices to life," first in writing, then as a mini-drama, we invariably get a visceral grasp of the situation, with all its uncertainty and pain. The dilemma expressed in the voices and role play is normally a symptom of a much deeper issue, and the resultant insight often provides the courage for deeper exploration of our shadows.

Louis eventually did bring his "Get out" versus "Stay where you are" dilemma to life in a role play. As he heard the voice of "Stay where you are" speaking its lines, it reminded him of his father discouraging him from his first college choice—a large public university 1,500 miles away. His dad had gently exhorted him to stay close to home: "You don't know what you'll find out there. Stay here. You'll be near home . . . and your mom can see you more often. We'll sure miss you if you choose to go *out there*." So he had chosen a local college, and had always regretted opting for family harmony instead of seizing the adventure of going to a larger university. In many ways his current dilemma was a replay of this earlier decision.

The third area of truth telling involves *speaking the facts and emotions* around our betrayals and unresolved wounds, and often evolves from speaking our fears around a dilemma. As just shown with Louis, when a current betrayal or injury is brought into the light, it often triggers memories of past injuries or betrayals that remain unresolved. This last form of honesty can be the gateway into expressing anger and grief.

EXPRESSING ANGER

Confronting the hard truths around a difficult issue, relationship, or dilemma in life often surfaces the anger buried in unresolved betrayals or wounds. Honesty exposes fear, and confronted fear often unveils anger.

To cleanse the anger we must first acknowledge it and then define the specific events and relationships about which we harbor anger. We must also get out of denial: "I'm fine. I've worked through all this. There's no problem here. Well, I may be a little frustrated, but I'm certainly not mad."

Before we actually confront our anger we need to understand the risks. Cleanly expressed anger requires honesty with others and setting boundaries in our lives. When we enforce boundaries—"I won't serve on your board," "I won't give you that raise," "I won't deliver that message to our customer," "You cannot have the car," "If you continue to abuse me, I will leave"—we risk the alienation and retribution of others. Relationships may die; people might not like us. We may lose influence in another person's life. We may be viewed as difficult, brash, insensitive, intimidating, or overbearing, or labeled as a rebel, maverick, or fool. We may have to take responsibility for our lives. We may end up alone.

The same risks of loss exist when we speak the anger about our wounds to another person: "I don't like it when you _____"; "When you _____, it makes me angry. I want you to stop, or this relationship must end." These are intentionally hard, abrupt, clear statements, where the blank lines are filled in with very specific facts (e.g., "when you arrive 20 minutes late for our meeting," "when you tell my banker that I am having marital problems," "when you slap me on the butt"). Cleanly expressing anger requires mature Warrior energy to speak the direct truth, without innuendo or trying to protect the other person's feelings. It requires clear, purposeful communication, without whining or rationalization. We have to mount and ride the stallion.

Anger might first be expressed in writing, perhaps in a letter or journal. This expression is for us and not necessarily for the other person. A therapeutic way of releasing this emotion is to state our deepest anger in a letter, as vitriolic and potent as we choose to make it, and then destroy the letter. The destruction is a form of letting go, which we'll explore later in this chapter.

The second approach is to "get clean" with the other person directly, using the Clean Talk model presented in Appendix C. This model is especially useful for less potent wounds where direct expression to the wounding person is possible and the anger is still present but has not escalated to rage.

The expression of deeply held anger is best done in a ritual way with supportive witnesses who assure the safety of the participant and the safety of others. A "clean" release might be made by hitting a punching bag or through strenuous physical labor. Other releases include visualizations, drawings, or dramas where we can express the anger in "ritual space" without harming anyone in the real world. These releases are best accomplished with experienced therapists or facilitators.

At an experiential retreat Susan was able, in a role play, to voice her anger toward her in-laws. She expunged her bottled rage over their judgments and pettiness—rage she had carried ever since her courtship. Once the anger was released, she began to feel sorrow for their narrow selfishness that made them, in her opinion, lonely, desperate people. By expressing her anger cleanly in a safe setting, she also found the resolve to hold her boundaries with them when they tried to encroach on John's and her lives. Upon her return from the retreat, she initiated direct conversations with her mother-in-law about her frustrations, using the Clean Talk model of Appendix C. Remarkably, this was the first time anyone had ever stood up to this matriarch, and it eventually led to a civil and polite relationship.

EXPRESSING GRIEF AND SADNESS

Expressing the whole, unadulterated truth, especially about our anger, often opens the clogged gateways to our other emotions. Grief normally resides just beneath the anger and is the portal into our body and our soul where the toxins and coagulants are most deeply stored. The combination of truth and grief acts as a flushing mechanism that gently washes the toxins and coagulants into the open where they can be acknowledged, blessed, and cleansed.

Rather than simply endure our grief—go through it and get it over with—we are called to become intimate with our sadness, to embrace our sorrow as a purifying gift. Repressed grief can destroy us; expressed grief can renew us. Once we have gone through the fires of sorrow, we can begin to nourish others.

Again, we must first understand the risks before going into our grief. The first is that because grief is inherently insoluble—the loss is a fact and can't be changed—the ensuing pain might feel purposeless, endless, and unbearable. A second risk arises when we express and begin to release our grief, and as a result become more prone to forgiveness. As we saw in Chapter 19, unforgivingness is a potent, though negative, energy source that can fuel obsessive commitments to get even and to build majestic, "I'll show them" towers.

Grief is also the primary gateway into a rich emotional life. Once we begin to feel, we can no longer rely solely on our cognitive skills. We begin to assume mature Lover characteristics—appreciation of beauty, a contemplative nature, spiritual connection—that may be foreign to us and surprising to our loved ones ("When did *you* become so caring and empathic?"). When we become more aligned with the "softness" of the Lover, we become more vulnerable and open to possible betrayals; we may be hurt again, or mocked by peers who expect our "tough guy" persona.

As with fear and anger, the acknowledgment of grief starts with cognitive expression, such as writing in a journal. Speaking our grief brings another, deeper layer of truth about ourselves into the light. Release of grief comes through the body and is normally manifested in tears. The longer the grief has been repressed, the deeper the tears, ranging from light weeping to racking, convulsive wailing. There is no one right way to grieve. The best path is to find the thread of grief in our body, and then follow it—wherever it leads.

When we get close to grief our Risk Manager might engage, warning our system of "dangerous territory ahead." The experience of deep grief makes us very vulnerable. Perhaps we approached grief in the past and were shamed: "That's nothing to cry about. Grow up. Blow your nose, wipe your eyes—you look silly." An adult on the verge of grief, especially in the presence of others, may go numb, devoid of any sensations, *knowing* something needs to happen, but inhibited from further delving into or releasing of the emotion. This is when a loving friend or small group can simply sit with the blocked person, just *being* with him, without time constraints or expectations. The support community simply holds the space for the person to grieve.

Mel was the jokester who always had a cutting one-liner or cynical remark whenever anyone in his small group started getting touchy-feely. But in a retreat exercise about relationship wounds, Mel shared, for the first time in the group, how his brother had died in a tragic accident when they both were teens. Overwhelmed and numb at the time, he had never grieved his brother's death, and his stoic parents, who themselves never expressed any grief, had simply encouraged him to get on with his life.

With support from a strong and tender Lover in the group, who simply mirrored back his story and reflected the pain Mel was expressing, Mel began to enter into the dark place of grief that he had stuffed for over 20 years. The group silently supported him as he sobbed out the blur of sadness, shame, and anger. When he had finished, the group honored him for his courage in sharing his story, and two other men spoke of similar losses.

Mel later described the experience as like "having a two-ton boulder re-moved from my chest." In subsequent meetings, Mel still had his wry sense of humor, but used it more for celebration and encouragement than for ridicule.

ACKNOWLEDGING AND RELEASING OUR JUDGMENTS

Though we may have been taught not to judge, the reality is that we all have judgments. Any time we can say, "I think _____," we're making a judgment. Our statement may or may not be true. Judgments are accept-able, if we acknowledge them as our judgments and don't assume them to be the facts or the truth. The Clean Talk model in Appendix C distin-guishes between facts and judgments.

A judgment, on its own, is not an energy constrictor, but it *fuels* the other energy constrictors, especially unexpressed anger and withheld for-giveness. Judgments are the salt that our disowned shadows love to rub into a small wound. For example, I might be angry when my new neighbor cuts down the trees that form a natural break between our yards. I start to ruminate about his insensitivity, how he likely has a telescope trained on my bedroom window, how he hates my kids who used to climb in the trees, and so on, to the point that I'll never forgive the jerk. The *reality* may be that his wife's serious allergies to the chemical spray required to keep the trees bug-free made him remove the trees—something that has *nothing to do with me.*

We often get a glimpse of others through their actions and immedi-ately jump to either anointing or damning conclusions about them. But when we accept that words and actions only give us a glimpse of other people, we can release our judgments and begin to see how their offense toward us may have actually been a cry for help, a backhanded expres-sion of love, a call for love—or had nothing to do with us whatsoever. Once we begin to own our judgments as judgments, and not facts, we can start to let them go, which invariably gets us to a place of clarity and, of-ten, peace.

FORGIVING AND BLESSING OTHERS

A common sequel to the expression and release of anger and grief is the willingness to forgive others. Forgiveness can start when we release our judgments, especially about the makeup and motives of other people. By unburdening our hearts of judgment and retribution, we make it possible for forgiveness to begin to flow toward the perpetrators and betrayers who have harmed us, and our own healing can begin.

Forgiveness has life-changing side effects. When we pardon those who have wronged us, vengeance ceases to be a driver in our lives, and we become free to enter healthy vocational pursuits and relationships. We can acknowledge and end codependent relationships: "I forgive you, I bless you, and I release you. I acknowledge that, *in my judgment,* our relationship was flawed and that I felt hurt. I have grieved my pain. I now choose to move on in my life."

As with anger and grief, forgiveness may begin by written or verbal expression. It may lead to an encounter with the wounding party, especially when the other person appears pained over wounding us. A common example in business is when we make an investment in a friend's endeavor and, through what we *judge* as mismanagement, he loses our investment. The relationship has a chance to heal permanently only if we can forgive him and release any harbored anger or judgments. When the other party seeks forgiveness, and we can give it genuinely, forgiveness is a sacred gift that can shatter guilt and shame, and totally defuse vengeance. A final step is literally to bless the person who has hurt us. In the biblical sense, this is Jesus' charge to love our enemies.

Forgiveness and blessing do not mean we have to stay in the same relationship with the person. In fact, forgiveness is often linked with boundary setting. For example, I might forgive my friend for losing my investment, but I don't have to invest again with him in the future. Both cleanly terminated relationships and clean ongoing relationships emerge when we learn from our mistakes, express our boundaries, and resolve to live in the truth, untainted by judgments or ill feelings.

Many leaders get to the place of speaking their truth and experiencing their grief, but struggle mightily with forgiving the predators and perpetrators who wounded them. They often say something like, "I can let go of what he did to me, but I'll never forgive what he did to my family." Without forgiveness, the anger and grief, like pieces of cancer that are not fully removed, fester, multiply, and eventually leak out again in destructive ways. Perhaps the life and teachings of Jesus are our best model for forgiveness. When his disciples asked how many times they should forgive others, he told them, "Forgive seventy times seven times." And even as he was dying he said, "Forgive them, Father, for they do not know what they are doing."[2] Until we learn to forgive and forget, we remain prisoners in the cage of our anger. Gandhi summarized this well: "The weak can never forgive. Forgiveness is the attribute of the strong."

FACING OUR UNWORTHINESS

As discussed briefly in Chapter 19, unworthiness is another block to the flow of energy. Unworthiness is normally buried very deeply in "successful" leaders, below the anger and grief, protected by layers of stoic, pretentious armor that has been polished and hardened by decades in shadow. At its most basic level the inner voice of unworthiness tells us either "You are not worthy to be loved" or "You are unlovable." All our mistakes and the wounds we have caused to others seem irreparable. Fueled by our shame and guilt, this demonic accuser says that we are not good enough to be in relationships with others or in communion with God. In this state, when we encounter our shadows we identify with them, and their message then becomes self-fulfilling.

Yet we are *never* called to identify with our shadows. At best they are only a part of our truth. Instead, we are called to feel sadness and tenderness toward them as we begin to face how poor, powerless, dependent, and broken we really are.

Receiving forgiveness and blessing from others, releasing negative energy, and receiving grace are forms of "chemotherapy" on the cancer of unworthiness. Confessing our shame and guilt to others dilutes the power of these imposters. When we are fully known, naked, and empty in front of both our fellowman and God, we can then begin to receive their affirmations of us.

The antidote for the conviction of unworthiness is to allow ourselves to receive forgiveness and love, both from others and from our Source, and thereby learn that we can forgive and love *ourselves*. But significant risks exist even here. Suppose we open our hearts and the love doesn't come? Suppose we lay out our lives and God rejects us? The thought of being unlovable or shunned by God can cast our spirit into the void of despair. But in order to receive our lives back, we must shed *all* the excuses that accompany the negative energy sources, including the fear that the love may not be returned and that we may end up rejected and alone.

This letting go and openness to receive love and grace requires immense trust. It cannot be reasoned or measured. It is the ultimate act of vulnerability to another person or a Higher Power: "I let go of all that I am carrying, and I open myself to your love."

The act of faith that is required to become open and vulnerable in the face of potential betrayal or condemnation is like intentionally poking holes through the cover we've placed on the energy inlet—in essence, blindly trusting that what comes flowing through will be love. And *we* have to poke the holes, opening ourselves; no one can do it for us.

In my retreat experience with midlife men and women burdened with deep shame or unworthiness, this act of faith is often the most difficult thing they have done in their lives. It requires supportive guides and witnesses who will encourage them as they open themselves to the love. The trust is that once the holes are poked, the Source takes it from there.

Then life can flow freely through us, and we will naturally make amends to those we have harmed—not out of a need to medicate our guilt and shame, but out of love for others and concern for their well-being. The key to making amends cleanly is the assurance that we are already fully forgiven—even if the other person has never really forgiven us—because we have forgiven ourselves and received the ever-flowing forgiveness of God.

Besides acting as antidotes to the toxins and purifying the flow of energy through us, the practices just discussed can also act as "well-care amplifiers" that enhance or heighten our experience of life and the flow of energy through us and out to others. They are like nutritional supplements that become a part of our daily health routine to strengthen our immune system.

Two other amplifiers act to enhance the flow of energy through us by opening and expanding the energy inlet, guarding against future toxins and coagulants entering our system, and breaking up dams at the outlet, allowing our love to flow out to others. The increased positive energy flow into us overrides the negative energy sources. Sediment buildup along the sides of the energy conduit is further reduced, and positive energy flows out to others as stewardship, service, blessing, vision, and love.

DISCIPLINES

Several personal disciplines act as energy amplifiers. The simplest, but far from easiest, discipline is to take time by ourselves in *solitude* and *silence*, distancing ourselves from the din and distractions of the world and simply experiencing our own company. Solitude is often the hardest discipline, because none of us want to be with someone we don't love, namely ourselves. To step off our addictive treadmill of activity and just feel what we're really feeling, examine what we're really thinking, is probably the most courageous act many of us will ever undertake. Many Eastern traditions have their foundations in solitude, silence, meditation, and reflection, with no outside stimuli, rationalizations, or activities to block a person from seeing and experiencing the real truth about themselves. Silence is the most spacious and empowering technique in the world—actually, it's the cessation of all technique.

Prayer and *meditation*[3]—simply being still and open to *what is*—allow the quiet voice of Spirit, the great Counselor, to be heard over the clamor of our daily lives.

Most of us in the West associate prayer with thoughts and words, which are an excellent starting point for communion with Spirit. But we need to expand this definition to include our bodies—for example, our breathing, heartbeat, and the *absence* of thought. In this way prayer becomes a way of life, rather than a specific or rote exercise we engage in on an occasional or regular basis. These contemplative disciplines often come naturally to mature Lovers. If you struggle with reserving time for solitude or muddle through prayer and meditation, consider retaining a mature Lover friend to guide you into these disciplines.

Study is the discipline most readily accepted in the West. We may continually learn about ourselves and Spirit by exploring psychological models, religious traditions, mythology, philosophy, and sacred writings, which can point us toward paths of deeper experience. While concentrated study is a Warrior discipline, it can also take us into multidimensional, nonjudgmental thinking, the realm of the mature Magician.

The disciplines of *journaling* and *fasting* are close cousins to solitude. They engender reflection on our lives and awareness of our bodies. A journal becomes a silent friend who listens to our deepest, most confidential thoughts, without judgment, approval, or condemnation—an instant camera for our lives, providing chronological snapshots of our thoughts and soul. As we express our angst and joy through writing, and later reexamine the entries, we begin to see patterns of behavior and perhaps glimpses into our blind spots. A journal can also be a release mechanism for flushing collected tensions and negative emotions. By letting our words of anxiety, anger, grief, shame, guilt, and unworthiness pour out on paper, we begin to release their negative energy and allow grace to flow into us. As importantly, journal entries can reinforce and magnify our experiences of joy, creativity, affirmation, and celebration.

Through the intentional discomfort of an empty stomach, fasting exposes, by association, the emotional or relational emptiness endemic in our disowned shadows. Fasting highlights our dependence on the complex chain of production and packaging that provides food to our lives, mirroring our dependence on a Source beyond ourselves for unconditional love.

In addition, fasting reminds us of how we fill or bloat ourselves with unnecessary "stuff." It gives us a hint of both the rigor and purity of a simple life. When we temporarily empty and cleanse our physical system by fasting, we are better able to sense the cleansing energy from our Source, which can flood through us at any time if we aren't clogging the inlet with our addictions and diversions. Fasting reminds us of our continual need to empty ourselves of pretense, and to realize that we are, ultimately, not the one in control.

Fasting is a subdiscipline of *forbearance*, which calls us to intentionally deny ourselves pleasures that might either distract us from communion with Spirit or encourage negative energy sources like greed, lust, and pride. Forbearance anticipates coagulants forming particularly at the inlet of energy and continually cleanses the opening. The restraint is not denial but rather a conscious choice to avoid circumstances, substances, and relationships that may clog the energy inlet or accelerate energy losses. This self-control is a Warrior discipline and usually includes physical or interpersonal discomfort. It helps us develop the psychic muscles of equanimity and courage for our inevitable encounters with adversity, temptation, and pain. By learning how to say no to ourselves, we can better hold our boundaries with others, risking their displeasure, wrath, or abandonment. Forbearance is crucial for developing the mature Warrior advisor and is a pivotal discipline within the recovery movements for countering selfishness, greed, gluttony, and lust.

Tied to self-control are the disciplines of physical *exercise* and *diet* to maintain our bodies. If we see our body as a temple for Spirit and one of the three gateways to aliveness (along with mind and emotions), then maximized awareness demands that we maintain optimal physical conditioning. Exercise and diet disciplines can be uncomfortable, but the "no pain, no gain" maxim applies if we view our physical health as a grounding component of greatness. Body awareness disciplines, including yoga and martial arts like tai chi and aikido, further strengthen the synergy among mind, body, and emotions.

Another difficult discipline in our culture of "more" is *simplicity*. Indulging in the distractions, diversions, comparisons, and pleasures of the material world leads us into a complex, future-focused life and draws us away from the wonder and completeness of the present moment. As with the other disciplines, simplicity requires the Warrior's courage to say no to increased complexity, and then to begin divesting the possessions and relationships that clutter and convolute our lives. This is difficult, because we can so easily rationalize why we need so much stuff.

A life of simplicity does not require asceticism. We don't need to discard our cars, phones, and computers if they support or enhance our awareness journey. We *do* need to release them if they seem to become critical to our lives or identities, either for their own sake (selfishness) or for comparison with others (pride and pretense). The real test of simplicity is when we have the discipline to divest of possessions or relationships that seem nice to have but have become debilitating baggage. The section in Chapter 21 on money and materialism presents additional tips for simplifying our lives.

The Tao of Leadership offers the following call toward a life of simplicity. The last paragraph is particularly challenging to aggressive tower builders.

A Simple Life

If you want to be free, learn to live simply. Use what you have and be content where you are. Quit trying to solve your problems by moving to another place, by changing mates or careers, by buying more stuff.

Eat food grown locally. Wear simple, durable clothing. Keep a small home, uncluttered and easy to clean. Keep an open calendar with periods of uncommitted time. Have a spiritual practice and let family customs grow.

Of course, the world is full of novelty and adventures. New opportunities come along every day. So what?[4]

The disciplines just described purge the psychic debris collected in our minds and bodies, heighten our consciousness, and hone our conscience—the ability to distinguish the right thing amid the commotion, confusion, and temptations of a self-serving world. Conscience is like a muscle that atrophies if not worked and strengthened. Just as maintaining physical health can be uncomfortable, strengthening conscience (and consciousness) can also be wearing and painful.

When practiced regularly, these disciplines act as a dual-purpose Geiger counter, measuring both the aliveness flow through us and the radioactive toxins that block this flow. As the disciplines become habits in our lives, the Geiger counter becomes more finely calibrated for sensing new toxins that seek to enter and pollute our system. For example, the more aligned we are with living a life of truth, the more inner angst we will feel when tempted to lie. We experience a consistent, resonating inner voice that counters our rationalizations and defenses and bellows, "This action isn't right!"

The rewards of discipline are rich, but the price is high. Most comfortable, wealthy, successful leaders in first-world countries falter in attempting these disciplines. They start with good intentions—like New Year's resolutions—but gradually succumb to the relentless pull of contentment and conformance. Their resolve is choked out by the temptations of the world, and they gradually rejoin the masses in their tower-building, tower-protection obsession. They long for spiritual connection, but not at the cost of their worldly security. Most get a lukewarm experience of both.

But if we allow ourselves to steep in these times of solitude and inner reflection, scanning our entire being (mind, body, spirit) for negative energy, while supported by a loving, truth-telling community, we will have both the vision and the courage to take the high road, the narrow path that leads to aliveness and joy. Both Richard Foster and Dallas Willard offer excellent suggestions for initiating and maintaining the disciplines of an aware life.[5]

COMMUNITY, CONTAINERS, AND COMPASSION

Many regimented people who love the challenge of individual responsibility will gravitate toward the personal disciplines. However, we cannot fully cleanse the conduit of energy on our own. We must be in honest, loving community with friends who will tell us the truth; illuminate our blind spots; affirm and bless us as we step into the fire of our anger, grief, and forgiveness; and help us stay tethered to our values. We need guides to hold the light as we navigate the dark canyons of our souls.

Guides shine the light of truth and affirmation for us as we enter into the darkness and perceived void of our souls. Having made the journey themselves, they forewarn us of the pain but assure us that it will end, that a light exists and we will see it. They encourage us to experience the whole process rather than trying to rush through it or leap over the grief or despair. Without these human guides and reliance on a Context larger than ourselves that sees, contains, and loves *all* parts, we will thrash in the darkness of our confusion and pain. While many business, professional, and ministry leaders have numerous acquaintances, few leaders have these kinds of friends, mentors, and guides.

Consider retaining a personal board of directors, a cabinet of external counselors who nourish and strengthen your mature inner advisors, while monitoring your shadow-driven blind spots (e.g., a return to addictions, languishing in a codependent relationship). Choose personal board members who have character and maturity in many areas, but who are *unlike* you. If you already have a strong Warrior in your inner advisory court, you likely don't need an outside Warrior. Instead, find a confidant who will complement your shadows. If you are prone to addictions, are out of touch with your emotions, or can't dance, find a mature Lover to coach you. If you tend to wallow in indecision and unworthiness, solicit a mature Sovereign to coach and bless you. If you slip into judgmental, black-and-white thinking, are easily fooled, or are gripped with anxiety, find a Magician guide. These guides and coaches will help you tap the genius buried in your disowned shadows and lovingly midwife the emergence of your greatness.

To face and embrace our shadows requires a safe, confidential, shame-free container for speaking our truth, experiencing our feelings, and receiving affirmation and blessing. A *container* is any gathering of people in which we can be confronted, held, nurtured, and affirmed; where we can try out riding our shadow stallions and greeting our emotions, knowing that seasoned guides and encouraging witnesses are present to support our inward journey.

A safe container holds the emotions, tensions, confusion, uncertainty —and the greatness—that accompany our deepest truths. It consists of participants working on their inner issues; guides who facilitate the exploration, experience, and transformation of shadows; and witnesses who honor and support the participants. To overcome past betrayals, the participants must feel safe with one another and with the guides. Example covenants of a safe container, agreed to by all the participants, are shown in Table 20.3.

The witnesses' role is to see, mirror, and affirm the participants as they work on their issues. Witnesses must observe and support, without judging or shaming the participants. Physical and soul-level safety allows participants to encounter their emotions and shadows, knowing that boundaries are in place and protection exists.

Possible containers include the meetings of the recovery movement (Alcoholics Anonymous and its derivative organizations for narcotics, sex, food, gambling, and other addictions), therapy settings, confidential small groups (like the forums within Young Presidents' Organization, The Executive Committee groups, and the Integration Groups within the Mankind Project), and religious small groups. The key ingredients are confidentiality, trust, truth, and experience.

Therapy and the recovery movement meetings offer opportunities for

Table 20.3 Example Covenant for a Safe Container

I Will Respect Confidentiality.
I Will Be Present in the Moment.
I Will Stay Around When Times Get Tough.
I Will Be On Time and Stay until the End.
I Will Speak My Truth.
I Will Ask for What I Want.
I Will Take Care of Myself.
I Am Willing to Make Mistakes.
I Am Willing to Laugh at Myself.
I Will Own My Feelings.
I Will Own My Judgments.
I Will Not Blame, Shame, or Fix Others.
I Will Ask Permission before Offering Advice.

shadow exploration in a community of open, wounded people led by experienced guides. Larry Crabb says that effective counseling involves "peeling the layers, sometimes gently, sometimes forcefully, to reach the real person underneath."[6] Executive small groups, like YPO forums and TEC groups, offer a confidential setting, with high affinity and minimal conflicts among members. As experience and trust develop among the participants, and seasoned guides either emerge within the group or are invited from outside, these executive groups have great potential for doing transformative soul-level work. Without experienced moderation or guidance, they often remain at head-level dialogue with occasional dips into emotion.

Great potential exists for intimate community in church small groups. Much of the resurgence in Christianity in the Western world can be credited to the fostering of smaller cell groups within the church that advocate prayer and study. These groups are beginning to encourage more truthful, intimate sharing of personal issues, the first step on the soul work journey.

While these groups are *spiritually* safe, they are not always *psychically* safe. They typically do not have a norm of confidentiality, and conflicts often exist among the members (like the presence of both a manager and an employee from the same company, or two potential competitors from the same industry) that inhibit full disclosure. Also, because Western religious traditions tend to be more cognitive, these small groups are often hesitant to explore potentially explosive emotional areas. Nevertheless, these spiritual small groups provide a basis for intimate, trusting community. The incorporation of safety covenants, the conflict resolution model in Appendix C, and soul exploration exercises can lead spiritual small groups to both deeper self-awareness and heightened God-awareness.

Several organizations offer soul exploration retreats. The typical format is to (1) separate the participants from the outside world; (2) build a safe container where truth is welcome and shadows can be invited into the light; (3) offer exercises and experiences where participants encounter their dilemmas, emotions, giftedness, and longings; (4) celebrate and share stories; (5) teach; and (6) link back to the world. Perhaps most importantly, these organizations promote follow-up among the participants in the form of confidential small group gatherings after each retreat. A list of these retreats and trainings may be found in the Notes.[7]

M. Scott Peck further explains the value of safe containers:

> "It takes a great deal of work for a group of strangers to achieve the safety of community. Once they succeed, however, it is as if the floodgates were opened. As soon as it is safe to speak one's heart, as soon as most people in the group know they will be listened to and accepted for themselves, years and years of pent-up frustration and hurt and guilt and grief come pouring out. . . . As the mutual intimacy multiplies, true healing begins. Old wounds are healed, old resentments forgiven, old resistances overcome. Fear is replaced by hope."[8]

If this discussion on containers and covenants seems daunting, consider that *one good friend* with whom you can share any element of your life without shame or judgment—who loves you—can be your safe container for inner work. Do you have such a person in your life? If not, make it a priority to find one.

Besides being supported *by* a community of friends and mentors, we need to be *in* community where we can return this gift of caring to others. In a confidential, open community we can offer the gifts of kindness and mentoring to protégés and peers. Our compassion gives rise to patience, tenderness, mercy, and humility in our words and actions, and affirms the worthiness of others. We become cheerleaders and advocates to other tunnelers, with no agenda and no thought of payback. When our energy conduit is clear, love flows through us and nourishes others. All that flows out from us to others is replenished in our own souls. The Source never runs dry. Henri Nouwen describes this wonder of caring:

> Every human being has a great, yet often unknown, gift to care, to be compassionate, to become present to the other, to listen, to hear, and to receive. If that gift would be set free and made available, miracles could take place.[9]

The Emotional Gauntlet

If thoughts are the language of the mind, emotion is the language of the soul. Figure 20.2 shows the path through our emotions to the center point of joy. Fear is the ogre at the mouth of the gauntlet, discouraging aliveness seekers from entering into the unknown territory of deeper emotions. Truth and a safe community are the antidotes for this fear, allowing us to go deeper into the soul canyons.

Anger is the next dragon on the journey, to be met with truth and navigated by the expression and release of the anger. Grief normally awaits the person who has faced his anger. Grief has its root in the heart of our brokenness, and warns of emptiness and pain. We steer through grief via our truth, forgiveness, and tears.

The deepest darkness, our conviction of unworthiness, represents the final edge we must cross, and resides in the bowels of our shadows. When we reach the place of unworthiness, we can do nothing by ourselves except to let go of our supposed control and receive forgiveness, blessing, and love. At this final stage, going into our unworthiness means confronting our brokenness, acknowledging how poor we really are. But instead of trying to deny it, attack it, or fix it—all futile endeavors—we simply accept it, weep over it, forgive it, and bless it. The miracle of joy emerges in this darkest hour.

Louis, the family business CEO torn between staying in or selling his business, entered the emotional gauntlet by experiencing and going through his fear of looking at a dysfunctional family system. After deeper exploration, he was able to express his anger toward his parents for manipulating him into giving up his college choice and feeling prematurely responsible for the legacy of the family business. He then grieved the losses of his college adventure opportunity and of never having had a "clean" relationship with his father while growing up.

Deep inside, Louis felt that the only way his father would ever love

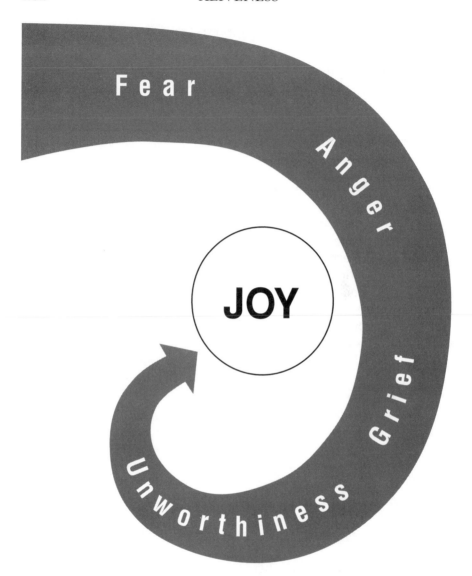

Figure 20.2 The Emotional Gauntlet.

him was if he sacrificed himself for the good of the family. This rescuer, perform-to-be-loved pattern became interwoven into all his relationships, including his marriage and his relationship with God. Beneath his fear, anger, and grief, Louis carried a deeply rooted unworthiness, a sense that he was unlovable unless he rescued or performed. In some cathartic retreat work he came to viscerally experience forgiveness toward his father, as well as self-love and the love of God. He felt loved just for who he was, without having to rescue or perform. Receiving this love led to tears of joy and a resolve to take responsibility for his life.

The ultimate message to this shadow self, trembling in the back of the bus, is a paraphrase of the Father's words to the prodigal son:[10] "My child, you are with me always. All that I have is yours. I love you just the way you are. I will love you always." And the sincere, visceral experience of this love opens the gateway to joy.

The most sacred and joyful experiences in my retreat work with wounded men and women are when a broken, yet courageous, individual expresses his anger; faces and navigates his shame; expunges his unworthiness; receives the blessing of God, the other participants, *and himself*, and steps through the portal of joy. He is ushered into an inner cathedral of innocence, joy, and celebration that has been there for a lifetime, waiting for him to come home. These are close encounters with the divine.

21

SURRENDER,
GRATITUDE, ACTION

Chapter 20 described antidotes, amplifiers, and cleansers for reestablishing the flow of energy into, through, and out of us. This chapter highlights the importance of a life grounded in surrender and gratitude. It also describes action steps that address the areas of midlife disillusionment introduced in Chapter 10.

Surrender

Healing of our disowned parts does not come by acting out psychodramas of our repressed voices or by navigating emotional gauntlets. Soul work processes and rituals bring the shadows into the light. Healing begins when we *surrender* our disowned parts—the sabotaging shadows and the repressed genius—to the Source of light.

We've already considered some forms of surrender: letting go of our unforgivingness and releasing the anger we feel toward others, along with any guilt or shame we're harboring; and surrendering our fears, our armor, our very souls in the act of opening to receive love from a Higher Power. Beyond this release of our psychic wounds, we are called to release our grip on our possessions and accept, even embrace, our powerlessness. In so doing we paradoxically begin to experience immeasurable freedom and peace, as described in this excerpt from *The Tao of Leadership*:

The Paradox of Letting Go

When I let go of what I am, I become what I might be.
When I let go of what I have, I receive what I need.
These are feminine or *Yin* paradoxes:

> ➤ By yielding, I endure.
> ➤ The empty space is filled.
> ➤ When I give of myself, I become more.
> ➤ When I feel most destroyed, I am about to grow.
> ➤ When I desire nothing, a great deal comes to me.

My best work is done when I forget my own point of view; the less I make of myself, the more I am.[1]

All of the great world religions teach surrender. In the West this movement toward total yieldedness to Source is called sanctification. In the East it's called awareness, becoming awake.

Surrender does not mean abdication. Rather, we are called to take responsibility for our lives, listening for divine guidance and remaining open to a total directional shift at any time, even though it may fly in the face of common sense. In the football vernacular, we have a game plan, but God can call an audible at any time—and we must obey.

At first this notion of surrender and dependence is abhorrent to those of us who have spent a lifetime building our towers. Why would I want to forsake a life's work toward security and return to a state of utter dependence? The answer is simple: peace. When all the success, money, significance, and security of the world feel flat and insufficient, we can release all we have and return to the place of dependence. The poor have an advantage they are often unaware of: Since they have so little to give up, they are already closer to God. In the Beatitudes, Jesus tells the crowds, "Blessed are the poor in spirit, for theirs is the kingdom of heaven."[2] Think of "poor in spirit" as meaning those who have surrendered their will, and "kingdom of heaven" as meaning the combination of communion with God and awareness.

Some religious traditions speak of being born again. We need to be born again and again and again. Tunneling into our souls is a lifetime journey; we will always find disowned or repressed parts of ourselves, or of humankind as a whole, that need to be reborn through surrender. As such our whole life is a continual cycle of self-discovery and then letting go.

Gratitude

Gratitude is a natural outgrowth of both solitude and community, a thankfulness for being alive, for nature, relationships, and God. Gratitude springs from the open, vulnerable heart that trusts in the provision of Source, regardless of our circumstances. As a result we find cause for wonder and celebration in every moment.

It's all too easy to lapse into cynicism and complaining when things go awry. Like the disciplines described in Chapter 20, gratitude is another "muscle" that needs to be exercised daily to become our strong, natural response to life, so that thanksgiving becomes the lead component of our communion with God and our connection with others.

Gratitude is always a choice. We can choose to be grateful even when our emotions and feelings are still steeped in hurt and resentment. The world and our disowned shadows draw us away from gratitude. Henri Nouwen explains the tension:

> I can choose to be grateful when I am criticized, even when my heart still responds in bitterness. I can choose to speak about goodness and beauty, even when my inner eye still looks for someone to accuse or something to call ugly. I can choose to listen to the voices that forgive and to look at the faces that smile, even while I still hear words of revenge and see grimaces of hatred.
>
> There is always the choice between resentment and gratitude.
>
> The choice for gratitude rarely comes without some real effort. But each time I make it, the next choice is a little easier, a little freer, a little less self-conscious. Because every gift I acknowledge reveals another and another until, finally, even the most normal, obvious, and seemingly mundane event or encounter proves to be filled with grace.[3]

Taking Action

This section reexamines the five areas of disillusionment presented in Chapter 10, offering suggestions and specific actions for penetrating the confusion or pain around these issues and returning to a purposeful, surrendered life.

IDENTITY AND PURPOSE

At their root level most "Who am I?" identity wounds stem from unworthiness and are healed through the antidotes of forgiveness and blessing. Love and surrender become the bedrock upon which our identity must be built or rebuilt in midlife. Attempts to recraft our identity independent of love and surrender invariably result in a frail or malleable identity, easily twisted or destroyed. As witnessed in this book's vignettes, most successful executives and professionals enter their autumn years with a very fragile sense of their own identity, much less an identity that rests in communion with its Source.

Most leaders and spouses in midlife transition who are seeking significance in the second half of their lives apply their proven tower-building talents of perseverance and discipline to craft their second-half identity and purpose. They seek a fix-it plan that they can digest quickly, so they can initiate the construction of their "tower of second-half meaning." They believe that by retooling and redirecting their gifts for wealth creation into wealth disbursement, they will find fulfillment and meaning. Their natural motion in life remains steadfastly upward and outward.

But consider that before we can freely move upward and outward into our life destiny, we must face and embrace our shadows and cleanse our clogged energy conduit. We have to admit our brokenness, accept our dependence, and do our soul work. We must go *down and in* before moving *up and out*. Otherwise, any new towers we might build will have shaky or rotted foundations. Once we adopt the antidotes and amplifiers presented in Chapter 20—once we clear the building site and lay a solid foundation—our identity and life purpose emerge naturally.

Several models and books[4] offer excellent tools for grasping our giftedness, personality nuances, and psychological profile. Appendix B offers one such assessment tool for evaluating our mature advisors and shadows. These cognitive tools reveal pieces of our unique and intricate mosaic and are an important part of the Understanding phase of the soul journey. But before we can plan the second half of our lives we must actually *do* our inner work—get out of being "big" and find our souls. Usually this means coming down from the top of our towers and dwelling in the real-life, no-pretense commonness at the bottom.

Hard-charging leaders, restless to enter a second half of significance, are encouraged to first "do your work." Climb down the ladder, leap from the tower, take a sabbatical, ratchet back your lifestyle, work no more than three days a week in your practice, migrate to a chairmanship and hire a CEO—in short, create space for *you*. Then build a support community, go into the back of your bus, do your soul tunneling, purge the sediment from your energy conduit, get "clean," and make amends for your wounding of others—and *you will find out who you are*.

MONEY AND MATERIALISM

As part of our fearless moral inventory we must examine our relationship to money. This is best done in a confidential community of peers who are willing to speak openly about their wealth or poverty and the role of money in their lives. We need to view money as a spiritual force, treated with respect but never idolized or ignored. Many affluent midlife leaders are cavalier and magnanimous in their words about money and possessions, but in reality are prisoners to their wealth.

As part of your downward and inward soul tunneling, look for the sediment of greed, selfishness, and avarice inhibiting your flow of energy. Determine the role of money in your life. This might include definitions like the following:

> ➤ Provide an environment, support resources, and flexibility so I can use my talents.
> ➤ Enhance personal growth, relaxation, recharging, reflection, education, and self-improvement.
> ➤ Open up time for deepening my relationships with loved ones.
> ➤ Help the less fortunate.
> ➤ Invest in people and causes that will make the world a better place.
> ➤ Provide security for my retirement years.
> ➤ Give my children a jump start as they launch their adult lives.

These are noble statements that few people will argue with. But do your actions mirror your intentions? Who is holding you accountable regarding your relationship to money?

Tower building is about accumulation of wealth; genius and greatness (as we will see in Chapter 22) are about disbursement of wealth. A clean-flowing energy conduit demands stewardship, not ownership, of our money and possessions. If we believe we own and control them, the reality is that they own and control us. Affluent people must walk the knife-edge of having wealth without being governed by it. They must continually ask themselves the question, "If it all goes away tomorrow, will I still feel alive, free, and grateful?"

There are ways to test this. Play out these more radical actions in your mind and perhaps consider them in your life.

1. Most of us give away money out of our abundance, with little pain. Determine an amount that would cause you pain to give away. Double it. Buy anonymously a cashier's check for the doubled amount and give it to an organization or person in need. Do this in such a way that the gift cannot be tracked back to you. Do not contact the recipient or even follow up on its use. Do not take a tax deduction.

2. Serve in a place of poverty for a minimum of two weeks. Live among the poor. Stay with them. *Do not bring any of your own money.* Rely on the poor to feed you and take care of your needs. Be dependent on them as you work with them as a peer or as their servant. If you choose, have a lifeline back to safety, but use it only if your physical well-being is seriously threatened. Can you endure being in a place of poverty and physical insecurity?

3. Get with a group of other people who are willing to speak openly about their wealth and possessions. Ideally, the individuals will have a wide range of personal wealth. Have each person write his net worth and last year's income on a card. Mix up the cards and pass them out so that no one has his own card. Then have each person speak on *what his life would be like* if the figures on the new card were indeed his new net worth and annual income. Listen attentively when the person who has your card describes what his life would be like if he had your wealth.

Money embodies a potent *spiritual* energy that, unacknowledged, can keep us away from our truth and our identity, comfortable and independent, and living in shadow. Affluent executives and professionals regularly ruminate about "How much is enough?" They focus on the "how much" part of the question rather than the "enough." Enough what? Comfort? Enough so I won't have to work again? So my spouse and children will be secure in case I die? So my friends will view me as successful?

Only rarely will I hear them describe "enough" as "so I feel fulfilled and alive." Consider that, if aliveness and fulfillment are our goals and we sincerely desire to escape the trap of comparison, the true answer to the "How much is enough?" question is zero.

RESPONSIBILITIES, BALANCE, AND BOUNDARIES

Chapter 10 painted the bleak picture of overcommitted leaders rationalizing life on a treadmill of ever-increasing responsibilities. As they approach meltdown they plead for balance, yet are unwilling to shed any of their perceived obligations.

The downward and inward approach to imbalance requires that we deal with our truth, anger, unworthiness, and boundaries. Until overburdened, exploited, workaholic leaders get their mature Warrior on line, setting boundaries and reducing responsibilities, they will whine and wallow in the mire of overcommitment.

Life imbalance is symptomatic of some combination of the Sovereign Weakling shadow, the Warrior Victim shadow, and the shadow Lover's codependence. These disowned shadows fear that unless they commit to projects or stay in relationships, they will be punished, rejected, shamed, and alone. They are captive to the approval of others.

The crucial step in regaining balance is to deal with the core wounds of feeling unworthy and unlovable, until we can say with confidence and directness, "No, I can't do that," "I must resign my position," "I am ending this relationship." Wearing our Warrior's armor, complemented by our Lover's compassion and our Magician's eloquence, we can communicate our boundaries cleanly, clearly, and tenderly, while remaining immune to the pleas, bargaining, rationalizations, and threats of others who demand our time.

When grounded in our mature inner advisors we are not responsible for others' happiness. We may cheer for them, perhaps help them, but always as our choice. Centered adults are never forced to do anything; they always know they are making a choice. Anytime you find yourself saying, "Yes, but I have to . . . ," you are slipping into the deflated shadows and succumbing to the treadmill way of life.

If you struggle with balance and boundaries, find and retain mature Warriors to be on your personal board of directors. Ask for their encouragement and accountability. Use them as an alcoholic in recovery uses his sponsor; call them whenever you are even considering a project or relationship that is at the fringe of your boundaries. Have Warrior friends guide you in definitively resetting your boundaries so that you have time for the disciplines outlined in Chapter 20. Give them permission both to bolster you and to cut short your whining and excuses.

I have been blessed with two Warrior friends in my life who exhibit the rare combination of bluntness and kindness as they puncture my rationalizations and fluff and encourage me to terminate lame projects or languid relationships. They helped me cut through the cheap sentiment and bogus strategic plans that blocked me from selling my company. They told me, "Determine your selling price, chop off 40 percent, find a buyer, and sell it. Nothing else is important." When the negotiations soured and I threatened to walk from the deal even though my sale price was being met, they plucked me from my whirlpool of confusion and fear of change, admonishing me, "It's hard, but the deal is right. Stay the course. Get it done." Their support led to a successful closing—of the deal and of a major chapter in my life—and a launch into a whole new adventure of executive coaching and retreat facilitation.

CONNECTIONS: MARRIAGE AND FAMILY

Resurrecting marital vitality begins with our willingness to work on ourselves, without trying to fix our partner. For the relationship to either heal and flourish, or to dissolve cleanly, both parties *must* get to the truth—about what's working, what's not working, individual needs, repressed emotions, boundaries, what each person wants.

We can't walk away from marriages and family relationships as easily as other relationships. But until we are no longer dependent on the relationship for our identity, until we know we are whole within or without the relationship, we are captive to (codependent in) the relationship and lacking integrity with ourselves. A common trend in our culture is to bail out of the relationship to "find myself." It takes great courage to find yourself—to do your inner work—while still in the relationship, and then determine whether to stay or leave. Both relational healing and relational closure require the counsel of all our inner advisors, not just the action-oriented Warrior or the connection-oriented Lover.

Before dealing with the wounds in a relationship, we must work on our own wounds and shadows. Only when we have aligned our mature inner advisors and retained outside mentors who bolster us in our areas of weakness (for most men, the Lover; for most women, the Warrior) can we initiate (Sovereign) communication with loved ones from a position of clarity (Warrior), tenderness (Lover), and wisdom (Magician). When we love ourselves and have our boundaries, we can love our partner enough to, if necessary, let him or her go.

Again, refer to the Clean Talk model in Appendix C for dealing with adversity or conflict in a relationship. It presupposes that facing conflict is the royal road to union. Truth doesn't solve issues; it gets them out of shadow. Truth quashes hidden agendas, exposes secrets, and gets the wheat and the chaff, the beauty marks and the warts, all out in the open. Truth is the entry point into shadow transformation and the entry point for relational healing. At first, the truth may induce *more* pain; eventually, it makes possible the release of pain. For lasting relational healing, we *must* stay in the truth.

To be in vibrant relationships we must strive to become Warrior-Lovers or, if you prefer, Lover-Warriors. If you are strong in only one aspect, get mentors and guides to help you strengthen the other. If your spouse is weak in one where you are strong, encourage (rather than bludgeon) her or him with your strength. Speak about your shadows to one another; admit how you sabotage yourself and others. Bringing them into the open, in front of the people you love, dilutes their negative power and invites their transformation into allies. Consult with outside advisors who have strong Magician skills, who can see and hold the big picture of your life without being swayed by your defenses, excuses, or emotions. You need wisdom, not a pity party.

For whatever reason, you may choose to stay in an unhealthy or difficult relationship (emotionally volatile spouse, rebellious child, cantankerous parent, sniping in-law). Choose to stay because of your sense of unselfish service to and love for the individual, and *not* as a victim or martyr (Warrior shadows), out of pity (Sovereign shadows), or as a codependent rescuer (Lover shadows). Acknowledge that your staying is a conscious choice, not a foregone conclusion. Keep working on your own personal issues and strive to maintain a life-giving support community to encourage you in the trials of your relationship.

At some point you may choose to leave the relationship—the Sovereign taking care of himself and the Warrior enforcing boundaries. Scan your shadows and energy conduit first to see if the decision truly arises from your adult self or if it is leaking out of your shadows. If you do choose to leave, do so cleanly and lovingly. Stay present and empathic amid the anguish and accusations of your partner. Find in yourself the capacity to love, forgive, and bless your partner, even if it's never spoken or never returned. Later, invest the time necessary to grieve the lost relationship. Continue to bless and love the other person as you get on with your life.

If you desire an open, mature relationship with your spouse and other loved ones, consider the books by Harville Hendrix.[5]

CONNECTIONS: SPIRITUALITY— YEARNING TO CONNECT WITH GOD

Midlife leaders longing for friendship—a safe place to tell their stories and receive loving support—can begin taking gradual steps toward community as described in Chapter 20. Beyond this human connection, many want a reunion with the spiritual side of themselves and a connection with Spirit beyond themselves.

A fundamental premise of this book is that the ultimate goal of both upward and outward spiritual quests *and* downward and inward soul-work tunneling is a sense of personal aliveness grounded in communion with our perception of God. Some pilgrims may choose to start with the spiritual path, relying on religious traditions, sacred texts, and spiritual guides to inspire them in their quest to know, love, and surrender to God. In this process they may commune with God, but normally only at the head level. For full communion, they need to know and welcome their *whole* self, which requires integrating soul work—self-exploration—with their spiritual quest. Those who focus only on the upward and outward spiritual quest and ignore or condemn their shadows are highly prone to being sabotaged by these shadows, no matter how fervent their outer faith.

The other route toward total communion with God is to begin with the soul work, understanding and embracing our shadows. At some point soul workers must complement this downward and inward, personal enlightenment work with belief in, surrender to, and dependence on a Wisdom larger than themselves. Without this spiritual surrender, self-enlightenment can become the goal and the pilgrim misses the joy and love of divine communion. Many enlightenment seekers deny the need for divine dependence and settle for an ever-improving, ever-more-content individual self. Others seek a sense of nothingness, the melting into some unfathomable void. Still others either strive to arrive at a place where they can feel peaceful most of the time or look for a series of emotional fixes. They resist the humility and obedience required for surrender to the Source.

Most people in traditional Western religions begin with the upward, cognitive spiritual path and need to deliberately open themselves to the downward, mystical soul path. Conversely, most people in the enlightenment community are comfortable with the soul path but are less open to the surrender and dependence called for on the spiritual path.

It doesn't matter which path you start on—spiritual or soul. But, at some point, to experience both intimate, loving communion with our Source (to love God with our *whole* heart, mind, body, and strength) and loving communion with our whole self (to love our neighbors *as* ourselves), we must go down *both* paths.

The first step in spiritual connection or renewal is an openness and desire to connect. If you are not open or ready to connect with Spirit, focus on creating safety for soul exploration. Rediscover yourself before trying to discover God, and in the process find out what it is *in you* that blocks your openness to a higher Source.

Once the desire exists to reconnect spiritually, deep wounds stemming from shaming or duplicitous religious experiences block many midlife seekers from opening fully to Spirit. Their Risk Manager reminds them of prior ridicule and judgment when they allowed themselves to become vulnerable, and warns them, "Don't go there. You'll just get hurt again." Many take the mask of bad religion and shadow-driven authority figures (e.g., parents and pastors) and place it on God. They envision a punitive, judgmental, damning God who rages at sin, demands mindless obedience, and occasionally doles out approval—just like their well-meaning but misdirected parents and pastors did. Many pilgrims cower in fear and unworthiness at the thought of reconnecting with, much less surrendering to, such a God, believing, "If I really do have an encounter with God, He'll condemn me for all I've done," or, "Look at what I am—how could God possibly love me?" Others bridle with anger at the duplicity and abuse and vow, "If that's the way God is, who needs it? I hate that God. I'll take care of myself."

The path to reconnection for seekers who are wary of religion is normally a combination of "test-driving" different traditions, while concurrently doing their inner work to encounter, rage at, weep over, forgive, and let go of the wounds and blocks that inhibit deep spiritual communion. An important part of spiritual renewal is forgiveness toward individuals or organizations that caused the wound. Once they've forgiven and released the bad experience, many spiritual pilgrims return to the tradition or denomination of their youth and find wondrous connection and communion.

Wounds around God can be approached in the same way as other wounds described. Speak the truth about the wound (for example, "I feel deserted by God"); speak the fears about going into the wound ("It won't work," "I'll find out God really *is* like that and I'll be truly condemned," "Maybe God's not even there"); and *experience* the anger, grief, confession, forgiveness, unworthiness—whatever comes up. In almost all cases the wound is not really about God, but a projection (parent, pastor, organization) onto God.

This is where Spirit takes over. If we have the personal desire and a safe, supportive community to go into these wounds, to their deepest, ugliest roots, God meets us right there, in the bowels of our pain, in the back of the bus, and says, "My child, I have loved you always. Welcome home. There is nothing you have to do to earn my love."

Regarding spiritual elders, guides, mentors, and religious traditions, consider the following allegory. Imagine that spiritual love is like the flow of pure water from an infinite well, available to all who thirst. The only cost is an openness to the Source, which *always* provides the water to thirsty pilgrims. Along come some well-intentioned zealots who cap the well, put a spigot on the end, construct a monument around it, and claim they have the only true source of pure water. They erect billboards proclaiming the water quality, the natural purification system of the shale beneath the well, and a host of other selling points for "their" water. Thirsty travelers often get so caught up in learning about the water that they never take a drink, while ardent sentinels guard the spigot so that parched pilgrims don't defile the monument by sneaking a drink without fully understanding and accepting the bottling process.

Down the road, other well experts are capping springs of the same water, adding their own spigots, erecting their own monuments and billboards, installing their own bottling process, while denouncing the other monuments. Meanwhile, some dry pilgrims, confused by the animosity among the monument builders, decide it's too much of a hassle to figure out who has the pure water, and buy sugar water from street vendors.

The water is what's important, not whom you get it from or its packaging. Spirituality is about connection, not membership—connecting with ourselves (including our shadows) and with others in community, and being in communion with Spirit. All are intertwined. All are one. The service and solitude disciplines amplify these connections. Religious traditions are an important, viable means—but not the end.

Spiritual awakening and amplification require guides, holy elders, and spiritual directors who lead you toward communion with Spirit. Be wary of supposed guides who try to mold you in their own image or paint their tradition, organization, movement, or approach as "*The Way* to God." Mature guides will help you find your own way to and realization of God, your calling into service, the right support community, and the right approach for you for communion with God.

Occasionally, a midlife seeker has little or no past religious baggage, but is simply open to communion with a Source beyond himself. These people are encouraged to go slowly, "test-driving" different approaches to God and different traditions while doing their soul exploration, concurrently asking God, whatever He/She/It might be, to reveal Himself and to act as a guide.

Both renewal and first-time seekers must be wary of feel-good, quick-fix spirituality. If the key to aliveness is a free-flowing connection to a source of Energy beyond ourselves, the combination of cheap religion and material pleasure short out this connection. Many people don't want a loving, universal, omnipresent God to whom they surrender themselves every waking moment. They want a plastic deity on the dashboard of their luxury car that bails them out of trouble, anoints their pursuit of material pleasure, and christens their tower. The parallel in the enlightenment traditions is feel-good, navel-gazing meditation and retreats that promote personal elevation independent of both spiritual communion and service back to the world.

Spiritual growth is often lonely, ordinary work that unfolds in the valleys of daily drudgery, with occasional visits to the mountaintop of transcendent encounters. The key to a rich spiritual life is to find joy in the drudgery. Very few people have the discipline, obedience, and surrender this requires.

The ultimate goal is not feeling good, but communion. Somewhere along this spiritual journey you will come to an edge of commitment and belief; the sampling period ends and you will choose the route to God that feeds you and best enhances this communion. Without this commitment, you risk becoming a spiritual dilettante who hovers around the fire of transcendent love, but never allows himself to become one with the flame.

Summary Thoughts on the Inner Journey

Many people in my Transition retreats ask, "How much work do I have to do? How will I know when I'm done?" *We're never done.* No ultimate healing comes from this work. The bottom of the egg is infinite; the back of the bus extends beyond where we can see. Our wholeness is a combination of our own labyrinth of personality, giftedness, and shadows and our connection to the shadows of other individuals, organizations, and nations. We are all one.

View this as good news: that we are wondrous, broad, deep, unfathomable human beings. We'll never know all of who we are—at least in this life. All we can do is nod to our collective shadows every day and bless them, "Hello. All of you are part of me. All of you are welcome." As importantly, we'll never know all of another person, community, organization, or nation, so we may as well stop judging them. And we'll certainly never know or even glimpse the fullness of God. Serenity comes as we find comfort in this place of not knowing and not judging.

Embark on the inner-work journey slowly. Many zealous tower builders attack soul work in the same way they approached tower building. They assemble a to-do list, build a time line, and try to be the first to achieve awareness. This is not a competition or a race to be the best inner-work pilgrim. It's not about "getting better" or "being fixed." Instead, the goal is to become more and more truthful about ourselves, knowing that we can never know all of our truth. Whatever we do find, we must accept it, offer it up, and then let it go, constantly surrendering ourselves to the Source. Inner work is more about abandonment and surrender of control than how many cubic liters of sediment can be scraped from the inside of the energy conduit.

Finally, continually ask yourself a few key questions.

1. *Is this working?* And if not, *What do I want to have happen?* Check in with all your mature advisors. Get the Sovereign's, Warrior's, Lover's, and Magician's views of your life situation. If these advisors are underdeveloped or certain shadows regularly sabotage your life, recruit a court of outside counselors to monitor your blind spots and help you scan your energy conduit for sediment buildup. Apply these questions to *every* aspect of your life—vocation, relationships, identity, spiritual journey—continually taking a comprehensive, fearless moral inventory.

2. *What's at risk?* This vital question is the entry into your truth and fears. Whenever you feel blocked or confused, what's at risk for you to take action, to make a decision, to step into the back of your bus?

3. *Who is my support?* The soul and spiritual journeys are dangerous and often futile when undertaken alone. Who are your friends, cheerleaders, guides, witnesses, confidants, outside advisors,

mentors, spiritual directors? If you have none, *find them.* Keep the communication with them clean and flowing. Charge them to watch your blind spots and hold you accountable.

With a cleansed energy conduit, awareness of and tenderness for our shadows, and a commitment to face and overcome the areas of disillusionment in our lives, we are poised to step into our greatness—a life purpose, aliveness, and love that connects us to others and engenders intimate communion with God.

22

GREATNESS

Chapters 20 and 21 laid the foundation for the final stage of the journey toward greatness, which was correlated in Chapter 13 with our ability to love. This closing chapter describes the gold we discover on our journey: the reality of our own genius, which is inescapably intertwined with the reality of love.

Incompetence, Competence, Excellence, Genius

Figure 22.1 offers a final model to guide you on the journey toward aliveness. Consider that our current life purpose matches our unique personality and giftedness at one of four successively higher levels.

At the lowest level, we live out of our *Incompetence*, performing tasks that we do poorly and that others can do much better. For me to be a tailor would be working at my level of incompetence. Susan, the neurologist, would be working out of her incompetence to labor as a bricklayer. I don't have the small motor skills to be a tailor and Susan doesn't have the strength to lay bricks. I could start finger dexterity exercises and go to sewing school, and she could retain a personal trainer and pump iron three

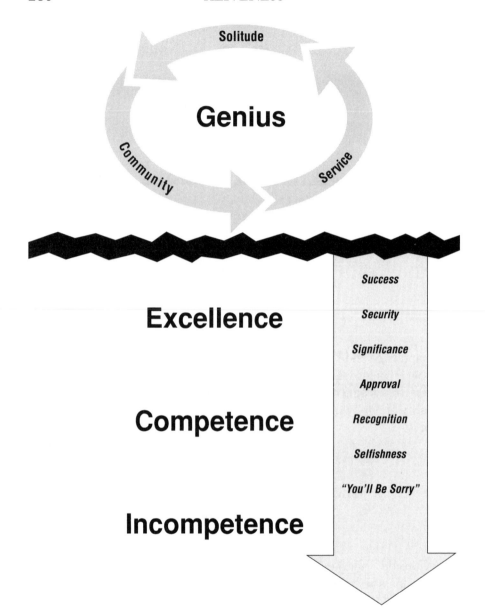

Figure 22.1 Levels of Life Purpose.

days a week, but our physical nature belies our ability to perform these jobs well. As importantly, I don't enjoy sewing, and Susan doesn't yearn to build patios.

Most of us have enough education and awareness to avoid the trap of incompetence in our primary vocations. Yet we often volunteer for or are pressured into service roles that are total misfits with our gifts and desires. This is common in youth sports, where the coach is drafted from among the parents because "The team needs a coach. No one else can do it. We're desperate. Can't you help us?" The parent doesn't know the game, doesn't really care about the game, and has a hard time relating to his own child, much less 11 other eight-year-olds. Yet, having weak boundaries and a desire to please, he reluctantly takes on the assignment. After a short time tensions build at all levels (kids with coach, coach with parents, kids with parents) and a dismal, frustrating season ensues.

Typically we find ourselves in frustrating roles of incompetence when we are pressured by others to "help out" in situations we are unskilled in and don't enjoy. We rationalize, "Oh, it won't take that much time. I guess I'll do it," and the aggravation begins. The solution is to consult our Warrior advisor, set a boundary, and simply decline the offer, realizing that we then risk the disapproval of others. Chapter 21 expanded on this boundary setting.

At the level of *Competence* we perform a task reasonably well, and may even find a modicum of enjoyment in the job. However, others could execute the same task at an equivalent or higher level, in less time, at less cost, and with more enjoyment. In my own work as an executive coach and writer I have become capable at word processing. I have learned the nuances of my word processing software and can type rapidly. Yet service bureau staff and freelance executive assistants are more efficient and are more affordable. To better leverage my time I should delegate my word processing assignments to one of these sources. Similar delegation rationales could be applied to Peter's scrutiny of advertising copy, Fletcher's tax return preparation, and Stan's car repair.

Many successful people in midlife never assess their giftedness while in their teens and 20s. They never find something they love. For example, a college student, forced to declare a major, may talk with a few friends and discover that an accounting degree virtually assures employment after graduation. So he enters the accounting program and after graduation joins a public accounting firm. He understands the skills required, completes his assignments, gets promoted, receives raises, and begins building a lifestyle around the compensation from this career. But he has little zest for the work other than for the compensation it provides. Thousands of other fledgling accountants (or lawyers, bookkeepers, secretaries, cooks, real estate agents—it could be any profession) across the country have similar or better skills. Larry's programming job with the large government contractor, described in Chapter 7, is another example.

Teachers, law enforcement officers, therapists, dentists, ministers—*all* professions employ many competent people who perform well in their jobs and receive fair compensation, but find marginal fulfillment in their work.

At the *Excellence* level we have mastered our job, perhaps risen to the top of our profession, and others affirm us for our unique talents. Each protagonist in this book has operated at a level of excellence in his career. Stan excelled at growing a culture of dedicated software professionals with a world-class customer service mind-set. Susan achieved national-level recognition in her specialty. Marty was a charismatic speaker and exceptional team builder within both the youth ministry and his church.

Ongoing excellence demands dedication and discipline, the hallmarks of successful tower builders. The rewards are usually recognition, approval, and financial security. During our commitment stage, excellence and its associated rewards are frequently our goals in life.

Beyond excellence is the level of *Genius*, which is the soul manifestation of excellence. Genius refers to our calling or destiny, and aligns closely with greatness. It embodies excellence and enjoyment, but is inherently fulfilling and therefore indifferent to personal recognition or rewards. Genius involves Sovereign stewardship of our gifts in unforced, flowing service to and love for our realms—our business, profession, ministry, family, community, church—every person or organization we touch in our lives. Genius is the pure manifestation of all four mature advisors working in unison: the Sovereign's love for the realm, the Lover's connection with the people, the Magician knowing the right thing to do, and the Warrior using his gifts with skill and dedication. When we are in our genius, love and energy flow into us unimpeded, assume our unique personality and giftedness, and flow out, unhindered, in service and love to others.

As shown in Figure 22.1, a jagged edge of fear blocks many of us from entering our genius. This edge represents the shadows and energy blocks accumulated over a lifetime of building our towers. In the early stages of tower building we're so focused on achievement, we don't sense the edge. We think excellence is the goal. Only when the tower (of accomplishment, wealth, and recognition) is at or near completion, normally in midlife, do we begin to reflect on our lives from our vanguard position of "success" and ponder, "Is this all there is?" This is when the edge becomes real and imposing.

What's Beyond the Edge?

Danaan Perry, in his "Parable of the Trapeze,"[1] characterizes our lives as a series of trapeze bars that we merrily swing on, imagining that we're in control of our lives. Then we see an empty trapeze bar approaching from the distance, with our name on it—our aliveness coming to claim us. In our heart we know we must release our grasp on the old bar and, for some moment in time, hurtle across space to grab the new bar. And it's terrifying.

We fear falling and being crushed on unseen rocks in the bottomless chasm between the bars. We forget those times in childhood when we took the leap across the void-of-knowing and *made it!* Genius calls us to do it anyway—no net, no insurance policy—because to hang on to the rickety old bar, our comfortable, numb, perfumed way of life, is no longer on the list of alternatives. And so for an eternity that can last a microsecond or a lifetime, we soar across the dark void where the past is gone and the future is not yet here—we are neither who we were nor who we will become. We must transcend our fears and give ourselves permission to *be* in the transition space between the solid bars. It can be the frightening precursor to enlightenment. Hurtling across the void, we may learn how to fly.

At the earlier crux point of success and recognition, the outer world is paying homage to our accomplishments, yet the passion has gradually seeped out of our lives. Many of us have caught the scent of our genius, a grander vision that calls us to forsake our false security, descend from our towers, and reengage life. This scent draws us to live among the common folk, act in a play, rake leaves, paint a mural, till the garden, announce a hockey game, write a book (!), whistle, dance, camp, do something totally different, stay right where we are, confess, forgive, weep—whatever it is, to *do it as a heart-beating, sweat-pouring, lump-in-the-gut adventure that makes us and everyone around us feel alive*. The aroma of genius challenges us to spit out the choking pablum of a nice, comfortable life, with its excuses and rationalizations, and chew on the meat, fat, and gristle of our passion—with no retreat, no reserve, and no regret.

True genius is not new terrain; we've had it all our lives. It's often part of either the mischievous streak that got us in trouble or the grand fantasies we'd play out in our imagination when we were children. To reconnect with it requires in part a return to the innocence of childhood, with the same vulnerabilities and risks of betrayal, but this time seasoned by adult wisdom. Vaulting into our genius requires a reopening to the creativity, spontaneity, artistry, resourcefulness, and compassion that were originally wired into our beings, but were somehow short-circuited back into our shadows, as modeled in Figure 22.2. Genius is revealed by going into the back of the bus, making peace with our shadows, exhuming our buried gift-edness, and rediscovering and blessing all of ourselves. In blessing and baptizing our disowned darkness and gold, in cleansing ourselves of the negative energy buildup that blocks or slows the flow of love and grace through us, we become fully alive again.

Most of us in midlife only get a whiff of our genius, a momentary hint

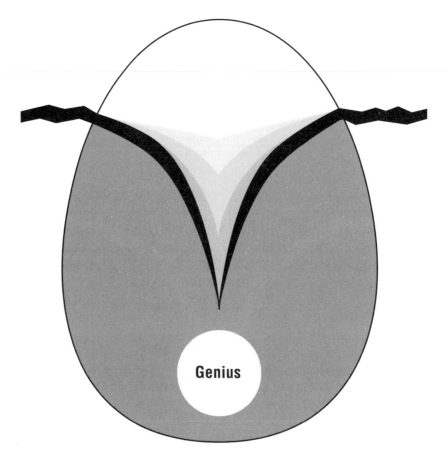

Figure 22.2 **Genius within the Darkness.**

of what our life might be if we abandoned the pursuit of wealth, notoriety, and security, and simply gave our heart and our gifts, in every moment, to whoever crossed our path, without concern for recognition or remuneration. Our aspirations of genius are quashed when we close off the energy inlet, permit sediment buildup in our energy conduit, and turn to the negative sources of energy. All these masking perfumes draw us away from the natural scent of love and service, the raw roots of our greatness.

In college Allen hungered to enter the Peace Corps, where he could leverage his craftsmanship and innovation skills helping poor, yet eager villagers in a third-world setting. But the call to serve was only a small ember, easily snuffed out when his seven-year girlfriend advised him, "Don't expect me to be around when you get back." Naturally shy and insecure around women and fearful of a solitary life, he buried his Peace Corps plans, married her, got his MBA, fathered four children, and made big bucks as an independent programmer/consultant in Silicon Valley.

The marriage and lifestyle were textbook upwardly mobile America with the minivan and the luxury convertible, the lawn service and book club, pool parties and vacations at Lake Tahoe. But the ember never really went out. His latent yearning to serve began to smolder again in his mid-30s, marking the advent of a decade of vocational unfulfillment, recreational drug use, pornography, and the gradual decay of his marriage.

They divorced in his late 40s after the kids left home, and Allen finally started to follow his original dream. He's now learning Spanish and just spent six months in Central America, building more efficient wood-stoves for people in small villages, helping them reduce their fuel waste and the number of infant deaths from smoke inhalation. He's still paying alimony and college tuitions, and his tower-building friends think he has gone nuts. This time he doesn't care what they think. He is rearranging his life to continue as a programming mercenary six months of the year while maintaining a relationship with his adult children. He plans to spend the rest of the year in some kind of third-world service. Twenty-five years after he shoved his genius ember to the back of the bus, he's beginning to honor his inner gifts and his dream.

The downward-pointing arrow in Figure 22.1 emphasizes how security, significance, approval, recognition, and selfishness conspire to keep us at levels of excellence or competence and safe from the possible side effects of accepting our genius: the risks of failure, rejection, obscurity, ostracism, and aloneness. When we've labored for decades in building our tower and have finally become "somebody," our ego tells us, "You've worked hard. You've earned this. You deserve the good things that are coming to you." A weak or narcissistic ego is going to rebel against moving from being the main attraction at the level of excellence to possibly becoming a sideshow novelty in genius.

As described in Part II, many midlife leaders attack their disillusionment with increased diligence, focus, and commitment. They try to leverage their intellect and *think* their way through the confusion to a new life purpose. The thought process goes something like, "I've grown tired of being a real estate entrepreneur (attorney, doctor, minister, professional, etc.). I'm a smart guy; I'll just scan the horizon and find something I love."

Most need a train wreck, or at least a derailment (the proverbial "two-by-four upside the head"), to blast them out of their comfortable deaf, dumb, and dead state. Crises like bankruptcy, getting fired, intensified competition, a crippling lawsuit or divorce, deep depression, or a brush with death force them to reevaluate their commitment to their work and their purpose in life. When the affirmations of the world (success, security, celebrity) evaporate in crisis, they become more open to a radical shift in occupation. Sadly, without such a crisis, most control-oriented leaders focus on figuring out their problems and never open and explore the dark cave in their heart that holds the jewels of their greatness. Instead, they stay in the womb of security, choosing comfort and independence over fulfillment. And that's when they die.

Greatness and genius require us to take a stand—to say, "This is what I believe. Succeed or fail, I will see this through." Genius demands unswerving commitment and a knowledge of "who I am." We can't stand for something honestly and effectively without knowing who we are—but we can't know our full identity, in all our brokenness and all our glory, until we go into our shadows and receive everything that's present.

The Western world equates genius with exceptional talents or high intelligence. We should instead view genius as the personal imprint we put on the flow of energy through us and out to the world. As such, genius is our unique expression of Spirit to the world, often unconsciously, not even being aware that we're doing it. Anthony deMello says, in his book *Awareness*, "You mean I helped you? I was enjoying myself. I was just doing my dance. It helped you, that's wonderful. Congratulations to you. No credit to me."[2]

The key ingredients for unearthing genius are an open energy inlet for receiving the grace of God; disciplines and a support community to keep our lives clean and flowing; a self-love grounded in surrender to and dependence on God; the flow of grace through us and out to others; and an openness to whatever arises in every moment. The seeds of genius germinate during times of solitude, are watered and nurtured by supportive guides and community, and blossom in service. Solitude, community, and service also help us stay above the jagged line of fear shown in Figure 22.1.

Service

Our Sovereign advisor continually poses the great rhetorical question, "What is your kingdom for?" The answer always has its roots in service, where every aspect of our life is a form of giving—not out of martyrdom, guilt, or the need for recognition, but from the natural flow of grace and energy through us, a torrent of blessing that fills others and urges us to risk emptying ourselves to the dregs in the giving of our gift. After building our towers during the first half of life, the movement into genius mandates a transition from self-aggrandizement and accomplishment into a give-back role of service. Albert Schweitzer said that service is the highest activity to which we can aspire: "I do not know what path in life you will take, but I do know this: If, on that path, you do not find a way to serve, you will never be happy."

Secure in our own self-worth, we can serve wherever we are placed, in every moment putting our whole self into our efforts without whining or second-guessing. We do our best with or without inspiration, with or without praise or recognition, in the day-in, day-out toil of living—cleaning the toilet, finishing the budget, staying with a friend's sick child, seeing an unscheduled patient, listening to the stories of the elderly—over and over, for as long as it takes. Joyous service celebrates our aliveness in the midst of the toil and allows love to flow through us, whatever we are doing. Victims and martyrs can be in identical situations and feel used, abused, or unappreciated, since they derive their identity and self-love from the reactions of others. I spent four weeks in and out of a hospice the year my father died. The full-time staff, most of whom work for a fraction of what they could earn in for-profit settings, exuded a serenity and loving loyalty that reflected their inner worth and flowed out as selfless giving to terminally ill residents and their families.

This call to discipline and ordinariness is where many aspiring geniuses falter and slip back into the competence and excellence realms. This is often evident among successful tower builders who make the difficult and noble transition from worldly success to a life of service. They apply the same ardor to their service endeavors that they invested in their tower-building careers. After they become successful and important in their service roles, "statesmen" for the causes of others, many abandon their solitude disciplines, release their tethering support community, bask in the adulation that comes with being known for their service work, and gradually succumb to comparison and measurement. Absent a truth-telling community to hold them accountable, they fall back into the same traps of success they encountered in their careers, as service becomes the new manifestation of their ego and a lip-service act of love. They have merely traded their old tower of worldly accomplishment for a gaudy cathedral of service.

The great servant leaders are equally at ease with the princes and paupers of the world. They can serve outside their comfort zones, in jails, in poverty and squalor, in environments where they are derided or even hated. They can operate behind the scenes with equanimity, content to serve anonymously, without fanfare or recognition. They focus on the needs of the present, whoever crosses their path, unconcerned about immediate rewards, much less a legacy. They don't need to have buildings named after them or be in the philanthropists' hall of fame.

People through whom life freely flows serve and love others as naturally as they breathe. Service becomes more a mind-set than a measurable act, performed as a dance of joy, not an obligation or responsibility. Once we have embraced the flow of energy into our beings, endured the often agonizing work of purging the toxins and coagulants from our souls, and finally built our lives on solitude, community, compassion, and a commitment to whole-person health, our entire life becomes an unconscious act of service. We are constantly giving, yet never victimized, never empty.

Taking the Leap

When the trapeze bar of our genius appears in the mist, the chasm between our current life and our calling can be terrifyingly wide. If we've invested ourselves heavily in one direction, building a sizable tower, the chains of control, notoriety, comfort, leisure, and affluence bind us and warn us, "You can't. You'll look foolish. You'll fail. Look at all you'll give up. Everyone will desert you. You'll be alone. Stay where you are."

Perhaps you're starting to feel inspired to quit your day job, sell your possessions, and move to a life of service—and that may indeed be your destiny. First, try some low-cost probes.[3] Experiment with a couple of mini-versions of the new trapeze bar while you are still holding your current bar. Have a courtship with your calling, rather than a shotgun wedding. For example, invest a few weeks next summer as a volunteer at a nearby camp. If it doesn't work, you've allowed yourself an honorable exit.

Concurrently, refer to Chapter 20 and scan your energy conduit—the inlet, the sides of the pipe, and the outlet—for clogged flow or sediment buildup. Is this really an escape from other problems you don't want to deal with? With whom do you need to make peace—perhaps starting with yourself? Where do you need to get clean, to make amends, to forgive? What other shadows need to be illuminated and transformed into allies? How secure are you in your own self-worth? How receptive are you to a Source of Love beyond yourself?

Are you contemplating this leap into a life of service out of surrender to a higher calling—or for the ego-bathing recognition and significance that often come from "giving back"? If you're not sure, try this test: Suppose no person ever acknowledged you in your new work. Suppose you never knew if your work actually helped another person (at least in your lifetime). Would you still make the leap?

Genius realization does not mandate a replanting. Consider overhauling the approach you are taking in your current vocation. Look for ways to apply your giftedness and passion right where you are—in your vocation, marriage, relationships, place of worship, and community.

Brad had served for 12 years under the tyrannical reign of his father in their struggling family business. His gifts lay in championing collaborative management, extensive training programs, and high-payoff incentive systems for employees. By contrast, his father ran the company with an iron fist and treated employees as ungrateful mercenaries, offering neither training nor incentives. The company was slowly dying through both customer and employee attrition, and Brad was prepared to jump ship and start his own company. In an emotional summit meeting with his father, he painted his view of the company and volunteered to lead a total overhaul of their approach to business. He knew this remake could take up to 10 years and he would miss the entrepreneurial window that beckoned him. But he knew he could make a difference "at home" as well. His father grudgingly agreed—and the business now thrives under Brad's leadership.

If you are still convinced that it is your time to leap from your tower and launch a new adventure into your genius, do so cleanly. Close off open endeavors or relationships that will not swing with you to the new trapeze. While you are not responsible for the happiness of others, you are responsible to clean up your own messes. As discussed in Chapter 21, if a relationship must end, do so honorably, with the integrity of the Sovereign, the compassion of the Lover, the thoughtfulness of the Magician, and the truth of the Warrior. If you find yourself making excuses or rationalizations, or be-coming angry or blaming, you're probably neither clean about nor ready for the transition.

Lastly, before you embark on changing the world, consider this re-minder to start by changing yourself:

Change the World by Changing Me

"I was a revolutionary when I was young and all my prayer to God was, 'Lord, give me the energy to change the world.'

"As I approached middle age and realized that half my life was gone without my changing a single soul, I changed my prayer to, 'Lord, give me the grace to change all those who come in contact with me. Just my family and friends [people in my company/people in my ministry] and I shall be satisfied.'

"Now that I am an old man and my days are numbered, my one prayer is, 'Lord, give me the grace to change myself.' If I had prayed for this right from the start I should not have wasted my life."

—Anthony deMello[4]

Risks of Living in Our Genius

True genius means being loyal to our calling—not being big or doing big things, not acquiring compliments, though all of these may come. Genius involves long stretches of ordinariness and requires us to find joy in pa-tience, simplicity, labor, and powerlessness. It demands commitment to the needs of the moment, no matter how great the pressure or intense the pain, without becoming cynical, bitter, indifferent, or lazy. Many times our efforts will seem meaningless or futile, but we must persevere. We must stay in the fire.

Ironically, the same skills, determination, and commitment used in our early tower-building years can serve us equally well as we manifest our genius. The difference now is that it's not for the goal of creating a tower, but simply living all that we are in the present moment, with no promise of visible success.

Genius comes with a price. We must be willing to risk it all and lose it all, accepting failure as simply part of the journey and, like the train wrecks and derailments, often a gift in disguise. In retrospect, the crisis in my company and my subsequent depression were vital for me to wake up and do my soul work. Being open to ordinariness and failure defies the common sense of our culture and requires us to rely on a spiritual sense of trust. It demands that we constantly strengthen, through the amplifier disciplines and enriching community, our conscience and intuition "muscles."

Living in our genius, guided by our mature advisors, mandates direct exposure to the negative realities of the world—the squalor, poverty, betrayals, rage, rape, atrocities, the desperate cries for help of a ravaged world. No more denial, diversions, or escapes. The truth becomes crystal clear, both the noble and the evil. We can no longer hide behind affluence and politeness. We become aware of the wonder, but also the suffering. To experience ecstasy we must equally embrace agony. To be pure we must confess sin and become a contemplative-activist. Life in the world becomes a furnace, and we must either endure the flames or retreat to the mediocrity of the tepid sidelines.

Genius is symbiotic with integrity—being whole in oneself with uncompromised values. Integrity is simply doing the right thing at the right time, regardless of the personal consequences. When we begin to make an impact on others by living our values and following our calling, we will inevitably face agitation, ostracism, and, potentially, persecution from an envious or indicted world. When we march to the drum of integrity, others will try to disrupt our cadence or silence our rhythm. Our Warrior truth—also part of the gold buried in our shadows—must be spoken, and will likely create enemies. To withhold our truth so that we'll be liked draws us back into the victim, pleaser role, so common at the levels of competence and excellence described earlier.

Roger, a modest yet brilliant engineer who loved to tinker in the lab, helped cofound a technology company. Within four years the company had grown to $20 million in sales, and Roger, as VP of engineering, managed a 40-person research and development team. And he hated it. Constantly in meetings, overrun with paperwork and personnel headaches, and asked to chair the strategic planning process, he had abdicated his real passion, product development, to his subordinates. He had tasted his genius and he wanted it back. So he resigned from the board, worked with the CEO to hire a new VP of engineering, and demoted himself to the lab—returning to his genius.

Fran had worked in the contracts office of her private company for 10 years and excelled in her work as liaison between customers and the sales staff. She prided herself on the accuracy and completeness of her work. When the end-of-quarter sales figures—upon which executive bonuses were calculated—were posted, she noticed major discrepancies between completed orders she had logged and those claimed by the sales VP. When she approached him about the discrepancy, he told her not to worry—"Everything is fine." When she persisted, he told her bluntly to let it go.

Fran knew the situation was not right, and went to the company president with her version of the situation. He listened patiently and told her he would get back to her. Within a month she received a termination notice with minimal severance. The executives had concocted an airtight alibi and "for cause" termination based on alleged insubordination and incompetence.

Fran could have initiated a lengthy lawsuit and carried a vendetta against the company and the executives. Instead, she let it go. She recognized the greed and dysfunction of the company, and felt blessed to be gone. She even forgave the executive team. Within three months she had joined a reputable manufacturing firm in a similar position and again felt fulfillment in her work.

As mature Magician-Lovers we must be able to "hold" the agitation of the world without being sucked into a vortex of fear. When we live in our genius, in the best case the world will see us as odd; in the worst case, as menacing or threatening. We will certainly be seen as different, and subject to derision or exile. The clamor of comparison and competition can overwhelm us, and we will be tempted to return to our old ways. Anthony deMello summarizes this danger in the following parable:

The Narrow Path

God warned the people of an earthquake that would swallow all the waters of the land. The waters that would take their place would make everyone insane.

Only the prophet took God seriously. He carried huge jugs of water to his mountain cave so that he had enough to last him till the day he died.

Sure enough, the earthquake came and the waters vanished and new water filled the streams and lakes and rivers and ponds. A few months later the prophet came down to see what had happened. Everyone had indeed gone mad, and attacked him, for they thought it was *he* who was insane.

So the prophet went back to his mountain cave, glad for the water he had saved. But as time went by he found his loneliness unbearable. He yearned for human company, so he went down to the plains again. Again he was rejected by the people, for he was so unlike them.

The prophet then succumbed. He threw away the water he had saved, drank the new water, and joined the people in their insanity.

The way to truth is narrow. You always walk alone.[5]

Alive and in Love

Check in with your mature Lover advisor for the rest of this chapter. Bring this energy of reflection, contemplation, and connection on line. If you are weak in Lover energy and struggle with abstractions and spirituality, then at least open yourself to the possibility of a Power beyond yourself, and a grand plan or vast context that is beyond our thinking, but nevertheless lovingly guides the unfolding of every event and every relationship—when not resisted or redirected by the self-serving ego.

A fundamental tenet of this book is the existence and availability of a spiritual Source of Love that is beyond us, around us, and in us—an energy that is vast and ubiquitous, yet simple and foundational; incomprehensible, and yet totally real.

The mystics of the Western world and many Eastern traditions accept this notion of a love Source and surrender to it. In so doing they begin to recognize and receive the fruits of the Source, manifested as peace, serenity, contentment, awareness, and truth. With these comes an acceptance that ultimately all is well, that we can relax into the Oneness of All.

In this book, I have referred to this Source as "God" or "Higher Power." If either of those terms trigger a reaction in you, plug in a word or phrase of your choosing (e.g., "Nature," "Energy," "the Universe"). Acceptance of the name is less relevant than openness to the concept.

As you reflect on the suite of advisors and shadows that both guide and sabotage your life, consider that all run on the sourcing fuel of love. The soul transformation process starts with an openness to the flow of grace from this ultimate Power, which says, in essence, "I see you and I love you just the way you are." The grace of this promise gives us *permission* to love ourselves. The second commandment that Jesus referred to was not to love others *instead* of ourselves, but to love them *as* ourselves. Before we can love and serve others, we must love ourselves, even in our imperfection. If we don't embrace our own defects, we can't love others with their shortcomings.

Grace is the word I use for the energy of truth and love that emanates from this Source. In some traditions this is called the unmerited favor of God. As shown in Chapters 19 and 20, if we are open to this energy, it flows into us, through us, and out to others. If this grace chose to speak, it might say, "I am with you, just as you are." I contend that at our deepest, most transparent level these are the words we most long to hear. They are the ultimate antidote to unworthiness.

As you consider the models and proposed action steps presented in this book, set aside your notions and judgments, and open yourself to the Source of the emanating grace. Consider that to be fully alive and living out of our genius on earth we need to receive the flow of this grace and truth over us, in us, and through us—all of us.

The acceptance of spiritual Love pouring into us from an infinite Source, coupled with our own self-love, yields a potent combination of illuminated aliveness. The Eastern traditions aptly call it awareness or enlightenment. Figure 22.3 models the flow of grace and light through us and out to others when we receive love from above and also love ourselves.

The Weakling Sovereign, Victim Warrior, Dummy Magician, and Stoic Lover all wallow in a sense of unworthiness that stunts aliveness. When we bless these parts, letting them know they are loved and worthy regardless of success, failure, or even future betrayals, they can release their guilt, shame, and fear of rejection, and become mature, grounded advisors.

Similarly, the combination of the perfect Love of God and our imperfect love of self lets us shed the masks of pretense created by our inflated shadows. The Tyrant Sovereign, Savage Warrior, Manipulator Magician, and Addict Lover can relax their need to control, to win, to be happy—and can simply trust. They come to realize that real power is not about them, that joy transcends the temporal pursuit of pleasure, and that while striving for success is honorable, achievement of success is irrelevant. The metric for life shifts to the rhetorical question, "Have I loved?"

The combination of these two loves creates a secure sense that the parachute of grace will protect us from above and the net of self-love will protect us within. This safety gives us the confidence and humility to step into our calling, our genius, to dare to be great, with no worldly assurances, only the promise that regardless of the outcome, "You are loved."

The more we allow ourselves to be bracketed by these two loves, the more we become aware of the presence of the Source in others. We marvel that we are all simultaneously broken and imperfect, yet whole and perfect. Whatever we see in another person, good and bad, is invariably true about us. With this realization comes the acceptance and for-

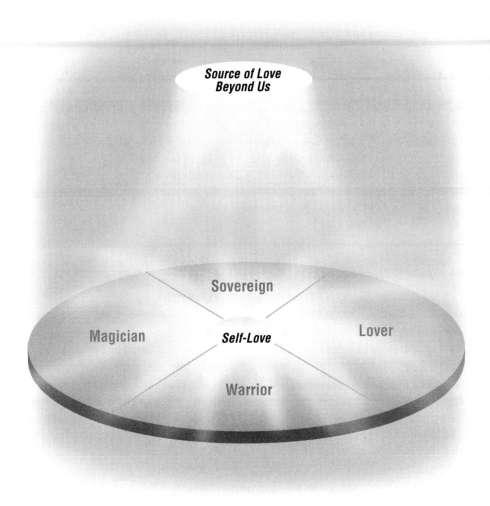

Figure 22.3 **Love from Beyond Us and Within Us.**

giveness of others, mirrored back to us as deeper acceptance and forgiveness of ourselves.

Without the combination of grace and self-love we are prone to wallow in guilt and unworthiness, and the deflated shadows run our lives. With
self-love, but without grace, we come to believe that our own love is sufficient, that we have an adequate internal source of light that illuminates our
path. Without yielding to a Source beyond ourselves, we can easily lapse

into control, narcissism, and arrogance, as we attempt to direct our own lives independently of others or of the divine.

Love gets us started on our journey to greatness. Love is not given to us to help solve our problems but, rather, leads us into our problems—including our shadows. When we love and receive love, we are led into the pain and joy inside ourselves and experience the anguish and wonder of the world. If we allow ourselves to fall in love with our Source, it leads us to a final, universal, grounding love that we can trust because we recognize that we're not the ones in charge, anyway. As a result, we don't have to take ourselves so seriously. This is why we can laugh like the holy fool and we don't have to secure ourselves, because we are already radically secured—we are beloved beings in a benevolent universe.

The Gold of Genius
and Surrender: Aliveness

By yielding to infinite, unconditional love from a Source beyond us and allowing the flow of self-love from within, we live in communion with God and our fellowman, experiencing deep personal awareness and a transcendent peace. No shadows can hide from this radiant awareness. Our lives have purpose and meaning in *every* moment, including the moments of ordinariness, drudgery, grief, and pain. We know that we can live in reality and never again be lonely. The hallmarks of our lives are the discipline of the Warrior, the wisdom of the Magician, the love of the Lover, and the gratitude of the Sovereign. Our genius flows out to others in the form of service. We begin to see life not as a problem to be solved or a question to be answered, but a mystery to be contemplated and savored. Even times of anguish, anger, betrayal, and misery are part of the human and divine tapestry, designed in ways we cannot comprehend to bring us into deeper communion with God.

As aware people, we find ourselves at home in a transcendent, paradoxical realm—in the world, but not imprisoned by the world. Because we are grounded in our Source, the world becomes our amphitheater, the stage where we dance out the passion and pathos of our lives, trusting God's loving choreography. As vestiges of fear, anger, grief, and unworthiness resurface, we welcome them onto the stage, face them, express them, receive their gift for us, and release them. In this way we are continually cleansing ourselves for the receipt of grace and the experience of joy.

Over time, as our fear diminishes (because we constantly keep it in front of us and bless it, there is no longer anything to fear), we experience less and less anger (fewer things can wound us). At the same time, we accept and experience more grief about the pain in the world—and more joy about the wonder of the world and relationships. The spiral continues upward and outward, as greater surrender begets greater aliveness.

The Protagonists—An Epilogue

In Part I the protagonists pondered their disillusionment and prepared for a journey into their souls. Through the ensuing chapters each pilgrim did some soul-level exploration and some took major transitional steps. Here's where they are today.

Thad eventually completed the insurance turnaround and left to join the executive team of a well-funded regional firm growing by acquisitions. Thad's job was business development: finding the candidate acquisitions, wooing the owners, negotiating the sale, and integrating the new firm into the regional fold. While not in the "king" role his father had predestined for him, he was part of the "royal court" of his new company, an integral advisor on vision and strategy, and a sage counselor to frightened—and greedy—owners who were about to be subsumed by Thad's larger firm. It was an ideal combination of Thad-the-Thinker and Thad-the-Catalyst/Inspirer.

Thad realized that the entrepreneurial home run he had missed was really his father's dream seeking fulfillment vicariously through him. His own genius lay in his Magician skills, both for coaching and convincing small company presidents to join his firm, and in advising the CEO of his own company, who relied heavily on Thad's business savvy. When he could let go of his egoistic ambitions, he found his true love—being an advisor, confidant, and mentor.

He and Rachael adopted an infant son, who became Thad's daily reminder of his call to love and be loved. He finally saw himself as a real man.

Stan initiated his second divorce. Due to the settlement and a handful of ill-advised business deals, he hovered near bankruptcy, but somehow emerged with a home and enough cash for a three-year sabbatical. He entered rehab for his sexual addiction and retained an executive coach to help him sort through the shambles of his life. He met and welcomed his shadows—the lust, the sadness, and his long-stuffed anger. In a ritual way he made peace with his father and "got clean" with his mother about the "special boy" label he felt was hung on him as a child.

After two years of sobriety, he met and married a lovely widow. He became an instant parent to her teen daughter, and stepped into his long-lost genius of guiding and mentoring young people. Now he mentors other midlife sojourners, and his family has a simplified lifestyle. He remains in a small group of midlife awareness seekers who watch his selfishness and anger blind spots. He and his new bride embrace a contemplative spiritual renewal, and more and more he is learning the wonder of surrender.

During the getaway weekend with her husband, John, Susan spoke her anger about his reclusion and her crushing responsibilities to provide for the family. She later worked through this anger and came to a place of reconciliation with her in-laws, as described in Chapter 20. She also listened to John's anger, which he had been terrified to express, about the way his family had treated both Susan and him. He had felt helpless to do anything, and her berating had driven him further away. It was truthful, painful, mutual confession—something they had needed for five years. They emerged with the resolve of loving each other during what would be a hellacious upcoming two years. She recommitted to her practice and attended workshops to explore and transform her anger. The breakthrough was a commitment to open communication with John, and the realization that she could no longer be superwoman. She still has no local support community, but regularly communicates with other professionals she has met on retreat weekends.

Peter is still in his company, but with a clear exit strategy. By serendipity he was invited to speak at a high school business class on marketing and found that he loved it. He now moonlights giving motivational addresses at local high school assemblies once a month, relishing the opportunity to inspire young people. On the personal side, he attended an intense men's initiation weekend and began to "get clean," for the first time, about the anger he carried toward his father and the deep unworthiness he has felt since childhood. Bathed in the love and support of the other participants, he felt the first, wondrous twinges of self-acceptance.

Fletcher and Lois have become very close and openly express their shadows to one another as they ponder marriage. Through the guidance of his small group and several men's retreat weekends, Fletcher came to grips with his addictions and began to attend Alcoholics Anonymous meetings. Flush with cash after the sale of his company, he still wrestles with the meaning of money in his life, but he's sold the flashy cars and downsized his lifestyle. The old habits are dying hard, but he sees a transitions counselor on a regular basis and is beginning to map his life more toward service than hubris.

Larry is still the soldier of fortune as a senior staff member in the large bureaucracy. But, like Peter, he has found renewed vigor and a hint of his genius by mentoring fatherless high school athletes in "the game of life beyond sports." After considerable personal work he cut off all his extramarital relationships and has been monogamous for 18 months. He and Beth are more in love than ever and have dialed back their lifestyle. He is building a nest egg so he might leave the monolith within the next three years, after his own kids graduate from high school, and devote himself full time to adolescent coaching.

In a make-or-break move, Marty approached the senior pastor and confessed that he was dying in his job as an associate pastor and had to break out on his own—support or no support. To Marty's surprise and delight, the pastor massaged the egos of the elder board and finessed a small grubstake for Marty to launch his own church. By a combination of his magnetic charisma, love for people, and two large anonymous donations, they secured real estate at bargain basement prices, broke ground, and, within two years, had over 1,500 congregants at the new church. Backed by an entrepreneurial support staff, Marty had finally found his vocational genius.

On the personal side, Marty entered his own dark night of the soul. His family life began to unravel as he became the lightning rod for his son's self-destructive behaviors. Both he and Sarah felt divorce would be a relief—the easy, logical exit. But they stayed in the process, and each of them worked on their own issues—the anger, the fear of abandonment, the blaming, their menagerie of shadows. With caring guides and timely interventions, the marriage is healing and his son has his life together. Of vital importance, Sarah is his biggest ally in leading the new church.

Greatness Personified

Steven Jimison caught your eye, smiled and giggled like any other normal infant, despite being diagnosed as "hypotonic," having relatively low vigor and muscle strength. Then, at 14 months, shortly after being weaned, he incurred his first seizure, a wracking convulsion that terrified his parents. Extensive neurological tests finally confirmed lysencephaly, a rare brain disorder that virtually assured that Steven would never be normal, physically or intellectually. Mitzi and John, Steven's parents, grieved deeply, yet resolved to give their son every opportunity to experience a full, loving life. Steven began to take seizure-control medication.

When Steven was three the family moved to Paris, where John had accepted a four-year assignment at an international agency. For unknown reasons, the seizures ceased, and by age seven Steven was potty-trained, riding a tricycle, and speaking bits of English and French. Buoyed by his progress and perpetual smile, his parents entertained hope that he might someday live a supervised but somewhat independent life.

Within two weeks of their return to the United States, Steven suffered his first seizure since they had gone abroad. As they searched for some link between the Parisian lifestyle and the absence of seizures, their hopes were dashed when a battery of medical tests concluded that the absence of seizures in France had been merely "a coincidence." Western medicine failed to pinpoint the cause of his convulsions. The specialists' recommendation: Use stronger medication to control the seizures and extend the boy's life. Though unsatisfied with the verdict and profoundly disheartened, John and Mitzi felt they had no choice but to comply. And the seizures only worsened.

At age 11 Steven lost bowel control and required adult diapers. At 12 he was taking 16 anticonvulsion tablets a day, one of which would put an adult into dreamland for hours. He regressed to being a one-year-old in an adolescent's body and required continual care. When he could function, Steven was always compliant, never complaining, never upset. You could see in his eyes the longing to play with his three brothers, and the realization that he never could. Yet beneath Steven's fuzzy brain and awkward body beat a champion's heart.

Steven developed a trademark mannerism whenever something good happened for someone else. He would witness and celebrate the triumphs of others—that would never be his own—by rocking from side to side, smiling, and clapping his hands. He would also waddle up to his brothers from behind and gently lay his hands on their heads as if blessing them, beaming at them when they turned to look.

Shortly before his twenty-second birthday, Steven suffered a rare type of seizure that occurs in the brain stem and directly affects the heart and breathing. His funeral mass was concelebrated by eight priests and attended by six more, along with six hundred other people whose lives had been touched by this man-child. At the close of the service, one of the priests recalled Steven's trademark hand clapping, particularly after he received communion, and invited the congregation to honor Steven for a difficult life well lived. What followed was a thunderous, joyful ovation that rocked the gates of heaven.

Steven Jimison's life epitomizes greatness. His disabilities had stripped him of the surface vanities—pride, ambition, achievement, prestige—that most of us have and wield in our relationships, and left him solely able to relate to people at the most elemental levels of trust and love. The wonder and greatness of his life are that everyone responded to Steven on a common plane. People recognized his dignity and worth as a human being, entitled to trust and love, regardless of his inability to contribute anything "meaningful" by normal measures. He lived his life under heavy burdens and requirements for care from others, with *no tangible output or benefit to anyone*—yet the world is profoundly a better place because he made all who came in contact with him better people. So, in his vulnerability and dependency, he served others by opening innocent, trusting space for their latent love. There is no more profound or potent legacy a person can leave.

Through the models, stories, and parables in this book, may you choose to meet, greet, bless, and reclaim the parts of yourself that have been rejected over the years. May you have the courage to navigate the emotional gauntlet of your own unexpressed fear, anger, grief, and unworthiness, and find the holy joy in the center. May you find, and be nurtured by, a truth-telling community, men and women with whom you can establish a lifetime covenant of accountability, transparency, and love.

Whether you lean toward an upward and outward spiritual life or downward and inward soul-level enlightenment, I pray that you can interweave these two great journeys into a single wondrous and mystical quest for personal communion with your God and revelation of the gold that lies within you. May you embrace a blend of spiritual and soulful traditions that guide you toward and support you in this place of communion, gratitude, and surrender. Like Thad, Stan, Jean, Brad, Fran, Roger, Steven, and millions of other known and unknown pilgrims "doing their dance," may your genius and greatness flow out to others as compassion, guidance, and service.

Then, in your heart, listen for the ovation in heaven.

RESEARCH
SUMMARY

Two hundred CEOs completed confidential questionnaires about difficult issues in their personal and business lives. Each CEO was asked to prioritize 53 issues, divided into six categories, as High Priority, Mid-Level Priority, Low Priority, or Not Applicable. In Table A.1, the first column shows the different issues, in their respective categories. The second column shows how many of the 200 CEOs consider the issue either a Mid-Level or a High Priority. The third column shows how many consider the issue a High Priority. The fourth column shows the percentage of CEOs who consider the issue to be a Mid-Level or High Priority in their own lives—something they need to address. The fifth column ranks the top 20 issues. The top five issues are shaded.

Table A.1 Research Summary

Category	Mid or High Priority	High Priority	Percent Mid or High Priority	Top 20
Personal				
I Have More Talent Than I Am Now Using	100	39	50.0%	4
No Peace in My Life	84	27	42.0%	6
Life on a Treadmill	83	26	41.5%	8
Don't Know Strengths and Weaknesses	75	24	37.5%	13
Saying "No"	69	12	34.5%	20
Low Self-Confidence	58	15	29.0%	
Physical Health	50	20	25.0%	
Haven't Made Peace with Past	48	11	24.0%	
Not Held Accountable	21	0	10.5%	
Marriage and Family				
No Romance or Sexual Passion	79	31	39.5%	9
Life Revolves around Kids	73	16	36.5%	17
Flat, Listless Marriage	66	27	33.0%	
Spouse in Major Crisis	62	30	31.0%	
Choose Work over Family	56	18	28.0%	
Tension with a Relative in Business	52	33	26.0%	
Not Contributing to Kids	40	6	20.0%	
Child in Crisis	31	5	15.5%	
Parent Aging	31	8	15.5%	
Vocation				
Financial Independence Is Very Important	141	70	70.5%	1
Career Is Identity	79	25	39.5%	9
Fear of Losing Financial Independence	79	34	39.5%	9
How Much Is Enough???	73	21	36.5%	18
Not Realizing Life Goals	68	24	34.0%	
Locked In—Missing Opportunities	62	28	31.0%	
Lonely at the Top	41	12	20.5%	
Hate My Career	30	11	15.0%	

Category	Mid or High Priority	High Priority	Percent Mid or High Priority	Top 20
Life Transition				
I'm Ready for a Change	126	76	63.0%	2
Vague Personal Mission Statement	121	38	60.5%	3
Shallow Life Goals	84	32	42.0%	6
No Idea What to Do with My Life	75	36	37.5%	13
No Life Significance or Fulfillment	62	19	31.0%	
No Career—What's Next???	59	39	29.5%	
Blur of Issues in My Life	56	17	28.0%	
Addicted to . . .	41	12	20.5%	
"I Have It All"—It's Hollow	34	12	17.0%	
Career Great, Rest of Life Uncertain	33	6	16.5%	
Trade Success for Family Relationship	19	6	9.5%	
Don't Seek Others' Advice	8	1	4.0%	
Other Relationships				
Want to Be a Mentor	76	19	38.0%	12
No Mentors in My Life	74	19	37.0%	15
Sensitive to What Others Think	72	19	36.0%	19
Need a Forum	56	17	28.0%	
Always Have to Be "On"	47	10	23.5%	
No Friends to Share My Heart With	35	10	17.5%	
Trample Relationships	31	3	15.5%	
I Feel Terribly Lonely	28	7	14.0%	
No One Is Straight with Me	21	2	10.5%	
Spiritual				
Little Solitude or Reflection Time	92	34	46.0%	5
Like to Know God Better	74	21	37.0%	15
Don't Want to Be "Ordinary"	62	28	31.0%	
Feel "Driven" versus "Called"	57	9	28.5%	
Spirituality: Spouse Different from Me	45	17	22.5%	
Like to Know God	29	10	14.5%	
Afraid of Dying	26	1	13.0%	
Tension: Success versus Integrity	22	1	11.0%	

B

LEADERSHIP SKILLS and SHADOWS ASSESSMENT

The Leadership Skills and Shadows Assessment created by Oncourse International measures a person's abilities and shadows across four primary areas of leadership. Each of these areas is associated with one of the inner advisors.

1. The ability to initiate, support, and create order (Being)—**The Sovereign**.
2. The ability to take action and enforce boundaries (Doing)—**The Warrior**.
3. The ability to assess, analyze, and contain (Thinking)—**The Magician**.
4. The ability to connect and feel (Feeling)—**The Lover**.

The adult self is able to call on these abilities, individually or collectively, in response to situations, opportunities, or crises.

Every person manifests leadership in one or more *realms* of his or her life. Businesspeople live much of their lives within the realm of their businesses. A husband and father, or a wife and mother, both individually and with the spouse, has leadership responsibility for the realm of the family. Other realms include extended family, church or synagogue, neighborhood, organizations of which one is a member, or any circle of friends. Leadership activities within any of these groups are a blend of iniation, action, containment, and connection in service to the realm.

Each advisor is further defined as a blend of three manifestations:

1. The mature manifestation or adult, which we strive for in our lives.
2. A deflated manifestation or shadow (or too little of the mature characteristics).
3. An inflated manifestation or shadow (or too much of the mature characteristics).

The online Assessment consists of 96 statements and typically takes about 10 minutes to complete and have scored. Simply go to the web site www.oncoursein.com and follow the instructions. The Assessment is *free* if you have a copy of this book with you when you take the Assessment. You may be asked to enter information contained within the book as a password.

Example statements in the Assessment include:

> ➤ I plan my life to avoid or smooth over conflict.
> ➤ I communicate the hard facts, even in difficult situations.
> ➤ I am able to motivate, empower, and bless others.
> ➤ I have a hard time delegating authority.

An individual replies to each statement using one of the following answers (1 to 5):

1. Strongly disagree.
2. Disagree.
3. Neither disagree nor agree.
4. Agree.
5. Strongly agree.

The Assessment is scored immediately after a reply has been entered for every statement. A complete set of summary notes is provided online that describes the characteristics of the mature advisor, the deflated shadow, and the inflated shadow for each of the four inner advisors: Sovereign, Warrior, Magician, and Lover.

The web site also includes a third-party assessment, where another person can evaluate you. The summary results of that assessment are e-mailed to you confidentially.

The Assessment is an excellent tool within a family unit, small group, or any leadership team. The statements are gender-neutral, so both men and women can use the self-assessment and third-party assessment.

Appendix

C

CLEAN TALK—A MODEL for DEALING with CONFLICT

Clean Talk allows two individuals to speak honestly about an issue or conflict they have with one another. It also allows each person to express himself about an issue he has within a small group. The following discussion assumes the model is used within a small group. The purpose of the model is not necessarily to achieve resolution, but rather for issues and conflicts to be brought into the open—for the individuals to "get clean." Cliff Barry conceived the model, and we collaborated on this description.

Often, when the first person in a small group has the courage to use Clean Talk to air an issue, the dam will burst and other minor or major issues among members of the group will surface. Once they are cleared using this model, members are "clean" to support each other on deeper personal or vocational issues without being subconsciously sidetracked about unresolved interpersonal conflicts.

Ideally, Clean Talk is conducted with the group members seated in an open circle with no table in the middle. If one member ("X") has an issue with another member ("Z"), X invites Z to join him in the middle of the circle. If X's issue is with the entire small group, he asks one person, Z, to represent the entire group and join him in the center of the circle.

The success of any conflict resolution model hinges on the participants' ability to mirror each other's statements and emotions without becoming detoured by their own innate defense mechanisms. X's job is to present the issue, including his feelings, judgments, and wants. Z's job is to listen attentively and to reflect back to X what X has said.

Participant X presents the issue using the following structure:

1. Stating the facts ("The Facts").
2. Expressing X's feelings about the issue ("The Feelings").
3. Expressing X's judgments about the issues or about Z ("The Judgments").
4. Stating what X wants ("The Wants").

Participants should be encouraged to describe their feelings using emotions—sad, angry (mad, upset, hurt), scared (afraid, anxious), ashamed (guilty, embarrassed), happy (glad, joyous), excited, tender, numb (empty), overwhelmed—rather than using words like "disappointed" or "resentful." Word coaching may be done by a member of the group.

As an example, assume that X lives three hours from the site of small group meetings yet always arrives on time. On the other hand, Z lives 15 minutes from the meeting location and has arrived 5 to 15 minutes late for the past several meetings. Z is normally apologetic when he arrives late, and then makes excuses (e.g., complains about the heavy traffic or the last-minute phone call he *had* to take). X has had enough of Z's excuses and wants to get clean on this issue. X invites Z to the center of the circle.

"Z, I have an issue regarding your lack of punctuality at our small group meetings, and I want to get clean with you about this. [Beginning of the Facts:] Today, you arrived 15 minutes after the designated start time, last month you arrived 30 minutes late, and two months ago you were 20 minutes late. That time you called to say you would be late, but there have been no calls to anyone prior to the last two meetings. You did say you were sorry for being late. I live three hours from the meeting site and have arrived on time for all the meetings." [End of the Facts]

[The Feelings:] "Z, when you arrive late like this, it makes me feel angry. It has been eating at me, and I haven't been a full contributor because of it."

[The Judgments:] "When you arrive late like this it makes me think that you don't care about me or the other members of the small group. It seems you are putting your own priorities ahead of ours. I hear you say you're sorry, but since the problem continues, I don't believe you. I question your commitment to this group."

[The Wants:] "Z, first I wanted to get this off my chest. I also want to hear from you your level of commitment to this group and your commitment to be on time to future meetings."

Most people in Z's position tend to craft their defense strategy while X is still speaking. They may launch into a litany of excuses or retaliate with anger toward X rather than mirroring to X the facts, feelings, judgments, and wants related to the issue. To do this in a clean fashion, Z would respond as follows:

[Mirroring the Facts:] "X, let me see whether I have this straight. First I would like us to get very clear on the facts. I do agree that I was 15 minutes late today and 30 minutes late to the last meeting, but I believe it was only 15 minutes two months ago. So, it looks like, with the one correction, we agree on the facts."

[Mirroring the Feelings, Judgments, and Wants:] "I see that you are angry about this. You believe that I am putting my priorities ahead of the small group and that I am not really committed to the group. You question whether I'm really sincere when I say I'm sorry. You want to get this off your chest. And you want to hear my commitment both to the small group and to be on time for subsequent meetings. Do I have this correct?"

X then has a chance to respond. If Z responded incorrectly, the two continue a dialogue until Z has mirrored back correctly all of X's feelings, judgments, and wants. Notice that Z is simply mirroring back to X. He is neither making excuses nor making a retaliatory attack. It is important that Z reflect accurately X's view of the issue. Z does not have to *agree* with X's view; he must simply reflect it back. After this mirroring, Z gives X a chance to get completely clean using the following statement:

[Is There More?] "X, is there anything else you want to say about this?"

Often, X will discover some other frustration around the issue that needs to be spoken. Sometimes X will have the insight that the particular issue is merely a symptom of a much deeper issue in his own life, unrelated to X. For example, perhaps X's spouse is always late, but he feels awkward confronting her. Or, he may have been late for an event during his youth and then shamed by an authority figure for his tardiness.

Often, after X's issue has been reflected back to him, the tension is dissipated completely. Resolution of the issue may or may not occur at this time. The important thing is that the issue has been surfaced totally and that X believes he has been heard. Z may or may not pledge his commitment both to the small group and to being on time for subsequent meetings. This is often worked out between the two of them outside of the small group meeting.

To review, the general structure of a Clean Talk session is:

- ➤ The two parties discuss the issue in the center of the group.
- ➤ A small group member may offer word coaching to the two members to help them stay within the structure of the Clean Talk model.
- ➤ X states the facts around the issue.
- ➤ X states how he feels about the issue.
- ➤ X states his judgments around the issue.
- ➤ X states what he wants.
- ➤ Z mirrors back the facts and gets agreement with X about these facts. Note that the only thing that X and Z must agree on is the facts.
- ➤ Z mirrors back X's feelings, judgments, and wants related to the issue.
- ➤ X verifies that Z has indeed heard him correctly.
- ➤ Z asks X if there is anything else that X wants to get clean about.
- ➤ The two parties dialogue in this way until X has aired all of his feelings, judgments, and wants and Z has mirrored them back to X's satisfaction.
- ➤ Z may then respond directly to X's wants or set a time when the two of them can seek to resolve the issue. Resolution does not have to occur during the small group meeting. Often, X just wants to be heard about the issue—to get it off of his chest. Venting the issue to Z in front of the group is often all that is wanted.

Table C.1 provides a summary of the model.

When to Use the Clean Talk Model

Use this model when you want to be in relationship with another person. Typically, a member of a small group wants to be in relationship (i.e., share parts of his or her life at a deeper, more vulnerable level) with the other small group members. Similarly, an individual typically wants to be in a deeper relationship with his spouse, children, extended family, and, sometimes, with his business associates or partners. We are typically *not* in ongoing relationships with a store clerk, taxi driver, flight attendant, waiter, vendor to our business, and others with whom we have infrequent, business, or non–personal-sharing encounters.

Table C.1   The Clean Talk Model

➤ The specific facts are . . .
➤ My judgment is . . .
(I think . . .)
(In my opinion . . .)
➤ This makes me feel . . .
➤ And I specifically want . . .
➤ Mirror back:
(Let me see if I understand you . . .)
➤ Is there more?
➤ Are you clean about this?

The model is *not* specifically intended for issue *resolution*, although that may result. Its primary use in a small group setting is so that a member can *fully participate* in the small group meeting or retreat without being distracted by an unspoken issue between the member and either another member or the entire small group.

The model is used when the member *cannot be fully present* (mentally, emotionally, relationally) in the meeting unless the issue is "cleared" with the member or the group. *Not being fully present* means carrying an anger, anxiety, embarrassment, or other emotion that blocks the person either from fully engaging with the meeting events, exercises, and discussions or from openly and fully listening to the presentations of one or more of the small group members.

For additional information on the Clean Talk model visit the web site www.oncoursein.com.

Appendix

D

OnCourse International—
RETREATS and COACHING

OnCourse International is dedicated to helping individuals and small groups develop self-awareness, more fulfilling relationships, and a deeper engagement with life. The company conducts trainings and retreats for:

> ➤ Existing small groups.
> ➤ Individuals and couples who wish to work in a group setting.

OnCourse is the umbrella organization for Jim Warner, who works either alone or with other independent counselors and retreat facilitators on various assignments. Jim is also often called on for speaking engagements.

Small Group Retreats

FOR EXISTING GROUPS

OnCourse facilitators lead multiday retreats for YPO (Young Presidents' Organization) forums, WPO (World Presidents' Organization) forums, church men's groups, and other small groups who seek to build a safe, intimate community where members can share the deep issues in their lives. At these retreats the OnCourse facilitator also acts as a mediator to help the group address and resolve conflict or dysfunction.

FOR INDIVIDUALS AND COUPLES

OnCourse sponsors group trainings open to individuals and couples. Most participants are in midlife and have a professional career (e.g., executive, attorney, physician, pastor). While similar in structure to YPO and other small group retreats, these trainings focus more on self-awareness issues and a second-half game plan, and less on community building.

At least two OnCourse facilitators colead each retreat. Prior to the retreat each participant completes a set of materials that gives the facilitators a feel for personal and group issues. Each member then has a confidential telephone interview with a facilitator. The preretreat work and the interviews help the facilitators develop a customized agenda for the retreat. This agenda is flexible and often changes after the retreat begins, based on the flow of discussions and experiences, and on participant needs.

OnCourse retreats help evoke greater self-awareness in participants and often lead to transformative change in their lives. Discussions and experiences are developed around "heart-level" topics such as members':

> ➤ Identity (both personal and professional).
> ➤ Blind spots and "shadows."
> ➤ Marriages.
> ➤ Sexuality.
> ➤ Passions and emotions including fear, anger, sadness, shame, and joy.
> ➤ Spirituality.
> ➤ Peace, contentment, significance, and fulfillment.
> ➤ Life transitions.
> ➤ Parenthood.
> ➤ Family relationships.
> ➤ Friendships and relationships with others.
> ➤ Personal mission statement and sense of destiny.

These retreats are typically three or four days in length and are held at a retreat center, private residence, or conference hotel that offers privacy for the group and access to nature (trails, streams, lakes, woods, beach, desert, mountains). A 12-month schedule of retreats is posted on the On-Course web site, www.oncoursein.com.

LifeCourse Plan

LifeCourse is a customized two- or three-day mini-retreat in which an OnCourse facilitator meets with one to four individuals or couples, helping participants develop a game plan for directing their lives toward greater fulfillment, meaning, passion, and joy. Before looking upward and outward (i.e., "What's next?"), participants look downward and inward—examining the pivotal experiences and periods of their lives that have shaped who they are and how they approach opportunities and problems.

Participants then develop a "situation analysis" of their lives—where they are today, what they would like their lives to look like, and what is blocking them from getting there. Each participant crafts his or her own personal transition blueprint—a set of specific, measurable resolution statements and action plans for resolving outstanding issues. Along with the transition blueprint, participants leave the LifeCourse mini-retreat with a "Where I Use My Giftedness" template, which can be applied against future opportunities or vocational options.

Information on LifeCourse retreats may be obtained by calling (303) 449-7770 or sending an e-mail request to jrw@oncoursein.com.

The Foundation of This Work

OnCourse retreats and trainings assume that participants are open to deeper personal awareness and yearn for increased meaning and significance in their lives. Whether in retreats or LifeCourse planning, participants seek greater intimacy and friendship—a sense of community—with other men and women. As part of both self-discovery and community building, participants are open to exploring their spiritual lives and to seeking a sense of peace, destiny, and surrender, grounded in knowing and experiencing God. People from many religious traditions, as well as those with no beliefs, have found the spiritual dimension of OnCourse programs to be both eye-opening and transformative.

Client Engagements

Most engagements, whether a small group retreat or a LifeCourse plan, begin with a telephone call to Jim Warner to discuss the group's or client's specific needs. Often there is *not* a fit, such as when a small group is seeking a facilitator for business-level discussions to supplement what is primarily a social or recreational retreat, or when an individual is simply looking for guidance in a job search.

Both small group retreats and LifeCourse sessions are attended by committed participants who devote themselves to the processes, experiences, and celebrations custom-developed by the facilitators for the specific event.

NOTES

INTRODUCTION

1. Richard Rohr, *Quest for the Grail* (New York: Crossroad Publishing, 1994).

Chapter 9 COMMITMENT, FOCUS, SUCCESS

1. Richard Rohr, *Quest for the Grail* (New York: Crossroad Publishing, 1994).
2. Ibid.
3. Stephen R. Covey, *Principle-Centered Leadership: Teaching People How to Fish* (Provo, UT: Institute for Principle-Centered Leadership, 1990) and *The Seven Habits of Highly Effective People* (New York: Simon & Schuster, 1989).

Chapter 10 DISILLUSIONMENT and BREAKDOWNS

1. Henri Nouwen, *Out of Solitude* (Notre Dame, IN: Ave Maria Press, 1974).
2. David Deida, *The Way of the Superior Man: Women, Work and Sexual Desire* (Austin, TX: Plexus, 1997). A journey into the heart of the contemporary masculine experience, offering a revolutionary look at what it means to be a man in today's world.
3. Paul Simon, "Slip-Sliding Away," from the album *Negotiations and Love Songs* (Warner Bros., 1988).

Chapter 12 The EDGE, NUMBNESS, and BREAKTHROUGHS

1. Joseph Campbell, *Hero with a Thousand Faces* (Princeton, NJ: Princeton University Press, 1972).
2. *Alcoholics Anonymous* (Hazelden Information Press, 1986) and *Twelve Steps and Twelve Traditions/B-2* (1996). Also see J. Keith Miller, *Compelled to Control* (Deerfield Beach, FL: Health Communications, 1992). This book identifies the major cause of relationship failure as the need to control.

Chapter 13 UNDERSTANDING the SOUL—INTRODUCTION

1. Henri Nouwen, *Out of Solitude* (Notre Dame, IN: Ave Maria Press, 1974).
2. Romans 7:15, in the *NIV Study Bible* (Grand Rapids, MI: Zondervan, 1985).
3. Bob Sloan, president of Executive Expeditions, Worldwide, is a psychologist, facilitator, and executive coach living in the Chicago area. Bob may be reached at (847) 452-8661 or exeww@aol.com.
4. Jim Dethmer is an executive coach who lives in the Chicago area. He may be reached at (630) 858-6612 or jimdethmer@khanquest.com.
5. Richard Rohr, *Quest for the Grail* (New York: Crossroad Publishing, 1994).
6. "Love cleanly and joyfully . . . love painfully" comes from Cliff Barry's workshops on understanding our shadows.

Chapter 14 Our INNER ADVISORS

1. For a comprehensive statement of Carl Jung's psychological theories, see Ira Progaff, *Jung's Psychology and Its Social Meaning* (New York: Dialogue House Library, 1981).
2. Robert Moore and Douglas Gillette, *King, Warrior, Magician, Lover: Rediscovering the Archetypes of the Mature Masculine* (San Francisco: Harper-Collins, 1990). Moore and Gillette provide a Jungian introduction to the four archetypes. Also see Robert Bly, *Iron John* (New York: Random House [Vintage Books], 1992), Bly's poetic, practical, and groundbreaking work on being a man; and Richard Rohr and Joseph Martos, *The Wild Man's Journey: Reflections on Male Spirituality* (Cincinnati, OH: Saint Anthony Messenger Press, 1991).
3. Shadow Work Seminars® were created by Cliff Barry and Mary Ellen Blandford, who help individuals harness the power of their shadows through seminars, facilitator trainings, and individual coaching sessions. They may be reached at (970) 203-0400; e-mail shadowwk@frii.com; or via their web site, www.shadowwork.com.

Chapter 16 The WARRIOR

1. William J. Bennett, editor, *The Book of Virtues: A Treasury of Great Moral Stories* (New York: Simon & Schuster, 1993).
2. Matthew 5:37, in the *NIV Study Bible* (Grand Rapids, MI: Zondervan, 1985).
3. Oriah Mountain Dreamer, *The Invitation* (San Francisco: Harper Audio, 2001).
4. Anthony deMello, *The Song of the Bird* (New York: Doubleday [Image Books], 1984). Used by permission of Doubleday, a division of Random House, Inc. Anthony deMello has been acclaimed as one of the most important inspirational and contemplative writers of our time. His books offer stories and parables from a variety of traditions, both ancient and modern. The reader is also referred to deMello's *Awareness* (New York: Doubleday [Image Books], 1992).

Chapter 17 The MAGICIAN

1. "If." Rudyard Kipling, *Rudyard Kipling: Selected Poems* (UK: Penguin Books, 1999). Also at www.poetryloverspage.com/poets/kipling/kipling_ind.html.
2. "World-class facilitators" Barry and Blandford have been mentioned earlier. Dan Webster is president of Authentic Leadership, Inc., which trains and inspires leaders to live authentic lives of great impact. More information is provided on the web site www.authenticleadershipinc.com. Information on the other retreat leaders is provided on the web site www.oncoursein.com. All these retreat leaders, executive coaches, and facilitators are highly skilled at helping individuals and small groups develop greater trust and explore their shadows.
3. Cliff Barry and Mary Ellen Blandford conceived the unique concept of the Risk Manager and teach about it at their regular retreats and trainings.

Chapter 18 The LOVER

1. Susan Howatch, *Glittering Images* (New York: Crest, 1996). A gripping novel of spirituality and morality, interweaving God, sex, love, shadows, forgiveness, and soul-level guidance.
2. Mark Gerzon, *Listening to Midlife: Turning Your Crisis into a Quest* (Boston: Shambhala, 1996).
3. Gail Sheehy, *Passages* (New York: Bantam Books, 1984); *New Passages: Mapping Your Life Across Time* (New York: Random House, 1995); and *Understanding Men's Passages: Discovering the New Map of Men's Lives* (New York: Ballantine, 1999).

Chapter 19 ENERGY

1. See Chapter 14, note 3, for information on Bob Sloan.
2. M. Scott Peck, *The Different Drum: Community Making and Peace* (New York: Simon & Schuster, 1987).

Chapter 20 TRANSFORMATION

1. Richard Rohr, *Radical Grace* (Cincinnati, OH: Saint Anthony Messenger Press, 1995).
2. "Forgive seventy times seven times" is a paraphrase of Matthew 18:22 from the *NIV Study Bible.* "Forgive them, Father, for they don't know what they're doing" is found in Luke 23:34 in the same Bible.
3. The following books are excellent guides to the disciplines of prayer and meditation. Thomas Merton's *New Seeds of Contemplation* (New York: New Directions, 1972) is a contemplation classic that reawakens the dormant inner depths of the spirit so long neglected by Western man. Daniel Goleman's *The Meditative Mind* (Los Angeles: Jeremy P. Tarcher, Inc., 1988) gives an excellent overview of the states of meditation and how they relate. Goleman is also the author of *Emotional Intelligence* (New York: Bantam Books, 1995). Jack Kornfield, one of the great American Buddhist teachers, explains Buddhist psychology and meditation practice in *A Path with Heart* (New York: Bantam Books, 1993). Nobel Peace Prize winner and Vietnamese monk Thich Nhat Hanh offers simple practices for daily awakening in *The Miracle of Mindfulness* (Boston: Beacon Press, 1975). Oswald Chambers' *My Utmost for His Highest* (Uhrichsville, OH: Barbour Publishing, 1992) is a classic daily devotional with 366 entries. Thomas Keating's *Open Mind, Open Heart: The Contemplative Dimension of the Gospel* (London: HarperCollins, 1994) offers an excellent introduction to Christian meditation. Anthony deMello's *Wellsprings* (New York: Doubleday [Image Books], 1984) is a collection of teachings and spiritual exercises that blend the ancient traditions of the East with the psychological and philosophical perspectives of the West.
4. John Heider, *The Tao of Leadership* (New York: Bantam, 1996).
5. Dallas Willard, *The Spirit of the Disciplines: Understanding How God Changes Lives* (New York: HarperCollins, 1988), and Richard J. Foster, *Celebration of Discipline: The Path to Spiritual Growth* (New York: HarperCollins, 1978). These two books offer guidance in all the disciplines mentioned in this book. Also see Thomas Moore, *The Care of the Soul: A Guide for Cultivating Depth and Sacredness in Everyday Life* (New York: HarperCollins, 1992), and Caroline Myss, *Anatomy of the Spirit* (New York: Three Rivers Press, 1996).
6. Larry Crabb, *Effective Biblical Counseling* (Grand Rapids, MI: Zondervan, 1977).

7. Soul exploration retreats and trainings include the Mankind Project's *New Warrior Training* (www.mkp.org); the Men's Council Project's *Leadership Training* (e-mail menscouncil@aol.com); The Hoffman Institute's *Quadrinity Process* (www.hoffmaninstitute.com); Upper Room Ministries' *Emmaus Walks* (www.upperroom.org); and OnCourse International's *LifeCourse Transition* and *Fully Alive!* retreats (www.oncoursein.com or see Appendix D).

8. M. Scott Peck, *The Different Drum: Community Making and Peace* (New York: Simon & Schuster, 1987). Also see his classic books on spiritual growth: *The Road Less Traveled* and *Further Along the Road Less Traveled.*

9. Henri Nouwen, *Out of Solitude* (Notre Dame, IN: Ave Maria Press, 1974).

10. "The Prodigal Son," a story contained in Luke 15:11–32 in the *NIV Study Bible*, is Jesus' parable of a young man who demands his inheritance, squanders it in reckless living, and returns home to seek the forgiveness of his father. Also see Henri Nouwen's *The Return of the Prodigal Son* (New York: Doubleday [Image Books], 1994), a touching reflection on this famous Bible story, inspired by Rembrandt's painting of the same title.

Chapter 21 SURRENDER, GRATITUDE, ACTION

1. John Heider, *The Tao of Leadership* (New York: Bantam, 1996).

2. Matthew 5:3 (from the Beatitudes), in the *NIV Study Bible* (Grand Rapids, MI: Zondervan, 1985).

3. Henri Nouwen, *The Return of the Prodigal Son* (New York: Doubleday [Image Books], 1992).

4. "Giftedness" books include the following: Ralph Mattson and Arthur Miller, *Finding a Job You Can Love* (Nashville, TN: Thomas Nelson Publishers, 1982); Richard Leider, *The Power of Purpose* (New York: Ballantine, 1985) and *Repacking Your Bags* (San Francisco: Berrett-Koehler, 1995); Richard Rohr and Andreas Ebert, *Discovering the Enneagram* (New York: Crossroad Publishing, 2000); Ron Richard Riso and Russ Hudson, *The Wisdom of the Enneagram: The Complete Guide to Psychological and Spiritual Growth for the Nine Personality Types* (New York: Bantam, 1999); David Keirsey and Marilyn Bates, *Please Understand Me: Character and Temperament Types* (Del Mar, CA: Prometheus Nemesis Book Company, 1984); Laurie Beth Jones, *The Path: Creating Your Mission Statement for Work and for Life* (New York: Hyperion, 1996); and Dan Webster, *The Real Deal: Becoming More Authentic in Life and Leadership and Increasing Your Personal Impact* (Self-published, order through www.authenticleadershipinc.com).

5. Harville Hendrix, Ph.D., *Getting the Love You Want* (New York: HarperCollins, 1988); Harville Hendrix, Ph.D., and Helen Hunt, *The Couples Companion: Meditations and Exercises for Getting the Love You Want* (New York: Pocket Books, 1994).

Chapter 22 GREATNESS

1. Danaan Perry, "Parable of the Trapeze," *Warriors of the Heart* (Seattle, WA: Earth Stewards Network, 1990). A copy of the whole poem may be obtained by calling (206) 842-7986.

2. Anthony deMello, *Awareness* (New York: Doubleday [Image Books], 1992). Used by permission of Doubleday, a division of Random House, Inc.

3. Bob Buford, *Half Time* (Grand Rapids, MI: Zondervan, 1994), *Game Plan* (1997), and *Stuck in Half Time* (2001). Buford's wonderful trilogy on transition offers many tips and tools for changing your life plan from success to significance. He also offers a participant's guide, leader's guide, and audio/videotape set for helping small groups address transitional issues. For more information go to www.zondervan.com or call Leadership Network in Dallas, Texas, at (800) 611-6501.

4. Anthony deMello, *The Song of the Bird* (New York: Doubleday [Image Books], 1984). Used by permission of Doubleday, a division of Random House, Inc.

5. Ibid.

INDEX